Alexandra Pirici *Attune*

Für die / For the **Nationalgalerie – Staatliche Museen zu Berlin herausgegeben von** / edited by **Sam Bardaouil & Till Fellrath**

Sam Bardaouil & Till Fellrath
Hg. / Eds.

SilvanaEditoriale

Inhalt / Content

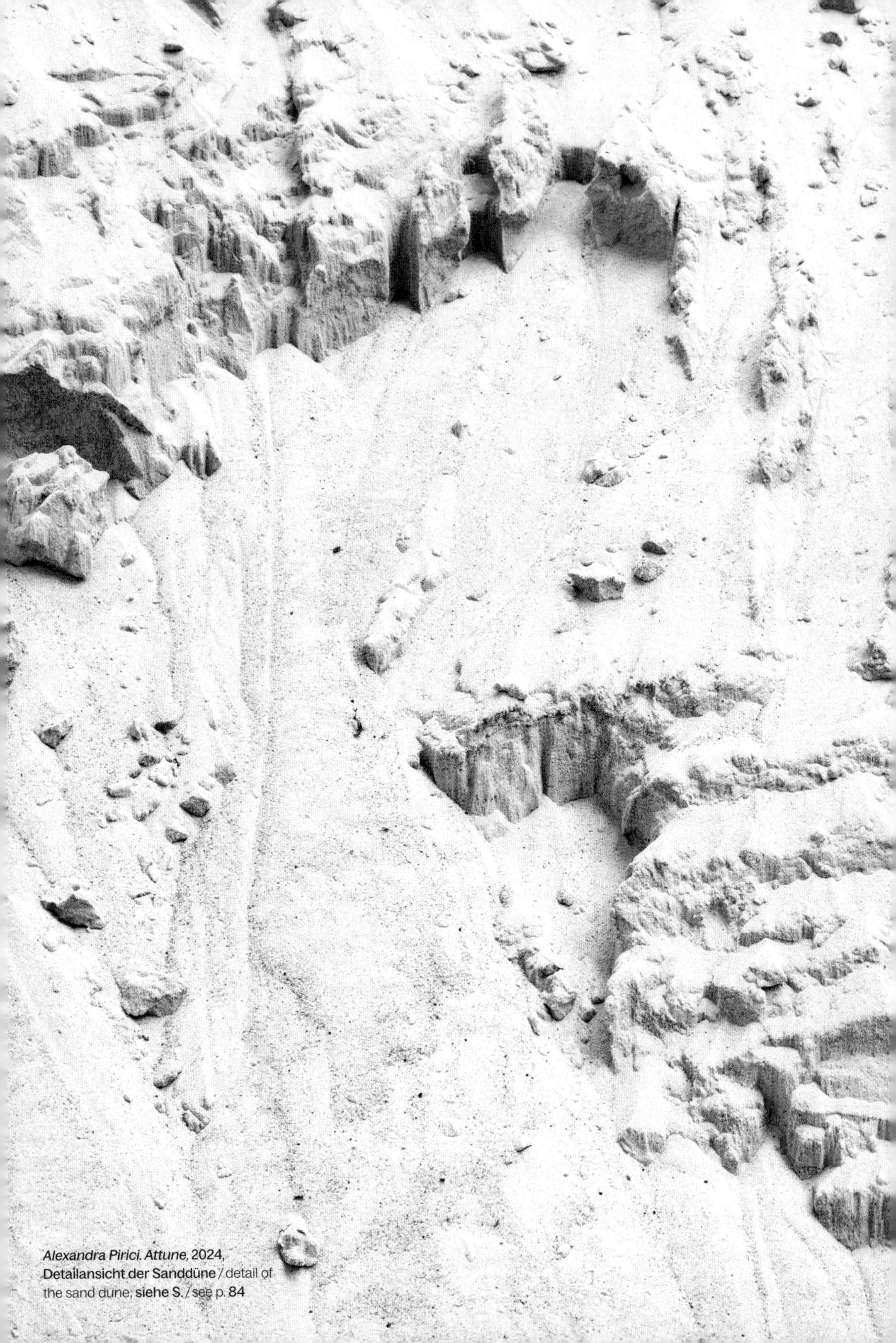

Alexandra Pirici. Attune, 2024,
Detailansicht der Sanddüne / detail of
the sand dune; siehe S. / see p. 84

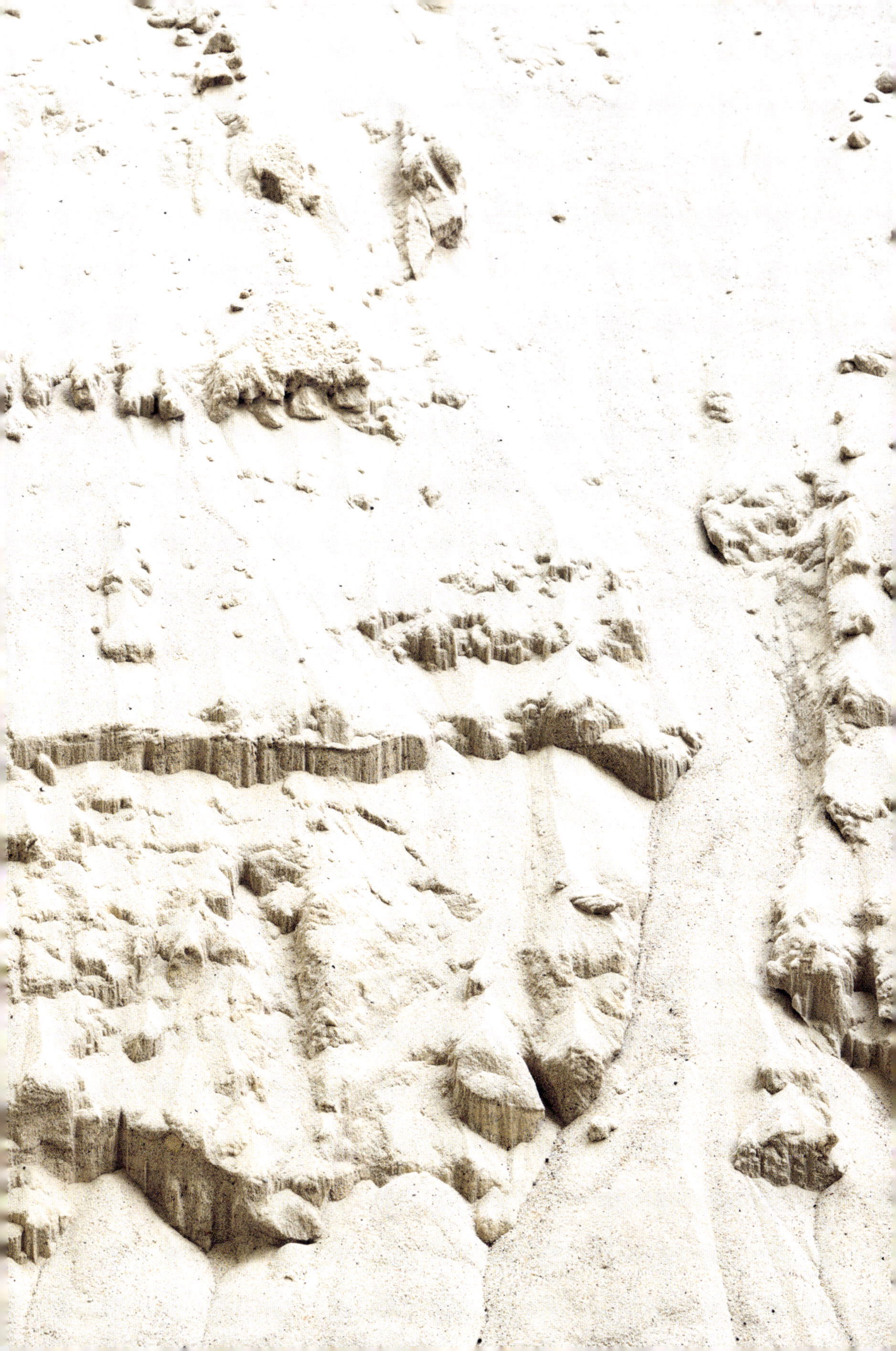

Vorwort/ Foreword

Kulturstiftung des Bundes / German Federal Cultural Foundation

„In der Fähigkeit zur Zusammenarbeit und in der Demut liegen unsere besten Ansätze und Chancen," sagt Alexandra Pirici in ihrem *Future ground* genannten philosophischen Video-Walk aus dem Jahr 2020, und sie fährt fort: „Auch wenn wir verzweifelt anerkennen müssen, möglicherweise nie zu wissen, wie das zu tun ist." Es ist ein Glück, dass dieses Risiko des Scheiterns Alexandra Pirici weniger zu hemmen als vielmehr zu beflügeln scheint, immer neue Ansätze für künstlerische Kooperationen zu erproben.

Was folgt darauf für die Fähigkeit zur Zusammenarbeit? Dass die Choreographin und Künstlerin Alexandra Pirici ihr raumfüllendes Haupthallen-Werk *Attune* in intensivem Austausch mit Performer*innen und Wissenschaftler*innen unter anderem von der Freien Universität Berlin und der Universität Bukarest entwickelt hat. Und dass in diesem Pluriversum von Gesang, Bewegung, Objektinstalla-

"Collaboration and humility are our best approaches and chances", says Alexandra Pirici in her 2020 philosophical video walk *Future ground*. She continues: "Even as we desperately acknowledge we may never learn how to do that." It is fortunate that this risk of failure, rather than inhibiting her, seems to inspire Alexandra Pirici to keep exploring new approaches to artistic cooperation.

What does this mean when it comes to collaboration? That the choreographer and artist Alexandra Pirici has developed *Attune,* her expansive work for Hamburger Bahnhof's main hall, in close consultation with performers, scholars and scientists from Freie Universität Berlin and the University of Bucharest among other institutions. And that within this pluriverse of song, movement, object installations and bio-chemical oscillations, collective forms of expression and knowledge interact with one another, thereby transforming the museum's typical

tionen und biochemischen Oszillationen kollektive Formen des Ausdrucks und Wissens ineinanderwirken, die dazu beitragen können, standardisierte Arbeitsteilungen eines Museums zu transformieren in einen – wie die Biologin Donna Haraway es fordert – „heißen Komposthaufen unerwarteter Kooperationen und Kombinationen".

Und was heißt das für die Demut? Dass es nicht einfach sein wird, im polyphonen System dieser Installation eine souveräne Publikumsposition zu beziehen. Eines aber wird deutlich: Der Vormacht des Auges erteilt Alexandra Pirici eine Absage. Vielmehr lädt sie das Publikum ein, sich in die postindustrielle Museumshalle wie in eine Landschaft hineinzubegeben. Überall ist Bewegung. Überall eröffnen sich Räume für flanierende Neugierde und eine Schärfung der Sinne, die für menschliche Performances ebenso empfänglich ist wie für das Farbspiel der Briggs-Rauscher-Reaktion oder der chemischen Gärten in den Glaszylindern, das exemplarisch die Biochemie bei der Arbeit zeigt, ohne deren selbstorganisierte nichtmenschliche Akteure das komplexe Leben auf diesem Planeten – so wie es uns bislang vertraut ist – unmöglich wäre.

Die Kulturstiftung des Bundes dankt Alexandra Pirici an der Seite ihres Performance- und Produktionsteams sowie dem gesamten Team des Hamburger Bahnhofs – Nationalgalerie der Gegenwart, insbesondere den Direktoren Sam Bardaouil und Till Fellrath und der Kuratorin Catherine Nichols, für die Erarbeitung einer Installation, die zu multiplen Aufbrüchen einlädt: in den Raum, in den Klang und in die Zeit, die wir brauchen werden, um über das Museum hinaus andere Formen der Weltaneignung zu erproben.

division of labor into "unexpected collaborations and combinations, in hot compost piles", as called for by biologist Donna Haraway.

And what does that mean for humility? That the audience will not find it easy to take up a confident position within the polyphonic system of this installation. Yet one thing is clear: Alexandra Pirici rejects the hegemony of vision. Instead, she invites people to enter the post-industrial space of the museum as though it were a landscape. Everywhere you look, there is movement. Everywhere you turn, spaces open up for a meandering curiosity and a sharpening of the senses that is as receptive to human performances as it is to the play of colors in the Briggs-Rauscher reaction or the chemical gardens displayed in glass cylinders. These exemplify the biochemistry without whose self-organizing, non-human actors complex life on this planet as we know it would never have been possible.

The German Federal Cultural Foundation would like to thank Alexandra Pirici alongside her performance and production team as well as the entire team of Hamburger Bahnhof – Nationalgalerie der Gegenwart, in particular the directors Sam Bardaouil and Till Fellrath and the curator Catherine Nichols, for bringing to life an installation that invites multiple departures: into the space, into the sound- and timescapes necessary for trying out other forms of worlding, beyond the realm of the museum.

Katarzyna Wielga-Skolimowska
Vorstand / Künstlerische Direktorin /
Chairwoman / Artistic Director

Kirsten Haß
Vorstand / Verwaltungsdirektorin /
Chairwoman / Administrative Director

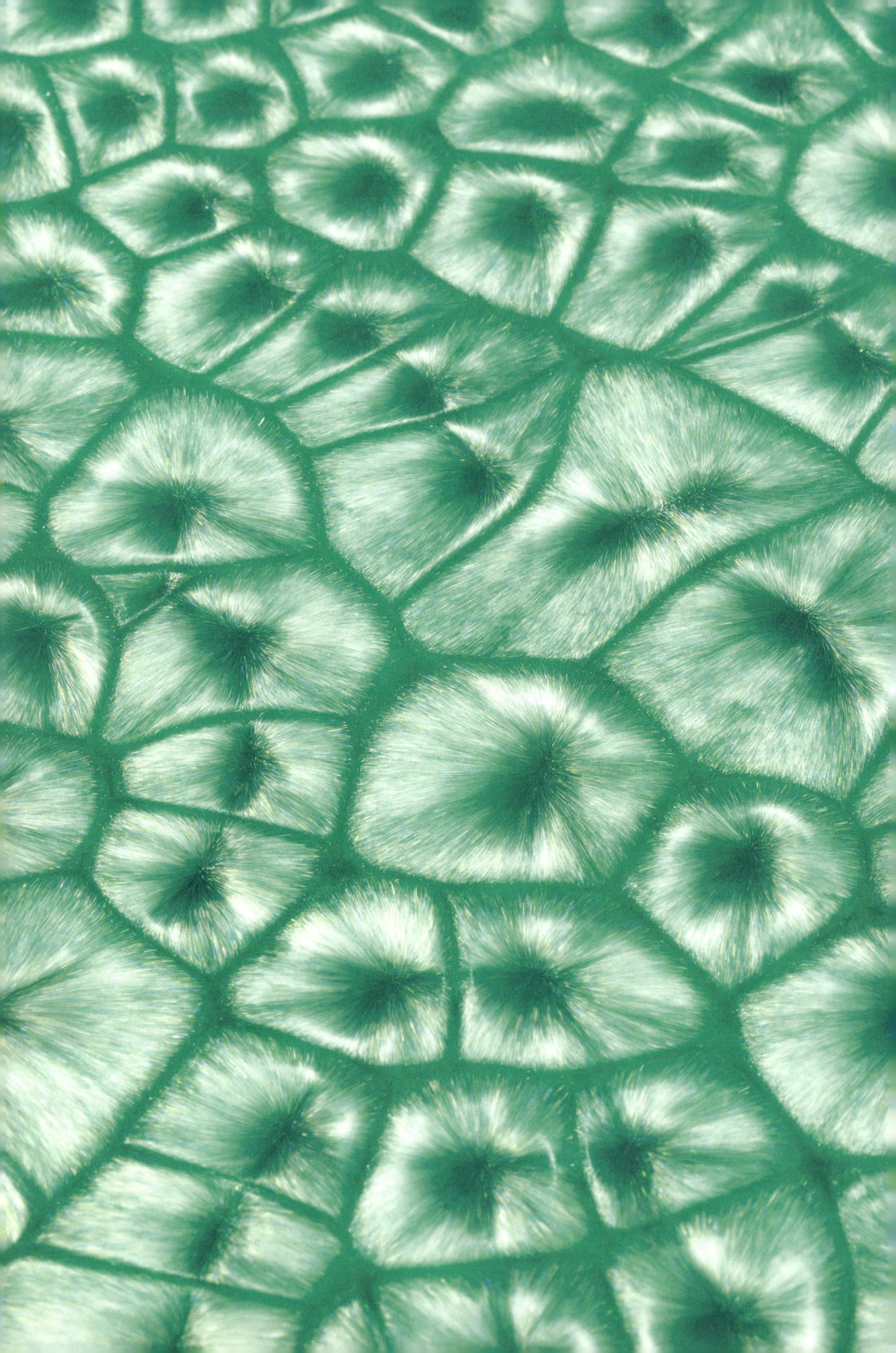

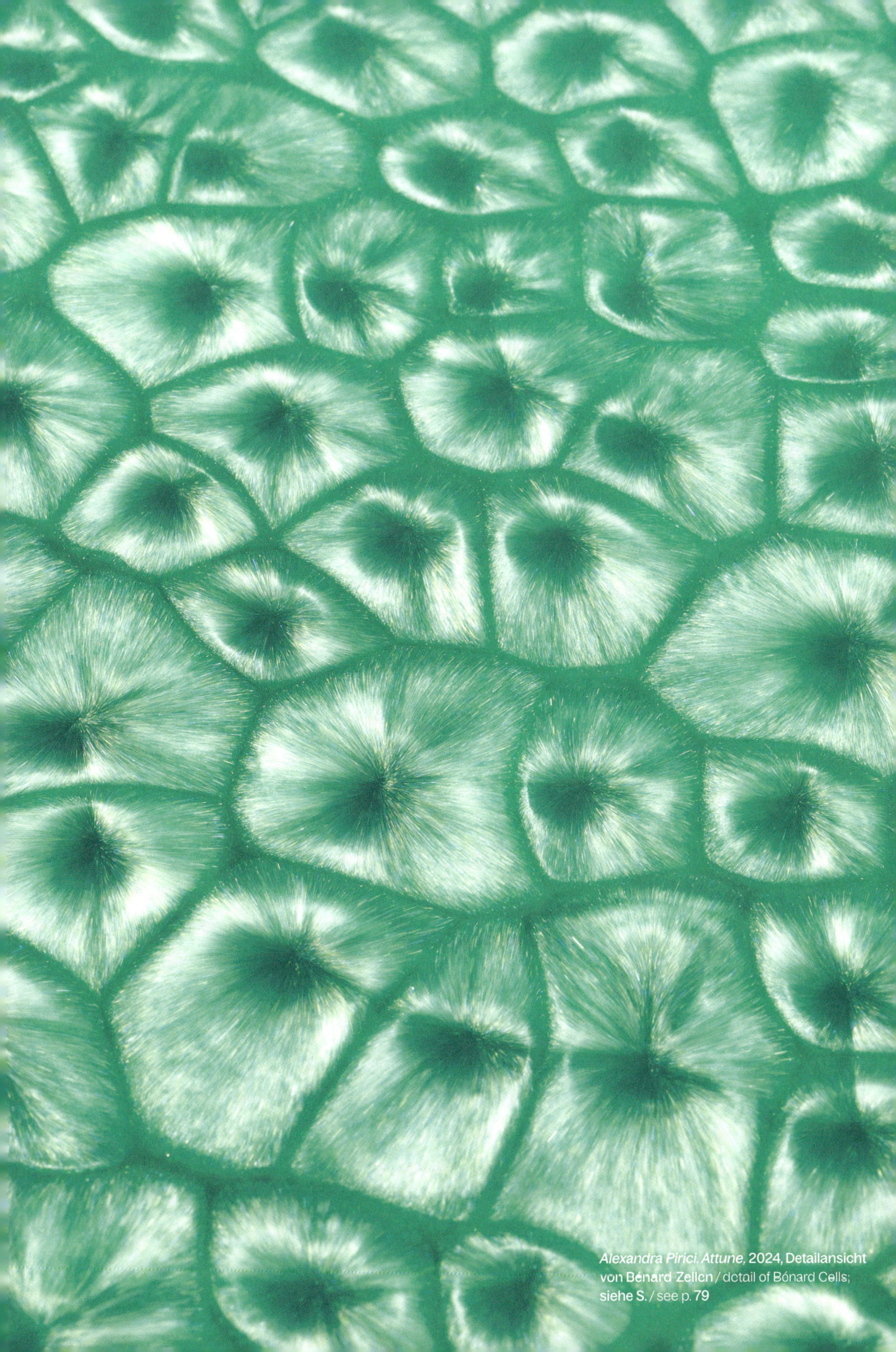

Alexandra Pirici. Attune, 2024, Detailansicht von Bénard Zellen / detail of Bénard Cells; siehe S. / see p. 79

Vorwort/ Foreword

Audemars Piguet Contemporary

Im Sinne des *embodied spectatorship* [verkörperte Zuschauerschaft] setzt Alexandra Pirici in ihren Arbeiten die Körper der Betrachtenden mit den Körpern von Performer*innen in Beziehung. Mit *Attune* hat sie nun zum ersten Mal eine skulpturale Umgebung geschaffen, die die Besucher*innen einlädt, die Historische Halle des Hamburger Bahnhofs – Nationalgalerie der Gegenwart in ihrem Ausmaß sowie ihrer architektonischen Kraft zu erkunden. Die Ausstellung in dem ehemaligen Bahnhofsgebäude aus dem 19. Jahrhundert bietet Besuchenden die Möglichkeit, eine philosophische Landschaft zu erforschen, die durch performative Handlungen und Gesänge aktiviert wird.

In früheren Arbeiten konfrontierte Alexandra Pirici monumentale Orte im öffentlichen Raum mit Performance, Humor und Kritik. Im Hamburger Bahnhof nutzt sie das enorme Ausmaß der Halle, um selbstorganisierende

Alexandra Pirici's practice engages the body of the viewer in a relationship with the body of the performer in what scholars identify as embodied spectatorship. For the first time, with *Attune,* Pirici has imagined a sculptural environment, inviting the spectator to navigate the scale and architectural prowess of the historic hall at Hamburger Bahnhof – Nationalgalerie der Gegenwart, once a 19th century train station. With this exhibition, the spectator has the opportunity to explore a philosophical landscape activated by performative actions and vocal musical pieces.

In previous works, Alexandra Pirici confronted monumentality present in the public sphere with performance, humor, and critique. At Hamburger Bahnhof, Pirici embraces the immense scale of the hall to exhibit self-organizing non-equilibrium physical and chemical processes in animate and inanimate matter. Her work enables visitors to experience the ways in which patterns and order emerge across the

physikalische und chemische Nichtgleichgewichtsprozesse in belebter wie unbelebter Materie aufzuzeigen. Ihre Arbeit ermöglicht es den Besuchenden, zu erleben, wie Muster und Ordnungen in der Tier-, Pflanzen-, chemischen und mineralischen Welt entstehen. Dabei regt Pirici unter anderem eine Neubewertung der Grenzen zwischen Menschlichem und Nicht-Menschlichem an. Die vielstimmigen Gesänge der Performer*innen spiegeln Muster von Abstimmungsprozessen, die in und zwischen allen Formen der Materie in bestimmten Daseinszuständen möglich sind.

Alexandra Pirici experimentiert in einem für sie noch nie dagewesenen Ausmaß. Sie hat Skulpturen geschaffen, die eine immersive Landschaft bilden, in der sich Elemente von sehr unterschiedlicher Größe gegenüberstehen: Einige sind klein und fordern die Betrachtenden auf, sich ihnen zu nähern, auf sie zuzulaufen, andere wiederum sind riesig. Die Performer*innen nehmen die Halle ein – ihre Stimmen füllen den Raum auf eine architektonische Weise, wie sie Komponist*innen vertraut ist, und ihre Körper stellen sich der Architektur entgegen. Man könnte sagen, dass Pirici ein neues Genre definiert, in dem Menschen, Objekte, Chemikalien, Pflanzen, Mineralien, Skulpturen und Architekturen miteinander agieren und sich aufeinander einstellen.

Audemars Piguet Contemporary ist stolz darauf, einen Beitrag zu Alexandra Piricis neuer Forschungsarbeit und der öffentlichen Präsentation von *Attune* zu leisten. Indem Audemars Piguet *Attune* gemeinsam mit dem Hamburger Bahnhof in Auftrag gibt, bekräftigt das Unternehmen seine Überzeugung, dass die Unterstützung von Kultur eine wesentliche Rolle darin spielen kann, uns miteinander zu verbinden und unsere Perspektiven zu erweitern. Alexandra Pirici bietet uns hier ein einzigartiges Erlebnis, das beides ermöglicht.

animal, vegetal, chemical, and mineral realms. In doing so, Pirici proposes among other things a reevaluation of the boundaries between the human and non-human. The polyphonic songs of the performers echo the patterns of attunement possible in and between all forms of matter in particular states of being.

Alexandra Pirici experiments on what is for her an unprecedented scale. She has created sculptures that form an immersive landscape, contrasting elements of vastly differing dimensions: some elements are small and call upon the viewer to walk and come closer, whereas others are giant. The performers take over the hall, their voices filling the space in an architectonic manner known to music composers, and their bodies confronting the architecture. One could argue that Pirici defines a new genre where human beings, objects, chemicals, plants, minerals, sculptures, and architecture perform and attune to one another.

Audemars Piguet Contemporary is proud to contribute to Alexandra Pirici's new body of research and to *Attune*'s public presentation. In co-commissioning *Attune* with Hamburger Bahnhof, Audemars Piguet reiterates its belief in supporting culture as an essential element in connecting us to one another and broadening our perspectives. Alexandra Pirici offers us here a singular experience to do so.

Denis Pernet
Kurator bei / Curator at **Audemars Piguet Contemporary,**
Ko-Auftraggeber von / Co-comissioners of *Attune*

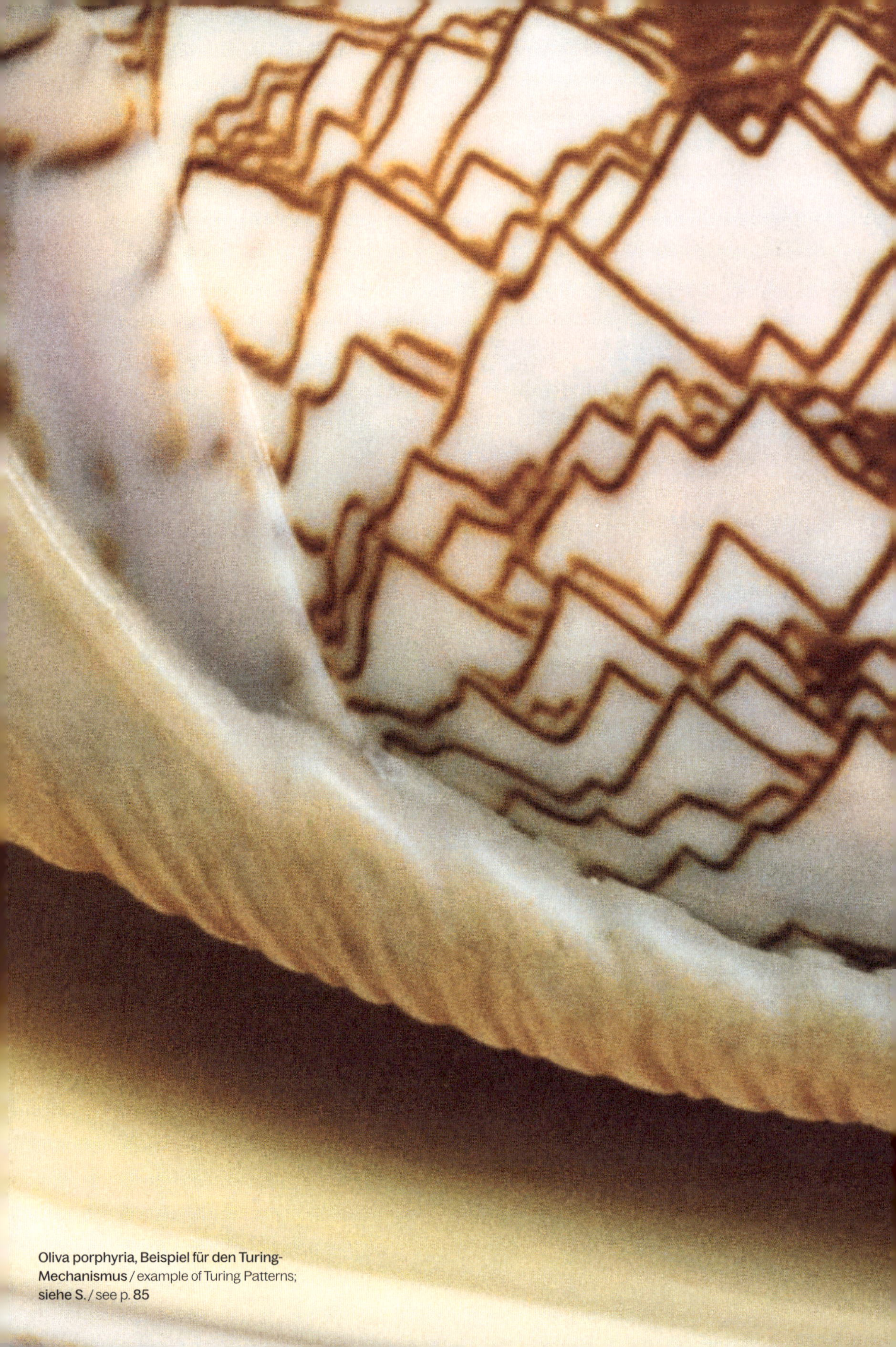

Oliva porphyria, Beispiel für den Turing-
Mechanismus / example of Turing Patterns;
siehe S. / see p. 85

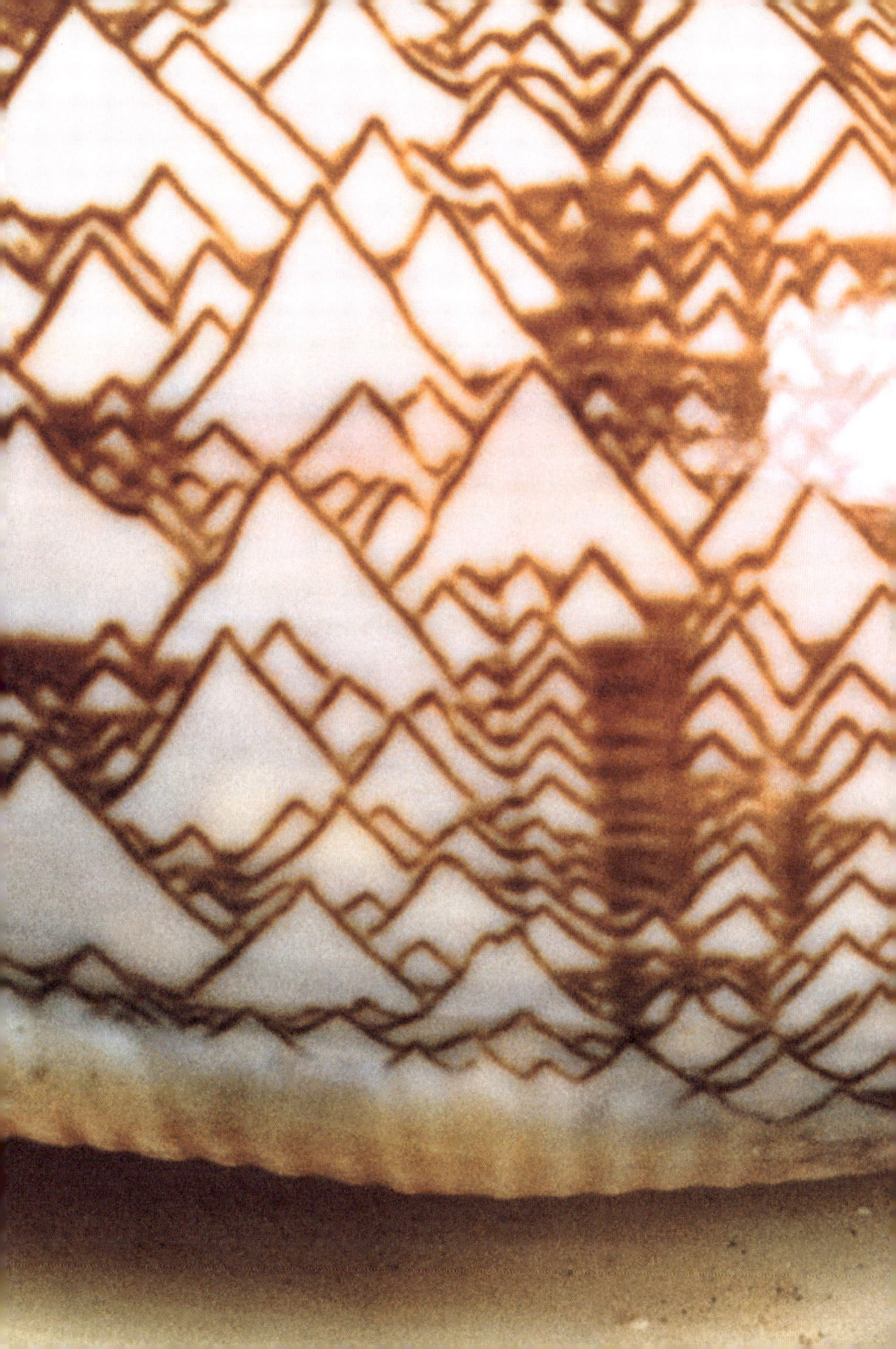

Alexandra Pirici.
Attune

Catherine Nichols

Nach Weihnachten flog ich von Berlin nach Westaustralien. An einem entlegenen, wind- gebeutelten Küstenabschnitt, an dem vor dem Indischen Ozean steile weiße Dünen die roten Weiten der Sandwüste ablösen, war ich mit meiner Mutter und meinem Bruder verabre- det – fernab unserer auf der anderen Seite des Kontinents gelegenen Heimat. Vor der Küste erstreckt sich ein über zweihundert Kilome- ter langes Korallenriff, an dem entlang sich zu bestimmten Jahreszeiten Walhaie, Buckel- wale, Meeresschildkröten und Mantarochen treiben lassen. In den Sommermonaten sind es eher Schulen der für ihre Scheu bekann- ten Riffhaie oder Schwärme bunter Papa- geien-, Clown-, Kaiser-, Doktor-, Wimpel- und Schmetterlingsfische, die hier umhergleiten und -flitzen. Wir trafen uns an einem kleinen, in der Wüste gelegenen Flughafen, zu dem mich das wacklige Doppelpropellerflugzeug aus Perth befördert hatte. Von dort aus legten wir die paar Hundert Kilometer bis zur Küste mit dem Auto zurück. Mein Bruder fuhr, meine Mutter hielt Ausschau nach Emus, wir plau- derten. In den hin und wieder entstehenden Gesprächslücken las ich in einem Buch über Komplexität und Selbstorganisation, das ich zum letzten Mal vor Jahrzehnten in der Hand gehalten hatte, als ich mich mit Hans Magnus

Not long after Christmas, I flew from Berlin to Western Australia. On a remote, windswept stretch of coast along the Indian Ocean, where steep white dunes give way to the vast red expanse of a sandy desert, I had arranged to meet my mother and brother – far away from our home town on the other side of the conti- nent. Just off the coast, a coral reef stretches for more than 200 kilometers. At certain times of the year, whale sharks, humpback whales, sea tur- tles, and manta rays pass through these crys- tal blue waters. Yet during the summer months, you're more likely to encounter schools of tim- orous reef sharks – or shoals of colorful parrot- fish, clownfish or angelfish, surgeonfish, ban- nerfish or butterfly fish – drifting or darting around. The three of us met at a small desert airport I had flown to from Perth in a rickety twin-propeller plane. From there, we traveled the remaining hundred-odd kilometers over to the coast by car. My brother drove, my mother kept an eye out for emus, as we chatted about this and that. In the occasional lulls in conversa- tion, I returned to reading a book on complexity and self-organization I had last picked up dec- ades before, back when I was studying the work of Hans Magnus Enzensberger and his recurring forays into the science of complexity:[1] *Order out of Chaos: Man's New Dialogue with Nature* by

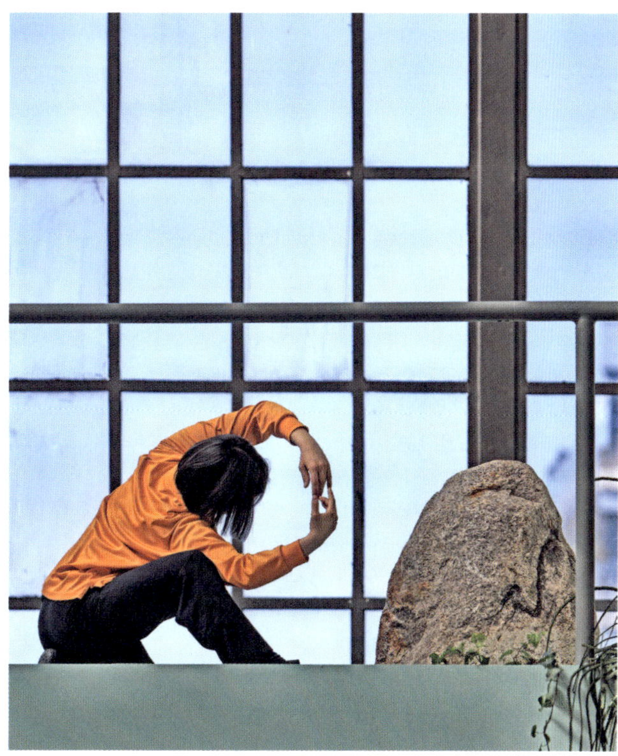

Ausstellungsansicht / Installation view, *Alexandra Pirici. Attune,*
Hamburger Bahnhof – Nationalgalerie der Gegenwart, 2024

Enzensbergers wiederkehrenden Auseinandersetzungen mit chaotischen Systemen[1] befasste: *Dialog mit der Natur. Neue Wege naturwissenschaftlichen Denkens* von Ilya Prigogine und Isabelle Stengers. Auf diese wegweisende transdisziplinäre Veröffentlichung zur Entstehung spontaner Ordnung aus dem Chaos waren Alexandra Pirici und ich bereits zu sprechen gekommen, als wir uns eines der ersten Male über ihr Ausstellungsvorhaben im Hamburger Bahnhof ausgetauscht hatten. Wie damals für mich, als ich – Enzensbergers Faible für die politische Philosophie des Anarchismus teilend – die Relevanz der Selbstorganisation für Politik und Gesellschaft zu erkunden versuchte, spielen viele der von Prigogine und Stengers angeführten Beispiele selbstorganisatorischer Prozesse in Physik, Biochemie und Molekularbiologie für die Künstlerin eine wesentliche Rolle bei der Konzeption ihres neuen Werkes *Attune*.

Bei der Vorstellung, im Auto ein Buch zu lesen, wird Ihnen womöglich übel. Doch die Straße war schnurgerade und vollkommen

Ilya Prigogine and Isabelle Stengers. This seminal study on the spontaneous emergence of order out of chaos had come up in conversation between Alexandra Pirici and me when we first began talking about her forthcoming exhibition at Hamburger Bahnhof. Like me, when, sharing Enzensberger's affinity for the political philosophy of anarchism, I mined the science of self-

1 Vgl. etwa Hans Magnus Enzensberger, „Das Ende der Inkonsequenz" [1981] und „Unregierbarkeit. Notizen aus dem Kanzleramt" [1982] in: ders., *Politische Brosamen*, Frankfurt am Main: Suhrkamp, 1985, S. 7–30 bzw. S. 97–113; „Vermutungen über die Turbulenz" [1989] in: ders., *Der fliegende Robert. Gedichte, Szenen, Essays*, Frankfurt am Main: Suhrkamp, 1992, S. 297–306.

1 See, for example, Hans Magnus Enzensberger, "Second Thoughts on Inconsistency" [1981] and "Ungovernability: Notes from the Chancellor's Office" [1982] in: *Political Crumbs*, London / New York: Verso, 1990, pp.1–16, 71–84; "Vermutungen über die Turbulenz" [1989] in: *Der Fliegende Robert: Gedichte, Szenen, Essays*, Frankfurt am Main: Suhrkamp, 1992, pp.297–306.

flach – eine dieser fast schon sprichwörtlich endlos langen, staubumwölkten Routen, die Australien durchqueren. Road Trains vor uns, Road Trains hinter uns, links und rechts – so dachte ich zumindest – nichts als Sand. Doch plötzlich geschah etwas fast Unglaubliches: Termitenhügel, die bei Prigogine und Stengers als Paradigma für Selbstorganisation stehen, materialisierten sich vor meinen Augen. Zu Abertausenden. Soweit das Auge reichte, ragten sie empor: mehrere Meter hohe Kathedralen aus rostroter Erde und zerkautem Pflanzenmaterial. Wir hielten an, liefen von Bauwerk zu Bauwerk, versuchten uns im gleißenden Sonnenlicht vorzustellen, wie jene sich scheinbar chaotisch bewegenden Wesen ganz ohne Anleitung eine solch vollklimatisierte, witterungsfeste Architektur zu vollbringen vermögen.

Als hätten Termiten auf den von Thomas Hobbes postulierten „Krieg aller gegen alle" verzichtet, sollen diese ursozialen Verwandten der Kakerlaken bereits in der Jurazeit begonnen haben, in friedlicher Zusammenarbeit und mit vielseitiger Intelligenz, wie Peter Kropotkin in seinem anarchistischen Gegenentwurf zum Sozialdarwinismus beschreibt, ihre „wundervollen ‚Haufen'", ihre „Gebäude", „ihre gepflasterten Straßen und brückenartig gewölbten Galerien; ihre geräumigen Hallen und Speicher" zu erschaffen.[2] Was sich in der Landschaft so plastisch formte, war aus dem Zusammenspiel von Unordnung und Ordnung entstanden, das, nach Prigogine und Stengers, der „Herausbildung einer neuen Struktur vorausgeht". So erbaulich die Vorstellung der auf gegenseitiger Hilfe beruhenden „Kollektivseele"[3] beziehungsweise Schwarmintelligenz einer Insektengemeinschaft auch sein mag: Der Grundstein eines jeden Termitenbaus wird vielmehr nach dem Zufallsprinzip gelegt, indem umherwandernde Termiten pheromondurchtränkte Erdklümpchen an einem beliebigen Ort fallen lassen. Das Pheromon zieht weitere Termiten an, die ebenfalls Erdklümpchen abwerfen. Nach und nach entstehen so an manchen Stellen Säulen, aus denen schließlich solch ausgefeilte Bauwerke hervorgehen wie jene, die uns nun umgaben. In instabilen

organization for its social and political implications, Pirici has looked to many of the examples of self-organizational processes from physics, biochemistry, and molecular biology assembled by Prigogine and Stengers in conceiving her new work, *Attune*.

The very thought of reading a book in the car may well make you nauseous. Yet the road was straight and flat, one of the many never-ending dust tunnels that stretch their way across the continent. Road trains ahead of us, road trains behind us, to our left and our right – or at least so I thought – nothing but sand and scrub. And that's when it happened. Something you'd scarcely believe. The termites' nests I was reading about as paradigms of self-organization suddenly materialized right before my eyes. Thousands upon thousands of them. Towering cathedrals of rust-red earth and chewed plant matter – as far as the eye could see. We stopped the car and got out. Slowly, incredulously, we wandered from one mound to the next, trying, in the glare of the blazing desert sun, to see, to imagine how such tiny, seemingly chaotic creatures could construct such intricate, fully air-conditioned and weatherproof architectural structures – without the slightest direction from above.

As though they had somehow renounced the evolutionary "war of all against all" postulated by political philosopher Thomas Hobbes, these supremely social, highly adaptive descendants of cockroaches are believed to have been cooperating on the construction of such wonderful nests, ornate buildings and paved roads, such vaulted galleries, spacious halls and granaries since the Jurassic period, as Peter Kropotkin describes in *Mutual Aid*, his anarchist alternative to Social Darwinism.[2] What became manifest to me in this desert encounter was the characteristic interplay of disorder and order which, as Prigogine and Stengers would have it, precedes "the formation of a new structure".[3] However uplifting it may feel to attribute to insect communities a "collective mind",[4] a form of swarm intelligence based on altruism or mutual aid, the construction of a termite mound is, as the authors point out, in fact a rather arbitrary affair. Roaming termites drop pheromone-soaked clods of earth in random locations as they move.

Situationen genügen wohl „einige wenige ‚Entscheidungen' [...], um ein System, das aus einer großen Anzahl von Entitäten besteht, in Richtung auf eine globale Struktur zu kanalisieren".[4] Was mir daran so spannend erschien – und was für die Arbeit Piricis zentral ist –, war die in wissenschaftlichen Kreisen wachsende Gewissheit, dass dieses die Evolutionstheorie Charles Darwins erweiternde Prinzip nicht nur für staatenbildende Lebewesen wie Termiten, Bienen, Ameisen oder Menschen gilt, sondern für Einheiten jeglicher Art, organisch wie anorganisch, belebt wie unbelebt, gleichermaßen für Atome, Moleküle, Zellen und Organismen.

Lange vermochten wir in der sengenden Hitze nicht zu verweilen, wir stiegen wieder ins Auto und fuhren weiter in Richtung Meer. In den folgenden Tagen, als das alte Jahr allmählich ins neue überging, schien sich die Zeit ein wenig zu dehnen. Frühmorgens wie spätabends wanderte ich am Strand entlang. Hin und wieder versuchte ich dabei, mir das noch im Entwurf begriffene Environment Piricis vorzustellen, das bald mit allen Sinnen in der Historischen Halle des Hamburger Bahnhofs zu erleben sein würde. Die wissenschaftlichen und technischen Herausforderungen des sich unter hohem Zeitdruck entwickelnden Projektes hatten uns bislang weniger Zeit zum Sprechen gelassen, als wir uns gewünscht hätten. Doch unter dem weiten blauen Himmel begann ich mich mit Alexandra in Gedanken zu unterhalten. Während ich über den filigran geriffelten Sand des Strandes schlenderte, die sich im Wind stets neu formenden Dünen, die sich wandelnden Wolkenmuster am Himmel, die nah um Ufer hin und her gleitenden Stechrochen beobachtete, knüpfte ich an die vielen begonnenen Gesprächsfäden an.

Immer wieder lenkten die angespülten Portugiesischen Galeeren, die an den meisten Tagen eine wellenförmige Linie entlang des Meeressaums bildeten, meinen Blick nach unten. Mit ihren mehrere Meter langen tintenblauen Tentakeln zwangen mich die langsam vor sich hin vertrocknenden Quallen, darauf achtzugeben, wohin ich meine nackten Füße setzte. Ich fühlte mich dabei an das Ineinander von Gehen und Denken erin-

The pheromone attracts other termites to the site, who likewise drop clods of earth. Little by little, these clods form columns, eventually giving rise to structures as sophisticated as the ones in our midst. In unstable situations far from equilibrium, it seems that a few clod-sized "decisions" may be enough to "channel a system formed by a large number of interactive entities toward a global structure".[5] What I find most compelling about this observation – and what is central to Pirici's work – is the growing conviction in scientific circles that the principle of self-organization applies not only to state-forming creatures such as termites, bees, ants, or humans, but to entities of all kinds, whether organic or inorganic, animate or inanimate, whether atoms or molecules, cells or organisms.

As captivated as we were, the scorching heat prevented us from pondering at length. Soon we were back in the car, continuing on our way over to the coast. In the days that followed, as the old year gradually faded into the new one, time seemed to slow down a little. In the early mornings and late evenings I traipsed along the beach, work never very far from my mind. Now and again my thoughts would wander to the performative environment Pirici has been developing for Hamburger Bahnhof's historic hall, a work designed to engage with all senses. The fast-paced production of such a scientifically and technically challenging work have afforded us much less time to talk than we would have liked. Yet here, all alone beneath the wide blue open sky, I finally found the space, the quietude, to converse, to think with Alexandra, if only in my mind. As I strolled along the delicately

---

2 Peter Kropotkin, *Gegenseitige Hilfe in der Tier- und Menschenwelt* [1902], Leipzig: Verlag von Theodor Thomas, 1910, S. 12–13.
3 Ilya Prigogine & Isabelle Stengers, *Dialog mit der Natur. Neue Wege naturwissenschaftlichen Denkens*, München / Zürich: Piper, 1990, S. 179.
4 Ebd.

---

2 Peter Kropotkin, *Mutual Aid: A Factor of Evolution,* New York: Heinemann, 1902, p. 14.
3 Ilya Prigogine & Isabelle Stengers, *Order out of Chaos: Man's New Dialogue with Nature,* Toronto / New York: Bantam Books, 1984, p. 181.
4 Ibid., p. 186.
5 Ibid., p. 187.

nert, über das Pirici in ihrem Videovortrag *Future ground* reflektiert, den sie 2020 gehalten hatte, während sie im Wald wanderte.[5] *Thinkmoving* nennt sie diese Handlung: sich denkend bewegend, sich bewegend denkend. Diesen gewählt ungeschmeidigen Neologismus nimmt die Künstlerin vorsichtig in den Mund, stellt ihn fragend zur Diskussion. Zwar seien solch holprig zusammengeschobene Wortschöpfungen keinesfalls die ultimative Methode, den mannigfaltigen Unzulänglichkeiten einer jeden Sprache entgegenzuwirken. Als ein erster Schritt in Richtung eines erweiterten Denkhorizonts mögen sie jedoch unerwartete Beziehungen herstellen und neue Haltungen hervorbringen. Den Blick auf den Waldboden gerichtet, das Knistern des unter ihren Füßen zerbröselnden Herbstlaubs im Ohr, reflektiert die hörbar atmende Künstlerin über das Potenzial des Begriffs *Thinkmoving*: als Aneignung von verkörpertem Wissen; als Erarbeitung einer multidirektionalen, multisensorischen Aufmerksamkeit; als Schulung einer sich stets neu in Bezug setzenden, sich neu verhandelnden Subjektivität.

Diese seien am Ehesten in der Lage, einen „future ground", einen anderen Boden hervorzubringen als jenen, auf dem wir uns aufhalten und der in den Mythen von linearem Fortschritt und ständigem Wachstum befangen wäre.

Eine solche in *Thinkmoving* begründete Herangehensweise erprobt Pirici in ihrer neuen Arbeit *Attune*. Das raumgreifende Environment greift zwar verschiedene Fragestellungen und künstlerische Strategien ihrer jüngsten performativen Arbeiten auf, darunter *Aggregate* (2017–2019) und *Encyclopedia of Relations* (2022). Doch die kühle, gleichermaßen archaisch wie futuristisch wirkende Landschaft, die sich im Hamburger Bahnhof entfaltet, besteht nicht nur aus von der Künstlerin choreografierten Bewegungen, aus Sprache

rippled sands, idly observing the dunes relentlessly shifting shape in the wind, the clouds forming patterns in the sky, and the stingrays gliding gently back and forth along the shore, I found myself returning to the many conversations we had embarked upon in months gone by, picking up the threads one by one.

Ever and again while walking, my gaze was drawn downwards by the undulating lines of bluebottles that washed up on the shore most days, slowly drying and dying in the sun. With their long, poisonous ink-blue tentacles, some extending up to several meters in length, these delicate hydrozoans make you watch where you put your feet. This heightened awareness took me back to Pirici's 2020 video lecture *Future ground*. Set in a forest, the video reflects on the interrelationship of walking and thinking.[6] Pirici refers to this mode of activity as *thinkmoving*: moving as thinking, thinking as moving. She uses this consciously cumbersome neologism cautiously, questioningly, as though she were somehow putting it up for debate. While such roughly hewn composite terms are unlikely to compensate for the significatory shortcomings of any given language, they can, as Pirici points out, nevertheless serve as a crucial first step in the right direction. Gazing down at the forest floor, crunching dry autumn leaves underfoot, the audibly breathing artist explores the potential of *thinkmoving* as she walks: as a form of embodied cognition, as a means of developing multidirectional, multisensory attentiveness, as a way to school a subjectivity capable of continually reassessing its relations to others and renegotiating its position in the world. If anything it will be this, she maintains, that brings forth a "future ground" – or at least a ground different from the one we're standing on now, mired as it is in myths of linear progress and constant growth.

As in many of her recent performative works, such as *Aggregate* (2017–2019) and *Encyclopedia of Relations* (2022), Pirici's new work, *Attune*, is grounded in the practice of *thinkmoving*. Indeed, her expansive environment at Hamburger Bahnhof takes up many of the same themes and artistic strategies as earlier pieces. Yet the cool, equally archaic and

und Musik, darunter polyfone Originalkompositionen Piricis für Gesang, sondern erstmals auch aus aktiven beziehungsweise zu aktivierenden skulpturalen Elementen, die menschlichen, mehr-als-menschlichen, aber auch maschinellen Akteuren einen Handlungsraum bieten.

Unter den raumgreifenden landschaftlichen Elementen befindet sich eine scheinbar aus dem Boden emporwachsende metallene pflanzenartige Struktur mit oberirdischem Wurzelsystem. Wie reife Früchte oder Blüten hängen von dessen zahlreichen Ranken unterschiedlich große Glaszylinder herab, in denen sich chemische wie physikalische Ereignisse anschaulich abspielen. An anderer Stelle breitet sich eine mehrere Eisenpfeiler umschließende Wanderdüne aus. Weiter hinten steht ein über eine halbrunde Rampe erreichbares, mit Kletterpflanzen bewachsenes Podest, auf dem ein großer, rätselhaft wirkender Findling thront. Hier, umgeben von vielgestaltigen Veranschaulichungen, in denen ebenfalls chemische und physikalische Reaktionen ablaufen, von Klängen und Bewegungen, spüren Performer*innen und Besucher*innen der Entstehung komplexer Strukturen nach: in belebter wie in unbelebter Materie. In Anlehnung an Anna Lowenhaupt Tsing, die in *Der Pilz am Ende der Welt. Über das Leben in den Ruinen des Kapitalismus* Landschaft als „Ausdruck von mehr-als-menschlichen Dramen" und somit als „ein radikales Instrument zur Relativierung menschlicher Hybris" auffasst, versteht sich Piricis Landschaft nicht als „Kulisse für historisches Handeln",[6] sondern sie handelt selbst. Nimmt man die Formierung dieser Landschaft in den Blick, sieht man, wie Menschen sich mit anderen Wesen und Dingen in „polyfonen Gefügen" verbinden, um mit verschiedenen, simultan ablaufenden Melodien und Rhythmen, mit Harmonien und Dissonanzen Welten mitzuerzeugen und mitzugestalten.[7] Jede „Stimme" in solchen veränderlichen „Liedern" kann ungehindert wandern, wie Merlin Sheldrake in *Verwobenes Leben. Wie Pilze unsere Welt formen und unsere Zukunft beeinflussen* schreibt. Und „doch kann man ihre Wanderungen nicht getrennt voneinan-

futuristic landscape she has developed consists not only of movements, gestures, language and original polyphonic scores for voice, choreographed and composed by the artist, but also of active and activatable sculptural elements. This new addition to her practice gives rise to a multilayered sphere of action for human, more-than-human, and machinic agencies.

Pirici's imaginary landscape comprises several elements, among them a sprawling metal vine-like structure that would appear to shoot up out of the ground. From the many tendrils of this vast vegetal machine, with its wildly bifurcating aerial root system, glass cylinders dangle down like ripe fruit or flowers, each displaying a different chemical or physical phenomenon. Diagonally opposite this bright, bubbling hybrid lies a light yellow-grey sand dune, which surrounds several iron pillars of the erstwhile railway station with its steadily shifting form. Spiraling up in the distance is a pale blue, vine-entangled platform, atop of which stands a large sandstone foundling. Here, amid the many chemical and physical processes, sounds and movements contributing to this environment, we become privy to the emergence of complex patterns and structures in animate and inanimate matter alike. Like Anna Lowenhaupt Tsing, who, in *The Mushroom at the End of the World: On the Possibility of Life*

---

5 Der Videovortrag *Future ground: A movement-lecture on nurturing different sensibilities, pleasures, and collaborations with land,* der anlässlich des Driving the Human Festival in Karlsruhe aufgenommen wurde, findet sich hier: https://zkm.de/de/media/video/Alexandra-Pirici-future-ground-a-movement-lecture-on-nurturing-different-sensibilities-pleasures-and, zuletzt abgerufen am 26. Februar 2024.
6 Anna Lowenhaupt Tsing, *Der Pilz am Ende der Welt. Über das Leben in den Ruinen des Kapitalismus* [2015], Berlin: Matthes & Seitz, 2018, S. 205.
7 Ebd., S. 42.

---

6 The video lecture *Future ground: A movement-lecture on nurturing different sensibilities, pleasures, and collaborations with land,* which was recorded for the Driving the Human Festival, is available online at: https://zkm.de/de/media/video/Alexandra-Pirici-future-ground-a-movement-lecture-on-nurturing-different-sensibilities-pleasures-and, last accessed February 26, 2024.

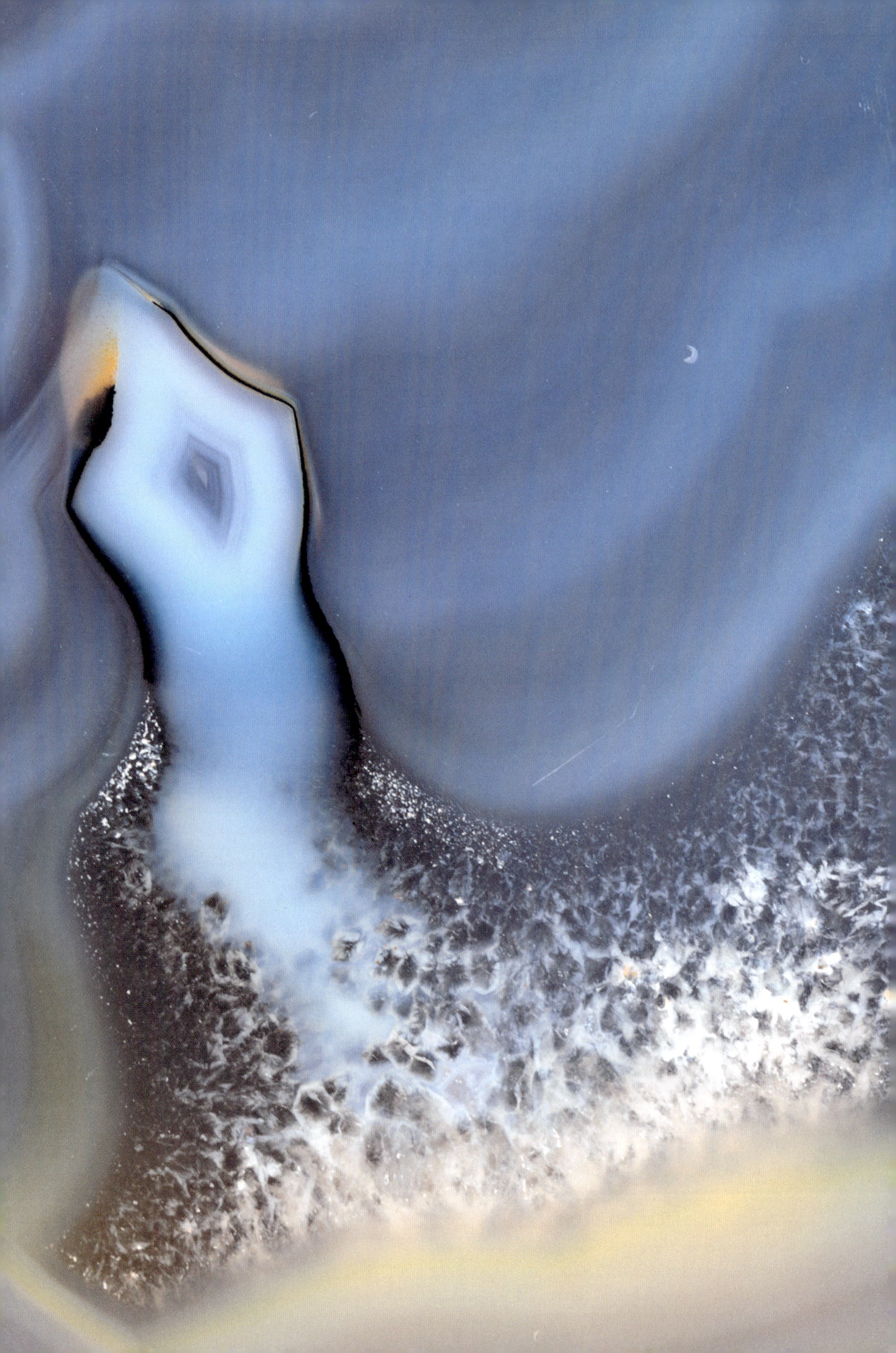

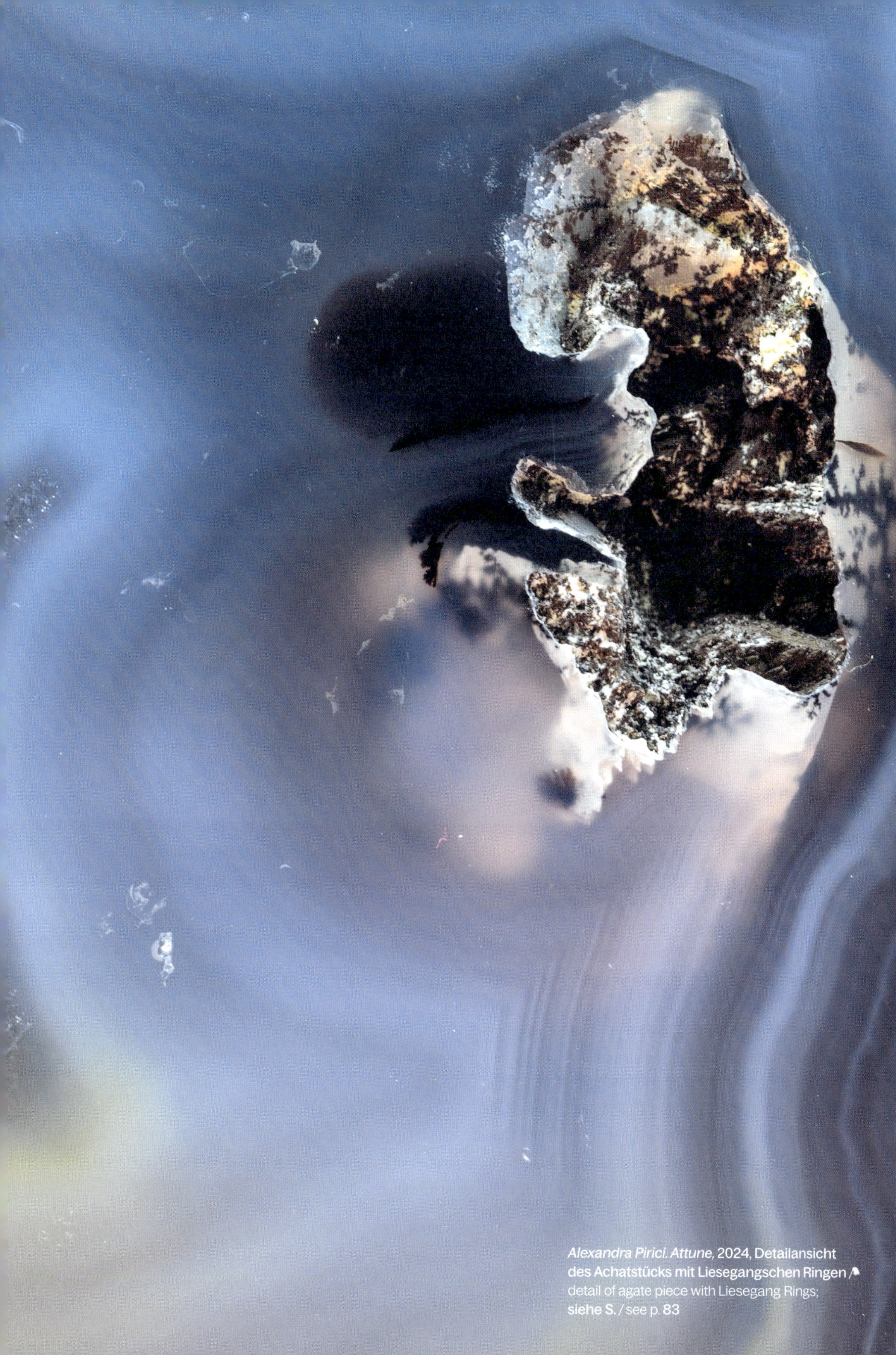

Alexandra Pirici. Attune, 2024, Detailansicht
des Achatstücks mit Liesegangschen Ringen /
detail of agate piece with Liesegang Rings;
siehe S. / see p. 83

der betrachten. Es gibt kein Leitmotiv. Es gibt keine zentrale Planung. Dennoch erwächst daraus eine Form."[8]

Die chemischen Reaktionen, mineralischen Formationen und physikalischen Phänomene, die in Piricis „polyfonem Gefüge" neben lebenden Körpern auftreten, laden die Besucher*innen dazu ein, über Materie zu reflektieren, die aktiv ist und sich selbst strukturiert. Wie von Donna Haraway in *Unruhig bleiben. Die Verwandtschaft der Arten im Chthuluzän* beschrieben, veranschaulichen sie in einem artenübergreifenden Gedeihen, einem „Sich-verwandt-machen" oder „Mit-werden",[9] wie menschliche und anders- oder mehr-als-menschliche Wesen und Dinge einander ähneln, sich gegenseitig beeinflussen und aufeinander einstellen. Im Mittelpunkt stehen dabei physikalische, biochemische, mathematische, künstlerische und gesellschaftliche Prozesse der Selbstorganisation, die seit der Popularisierung der Chaostheorie in den 1980er-Jahren in der Darstellung emergenter und chaotischer Systeme geläufig sind. Dazu zählen so unterschiedliche Phänomene wie oszillierende Reaktionen in der Chemie oder die Bewegungen der Körner einer Sanddüne, zellulare Automaten in der Mathematik oder das Schwarmverhalten von Fischen, Vögeln und Menschen.

Solche komplexen, sich spontan selbst organisierenden Systeme, die heute als wesentliche Motoren der Evolution betrachtet werden, bestehen aus Einzelteilen, die ohne externe oder zentrale Steuerung miteinander interagieren und so ein dynamisches übergeordnetes Ganzes bilden. Die Eigenschaften dieses Ganzen können durch die gründliche Untersuchung der Einzelteile weder verstanden noch vorhergesagt werden. Diese Erkenntnis untergräbt die tief verwurzelte westliche Vorstellung, das Universum sei ein messbares, mechanisches, sich seit dem Urknall linear entwickelndes Gefüge. Zwar hatte jene vorwiegend von René Descartes und Isaac Newton geprägte Weltanschauung erfolgreich einen „Dialog mit der Natur" eingeleitet. Doch deren reduktionistischer Blick und kalte, letztlich irreführende Metaphorik

in Capitalist Ruins, considers landscapes to be "sites for more-than-human dramas" and thus "radical tools for decentering human hubris", Pirici treats her own landscape not as a "backdrop for historical action" but as an agent in its own right.[7] Attune yourself to the environment unfolding around you and you may begin to read it as the set of "polyphonic assemblages" it is, as a confluence of melodies and rhythms, harmonies and dissonances that collectively bring forth and shape worlds.[8] As Merlin Sheldrake observes in *Entangled Life: How Fungi Make Our Worlds, Change Our Minds and Shape Our Futures*, each "voice" in the "song" of emergence is free to wander. Yet the wanderings of these voices "can't be seen as separate from the others. There is no main voice. There is no lead tune. There is no central planning. Nonetheless, a form emerges."[9]

The chemical reactions, mineral formations, and physical phenomena that appear alongside and engage with living bodies in Pirici's "polyphonic assemblages" invite us to explore matter as an active and self-structuring entity. Echoing Donna Haraway in *Staying with the Trouble: Making Kin in the Chthulucene*, they serve to illustrate – through multispecies flourishing and practices of "making kin" and "becoming-with"[10] – the ways in which human, other-than or more-than-human beings and things resemble, influence, and attune to one another. The examples of physical, biochemical, mathematical, artistic, and social processes of self-organization the artist chooses to explore are drawn from a repertory of phenomena that has commonly been used to elucidate the behavior of emergent and chaotic systems ever since the popularization of chaos theory in the 1980s. These include oscillating reactions in chemistry, the movements of grains of sand in a dune, cellular automata in mathematics, or the swarming of fish, birds, humans, and other animals.

Such complex, spontaneously self-organizing systems have come to be regarded as one of the driving forces of evolution. They consist of individual parts that interact with one another in unpredictable ways to form a dynamic whole – independent of any external or internal control. The properties of this new

haben die Menschen von der Natur isoliert, statt sie ihr näherzubringen, wie Prigogine und Stengers konstatieren: Aus „einem der größten Erfolge der menschlichen Vernunft" wurde die „traurige Wahrheit", dass die Wissenschaft alles, was sie berührt, entzaubert.[10] Eine Wissenschaft komplexer Systeme jedoch, die einen neuen „Dialog mit der Natur" ermöglicht, scheint imstande zu sein, das untergründige Gefühl der Entfremdung aufzuheben. Im Einklang mit Prigogine und Stengers spricht Piricis Werk davon, dass wir nicht mehr zwischen „einer Wissenschaft, die den Menschen zu einem Fremdling in einer entzauberten Welt macht, und dem wissenschaftsfeindlichen, irrationalen Protest" wählen müssen – zumal die Wissenschaft damit begonnen hat, die Komplexität der Prozesse „zu begreifen und zu beschreiben, aus denen die Welt besteht, mit der wir aufs engste vertraut sind, die natürliche Welt, in der Lebewesen und ihre Gemeinschaften sich gemeinsam entwickeln".[11]

Zurück in Berlin sehe ich die Konturen von Piricis werdendem Werk immer schärfer. Für die Künstlerin und ihre engsten Mitstreiter, Andrei Dinu und Bogdan-Constantin Enache, neigt sich eine Phase ausgedehnter chemischer Versuche dem Ende zu.

Die Reaktionen erweisen sich als reproduzierbar, skalierbar, bisweilen gar automatisierbar. Doch das wild wuchernde System ist bewusst ein offenes.

Eine berauschende Ungewissheit bleibt. Bald bricht die Künstlerin zum Ausstellungsaufbau Richtung Berlin auf. Bis dahin ist noch viel zu tun. Während ich diese letzten Sätze meines Textes schreibe, arbeitet Pirici an der Choreografie der performativen Handlungen und an der Komposition der Polyfonien, die sich im Laufe der Proben voraussichtlich noch verwandeln werden. Ein Spielraum für Improvisationen ist vorgesehen. Wird das Duett für Mensch und Findling, ein schon lang gehegtes Vorhaben, noch einfließen? Oder der Tanz für Sand und Mensch? Werden die Poesie des

dynamic whole can neither be understood nor predicted by examining the individual parts, no matter how thorough the analysis might be. This realization undermines the deep-seated western understanding of the universe as a quantifiable, mechanical entity to have evolved in a linear manner all the way from the Big Bang through to the present. Widely associated with René Descartes and Isaac Newton, this worldview may well have initiated a "dialogue with nature". Yet the reductionist vision and cold, ultimately misleading metaphors that inform it, have, as Prigogine and Stengers observe, isolated humans from nature rather than bringing them closer to it: what was initially a "triumph of human reason" turned into the "sad truth" that "science debased everything it touched".[11] A science of complexity, on the other hand, paves the way for a new "dialogue with nature" which, if Prigogine and Stengers are right, may well mitigate this overriding – and often enough debilitating – sense of estrangement. In line with their contention, Pirici argues that we no longer have to choose between "a science that reduces man to being a stranger in a disenchanted world" on the one hand, or "antiscientific, irrational protests" on the other. This is because scientists are beginning to understand the complexity of the "processes forming the world with which we are

8 Merlin Sheldrake, *Verwobenes Leben. Wie Pilze unsere Welt formen und unsere Zukunft beeinflussen,* Berlin: Ullstein, 2020, S. 86.

9 Donna Haraway, *Unruhig bleiben. Die Verwandtschaft der Arten im Chthuluzän* [2016], Frankfurt am Main / New York: Campus, 2018, S. 15, 52.

10 Prigogine & Stengers, *Dialog mit der Natur,* S. 16.

11 Ebd.

7 Anna Lowenhaupt Tsing, *The Mushroom at the End of the World: On the Possibility of Life in Capitalist Ruins,* Princeton: Princeton University Press, 2015, p.152.

8 Ibid., p.24.

9 Merlin Sheldrake, *Entangled Life: How Fungi Make Our Worlds, Change Our Minds and Shape Our Futures,* New York: Random House, 2020, p.54.

10 Donna J. Haraway, *Staying with the Trouble: Making Kin in the Chthulucene,* Durham / London: Duke University Press, 2010, pp.2, 34.

11 Prigogine & Stengers, *Order out of Chaos,* p.36.

kalten Steins, der leise Gesang der Pflanzen zu vernehmen sein? In der Weite der Nacht kreisen meine Gedanken immer wieder um Ursula K. Le Guins Vorstellung eines „Tanzes am Rande der Welt", der *Always Coming Home* zugrunde liegt – ihrer wegweisenden „Archäologie der Zukunft", in der sie Lyrik, Erzählung, Fabel, Gesang und Kunst ineinander verwebt. Um eine neue Welt zu erschaffen, so Le Guin, „muss man gewiss mit einer alten Welt beginnen. Um eine Welt zu finden, muss man vielleicht erst eine verloren haben. Muss man vielleicht selbst verloren sein. Der Welterneuerungstanz, der Tanz, der die Welt geschaffen hat, wurde immer schon hier getanzt, am Rand, am Saum, an der nebelverhangenen Küste."[12] Eine solche noch zu erkundende Küste, einen Ort des Weltverlusts wie der -erneuerung, scheint Pirici mit ihrer Arbeit anzusteuern. Oder gleitet sie eher an ihr entlang?

Die erkenntnistheoretische Umorientierung, die mit dem Verzicht auf lineare Denkmodelle einhergeht, versetzt uns in ein noch gründlich zu erforschendes Terrain, einen „future ground", der in der Abwesenheit einer wie auch immer gearteten Teleologie neue Künste, neue Techniken, neue Instrumente der Wahrnehmung, der Metaphernbildung wie der Erzählung erfordert. Wie, mit Anna Lowenhaupt Tsing gefragt, können wir über „progressive" politische Anliegen wie soziale Gerechtigkeit nachdenken, ohne uns der Vorstellung des „Fortschritts" zu bedienen?[13]

Wie lässt sich mit der Annahme umgehen, dass gerade die Unbestimmtheit, die Prekarität, das Unvorhersehbare, die Unkontrollierbarkeit das Leben erst ermöglichen?

Während für viele solche Ungewissheit Gefühle wie Angst und Unbehagen erzeugt, scheint Pirici mit ihrer im *Thinkmoving* gründenden Arbeit *Attune* gerade das Unbekannte als vielversprechende Offenheit, kollektiv anzugehende Aufgabe, als Beginn einer gemeinsam zu entwickelnden Erzählung zu

most familiar, the natural world in which living creatures and their societies develop".[12]

Back in Berlin, I see the contours of Pirici's work growing sharper by the day. As I write, a lengthy phase of chemical experiments for the artist and her closest collaborators, Andrei Dinu and Bogdan-Constantin Enache, is drawing to a close. The oscillating chemical reaction they have been testing has proven to be reproducible, scalable, and even automatable. Yet the rampant system they've come up with is a consciously open one, such that the thrill of uncertainty remains. Soon the artist will be making her way to Berlin to begin installing her exhibition. There is still much to be done before she arrives. As I formulate these final few paragraphs of my introduction, Pirici is working intensely to finish choreographing the performative action and composing the original polyphonies. Both will no doubt change over the course of the rehearsals. There is room, the artist says, for improvisation. Will Pirici hold onto her long-envisaged duet for human being and stone, I wonder. Or to the dance for performers and sand? Will the cold poetry of the stone, will the quiet song of the plants still play a role? As I sit conjuring up the work to come in the depths of the night, my thoughts keep circling back to Ursula K. Le Guin and her vision of "dancing at the edge of the world". It was this idea that guided her in writing *Always Coming Home*, her incisive "archaeology of the future", which, much as I imagine Pirici's new work will do, masterfully interweaves poetry, narrative, fable, song, and art. To make a new world, Le Guin writes, "you start with an old one, certainly. To find a world, maybe you have to have lost one. Maybe you have to be lost. The dance of renewal, the dance that made the world, was always danced here at the edge of things, on the brink, on the foggy coast."[13] If I am not mistaken, it seems to be a coast of this kind, a captivatingly unfamiliar place of world loss and renewal, that Pirici seems to be heading towards, or charting, with her all-consuming, fully immersive exploration.

The epistemological reorientation that goes hand in hand with the abandonment of linear models of thought plunges us headlong into a terrain that has yet to be thoroughly surveyed. It

empfinden. Eine solche Haltung geht für sie von Caspar David Friedrichs 1822 entstandenem Gemälde *Mondaufgang am Meer* aus, das in der Alten Nationalgalerie in Berlin hängt.[14] Zwei Frauen, die der Natur angehören, welche sie zugleich aufmerksam betrachten, sitzen ebenso wie der Mann neben ihnen ruhig auf einem Felsen und schauen auf das Meer hinaus. Ohne zu wissen, was die auf sie zugleitenden Schiffe mit sich bringen, sehen sie ihnen zuversichtlich, friedlich, erwartungsvoll entgegen.

thrusts us onto a "future ground" which, thwarting all forms of teleology, calls for new arts and new technologies, new modes of perception, new metaphors, and new narratives. Yet how, to return to the thought of Anna Lowenhaupt Tsing, might we think about "progressive" political concerns such as social justice without resorting to tropes of linear progress?[14] How might we come to terms with the notion that indeterminacy, precariousness, unpredictability, and uncontrollability may well be what make life possible in the first place? Whereas many people respond to such uncertainty with fear and unease, Pirici imbues it with hope and promise. By grounding her new work in the inherently open-ended, social practice of *thinkmoving*, she treats the realm of the unforeseeable as a task to be tackled together, as the beginning of a narrative to be jointly developed, of a story to be collectively told. The artist finds such an attitude captured in Caspar David Friedrich's painting *Mondaufgang am Meer* (Moonrise over the Sea, 1822), which hangs in the Alte Nationalgalerie in Berlin.[15] In the painting two women sit quietly on a rock calmly gazing out to sea. Like the man seated beside them, they seem to be an integral part of the natural surroundings they are attentively observing. Having no way of knowing what the ships sailing towards them might be bringing, the women nonetheless face them with confidence, quiet serenity and a keen sense of anticipation.

12 Ursula K. Le Guin, „Welten bauen" [1981] in: dies., *Immer nach Hause*, Wittenberge: Carcosa Verlag, 2023, S. 749–752, hier S. 752.
13 Tsing, *Der Pilz am Ende der Welt*, S. 43.
14 Alexandra Pirici, „Die Möglichkeit von Frieden" in: *Monopol*, 23. Februar 2022, https://www.monopol-magazin.de/alte-meister-alexandra-pirici, zuletzt abgerufen am 26. Februar 2024.

12 Ibid.
13 Ursula K. Le Guin, *Dancing at the Edge of the World: Thoughts on Words, Women, Places*, New York: Grove Press, 1989, p.48.
14 Tsing, *The Mushroom at the End of the World*, p.24.
15 Alexandra Pirici, "Alexandra Pirici on Casper David Friedrich's 'Moonrise Over the Sea'" in: *Monopol*, February 22, 2017, https://www.monopol-magazin.de/alexandra-pirici-casper-david-friedrichs moonrise over sea, last accessed February 26, 2024.

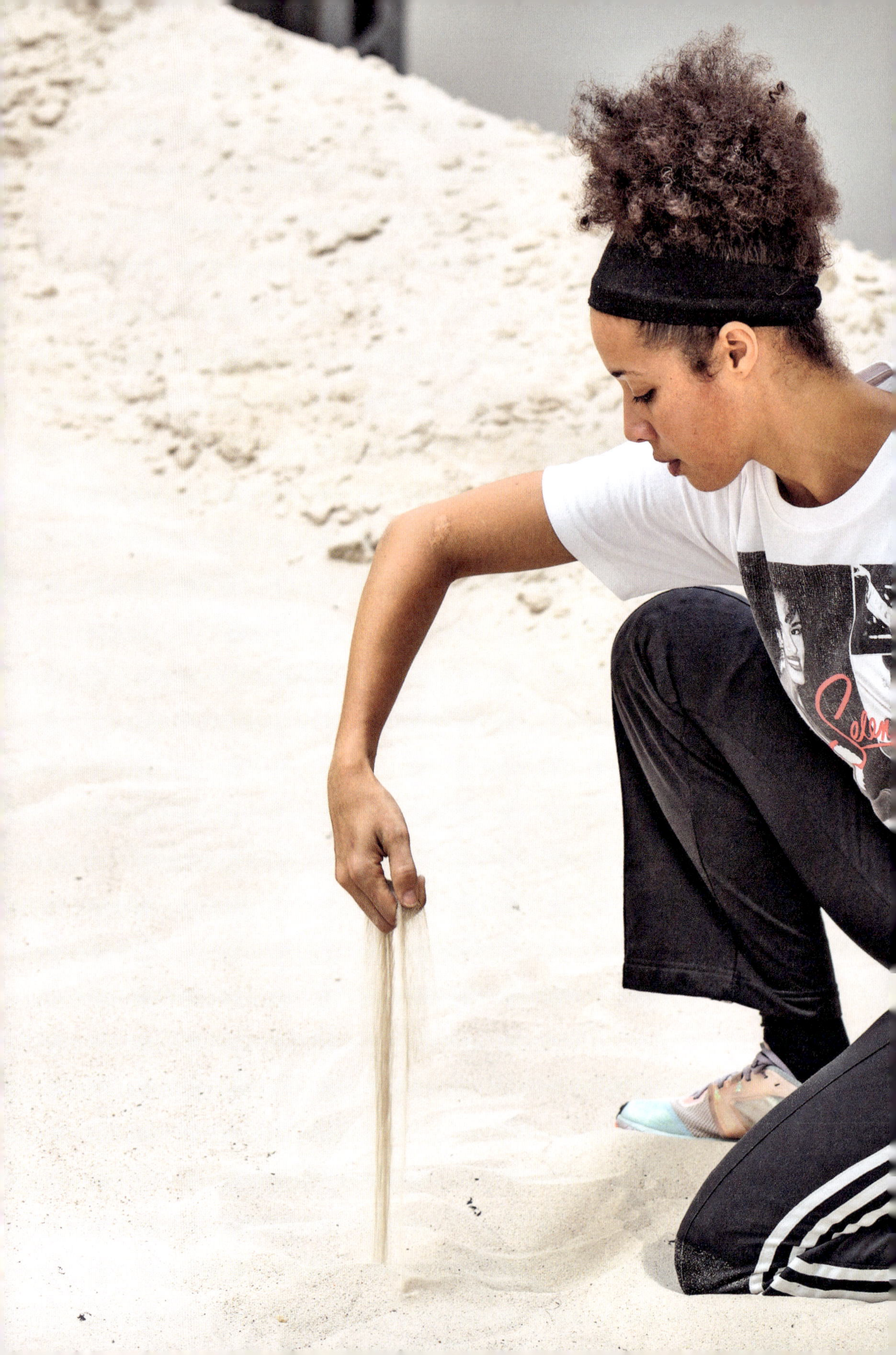

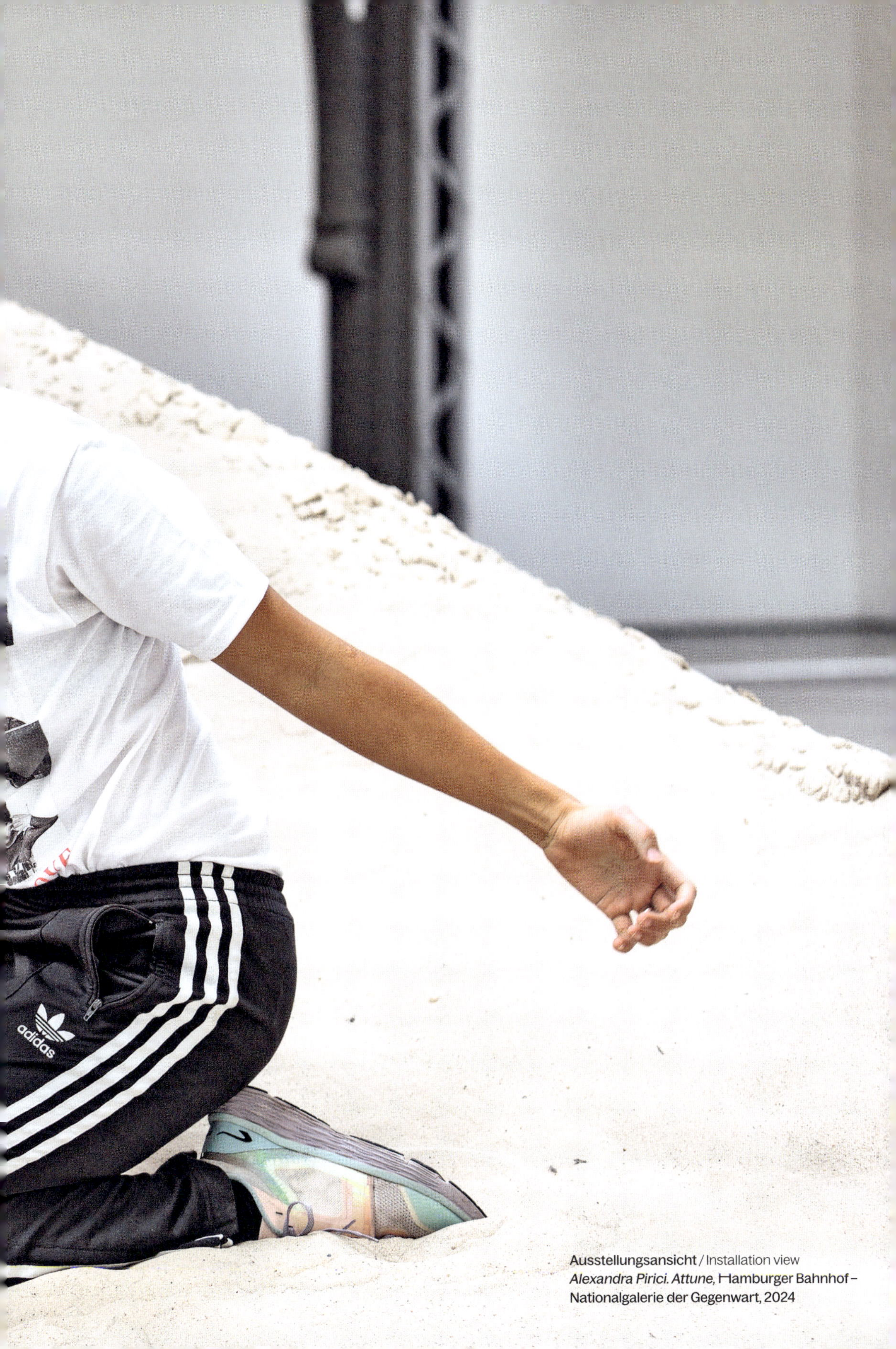

Ausstellungsansicht / Installation view
Alexandra Pirici. Attune, Hamburger Bahnhof –
Nationalgalerie der Gegenwart, 2024

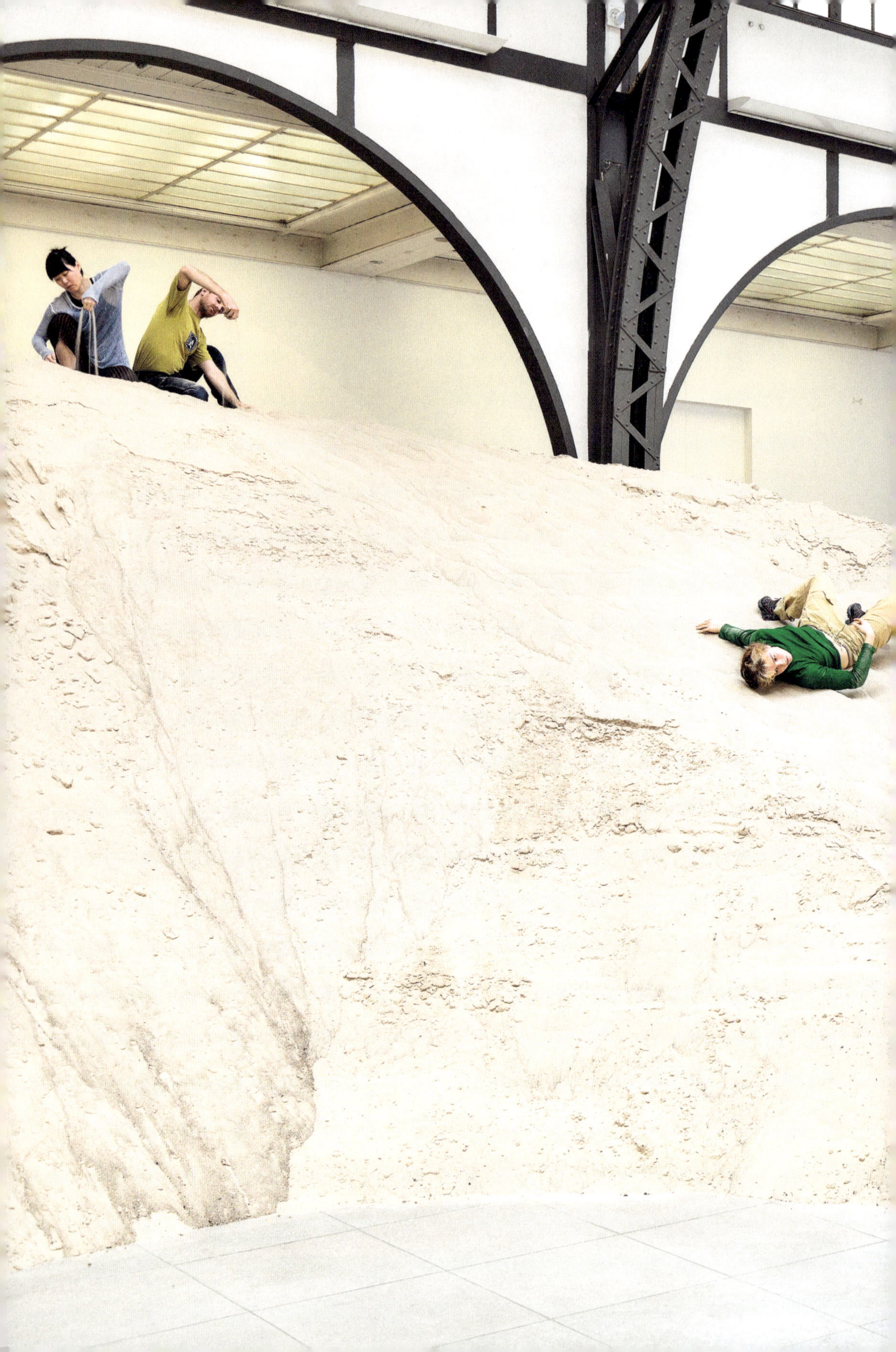

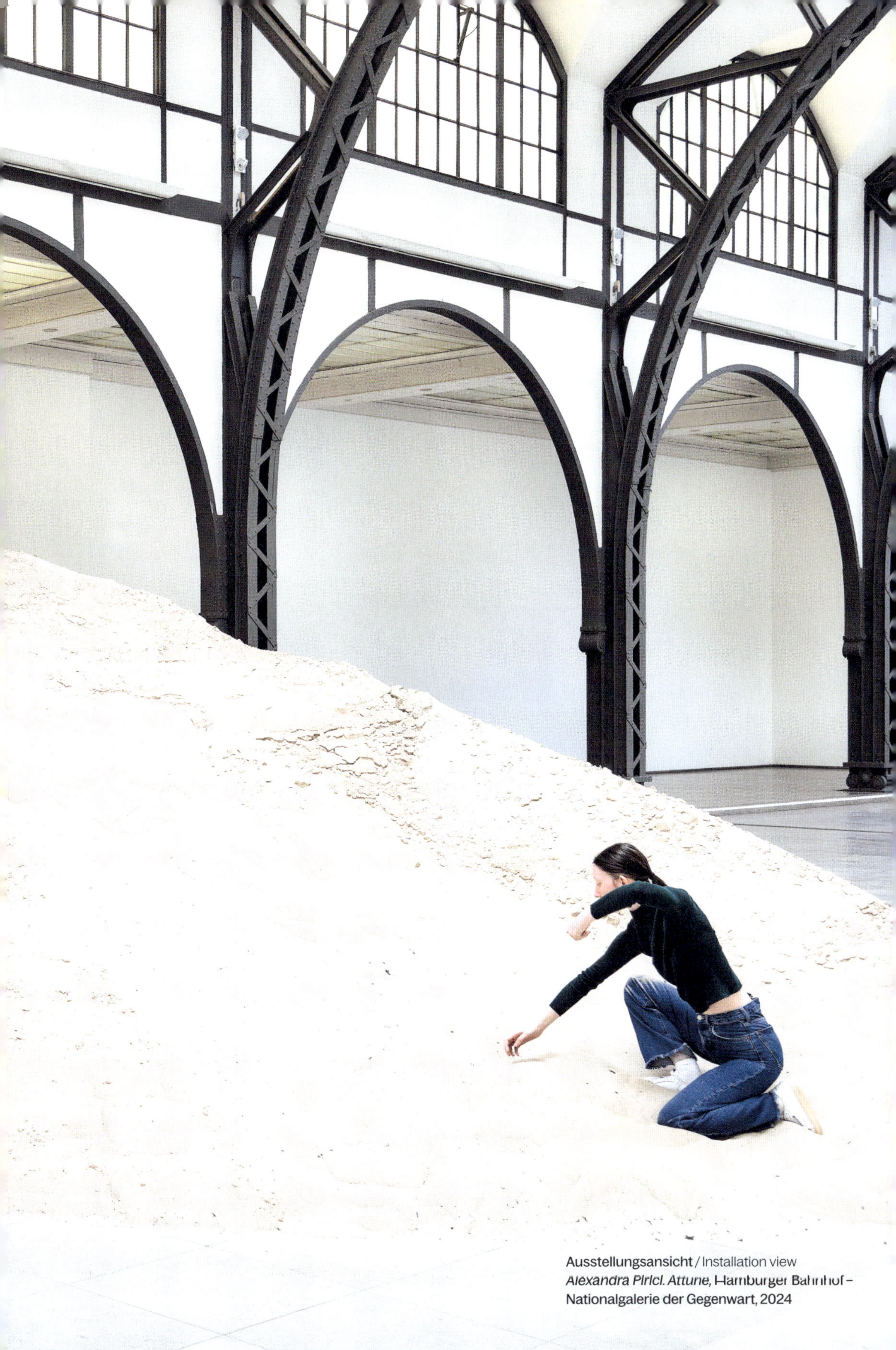

Ausstellungsansicht / Installation view
Alexandra Pirici. Attune, Hamburger Bahnhof –
Nationalgalerie der Gegenwart, 2024

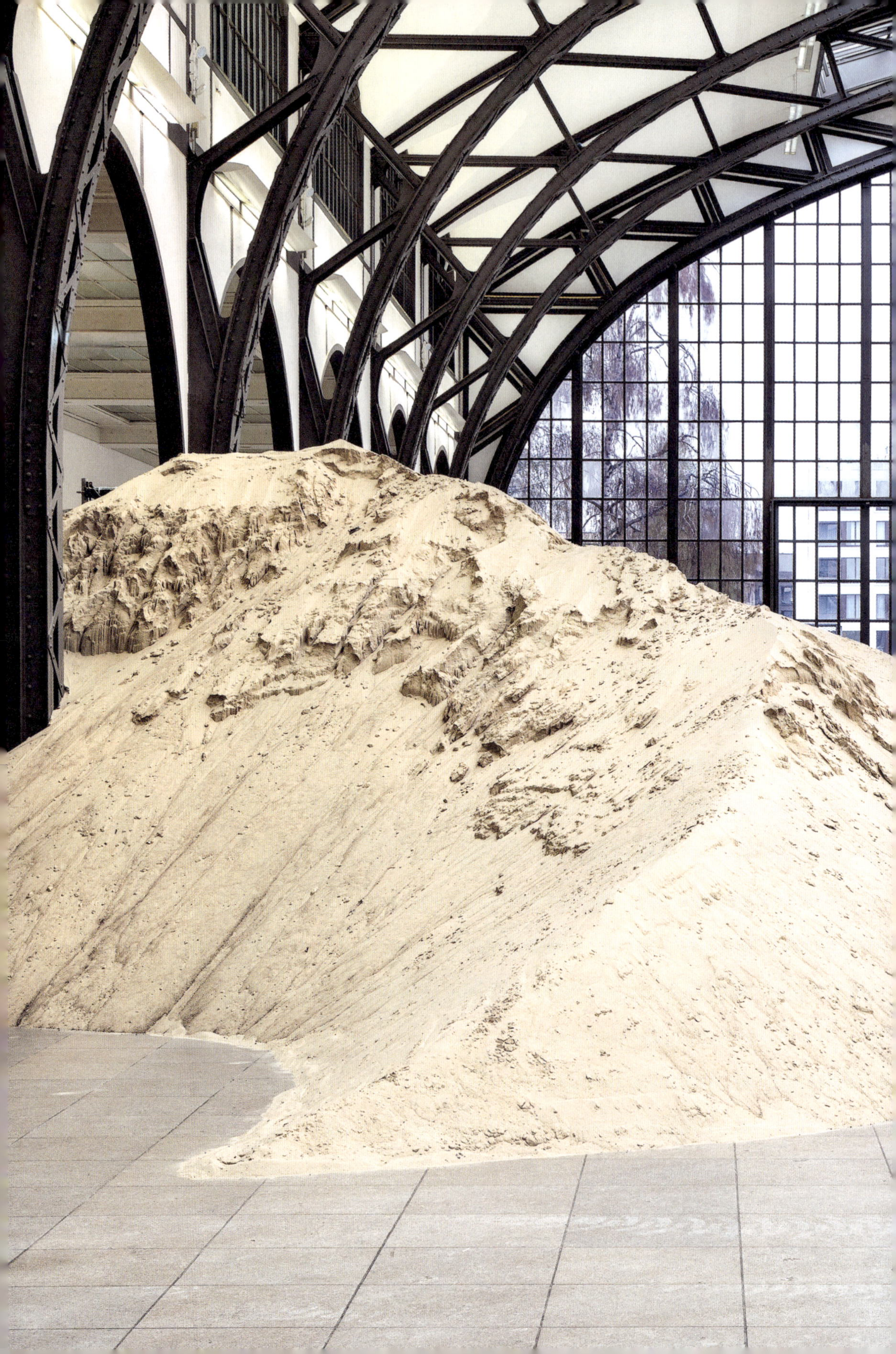

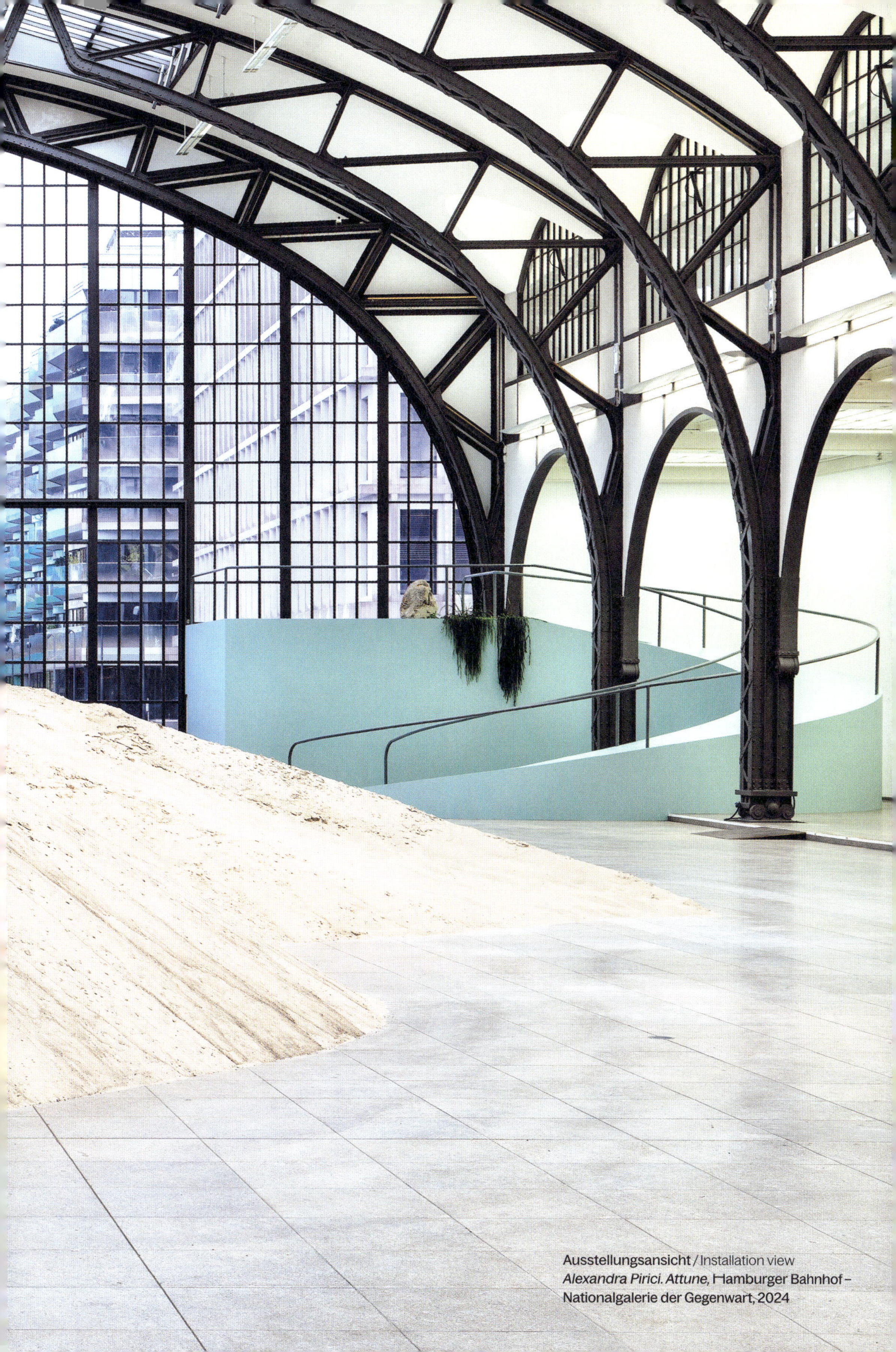

Ausstellungsansicht / Installation view
Alexandra Pirici. Attune, Hamburger Bahnhof –
Nationalgalerie der Gegenwart, 2024

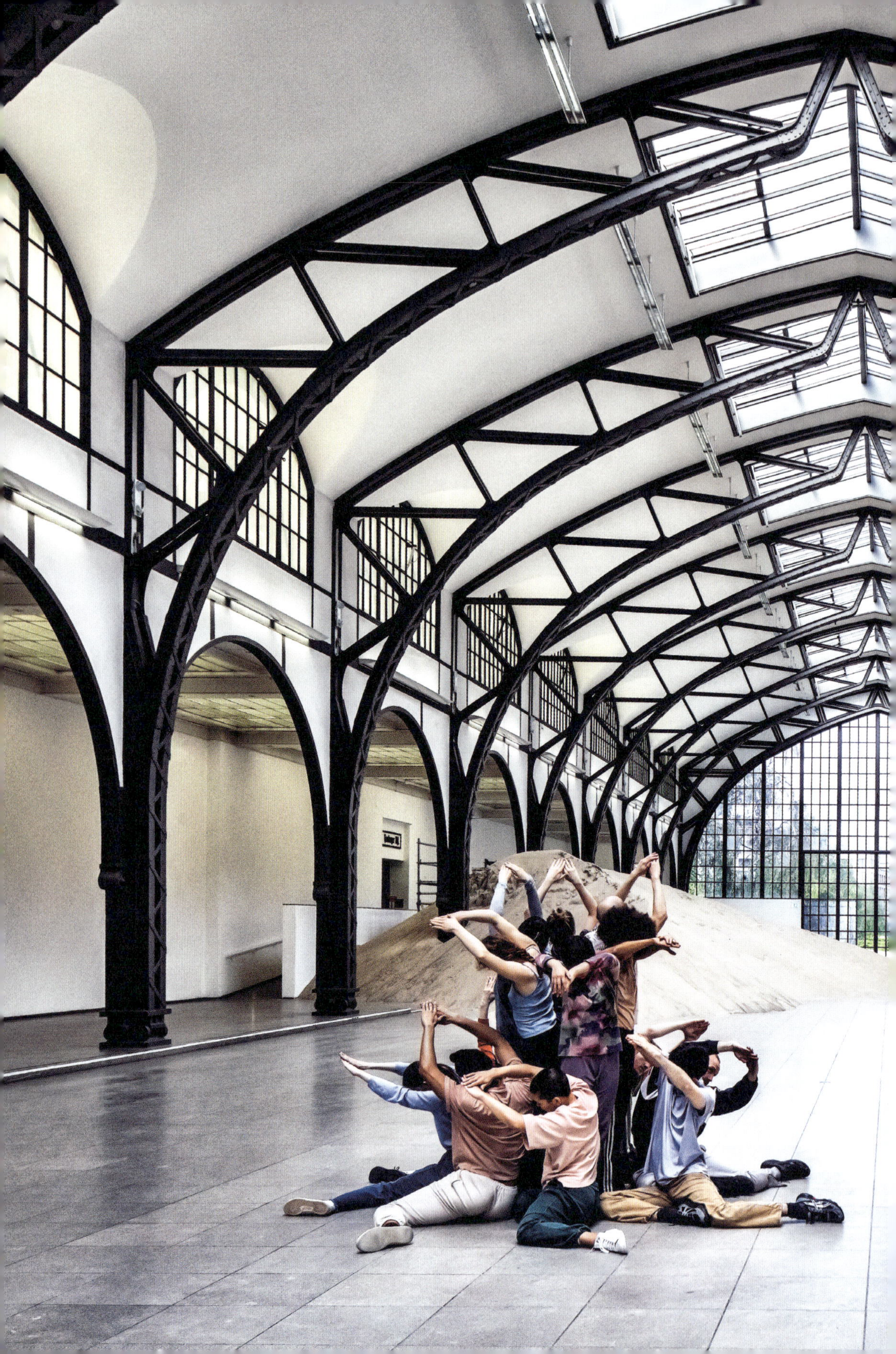

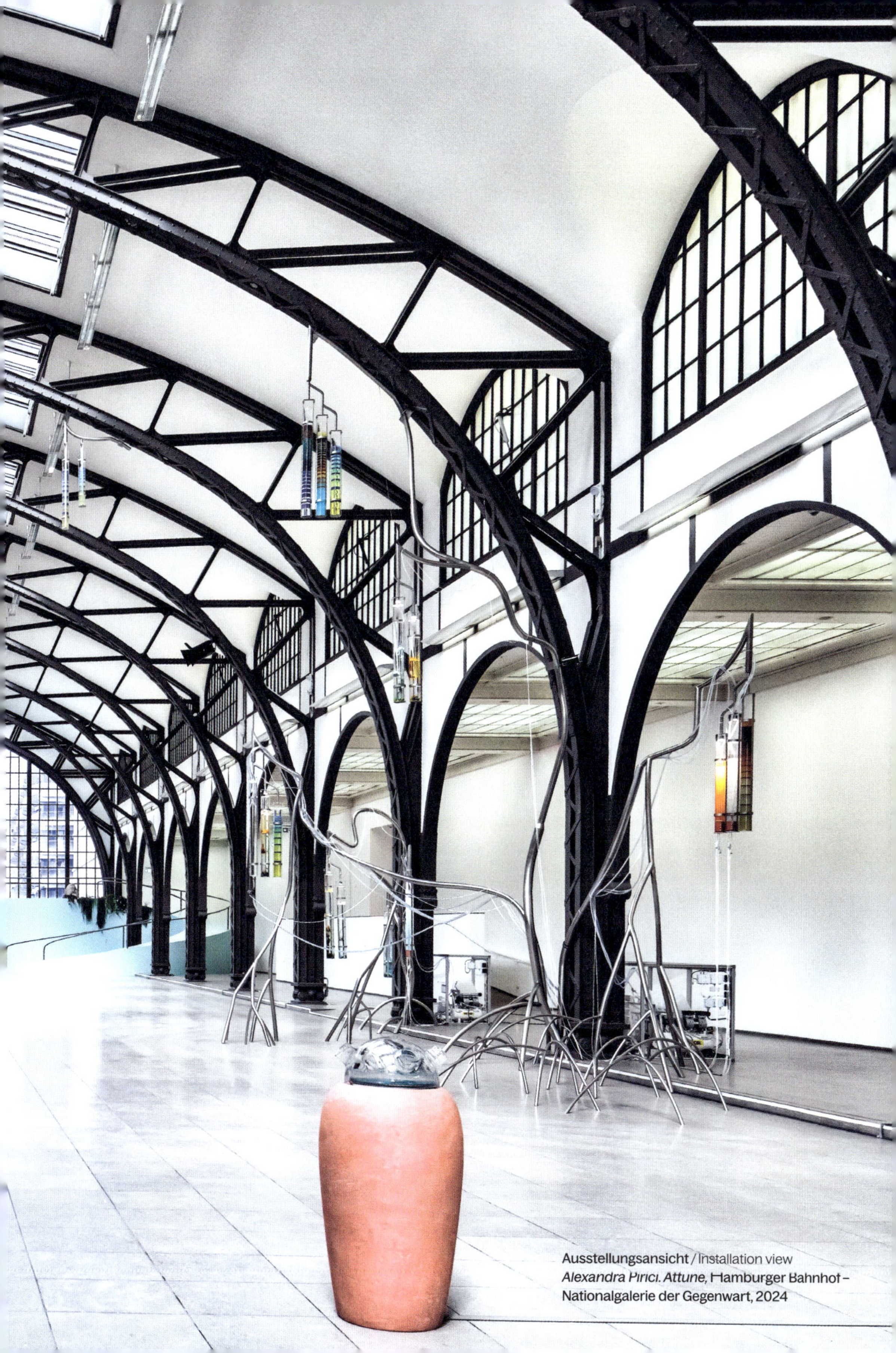

Ausstellungsansicht / Installation view
Alexandra Pirici. Attune, Hamburger Bahnhof –
Nationalgalerie der Gegenwart, 2024

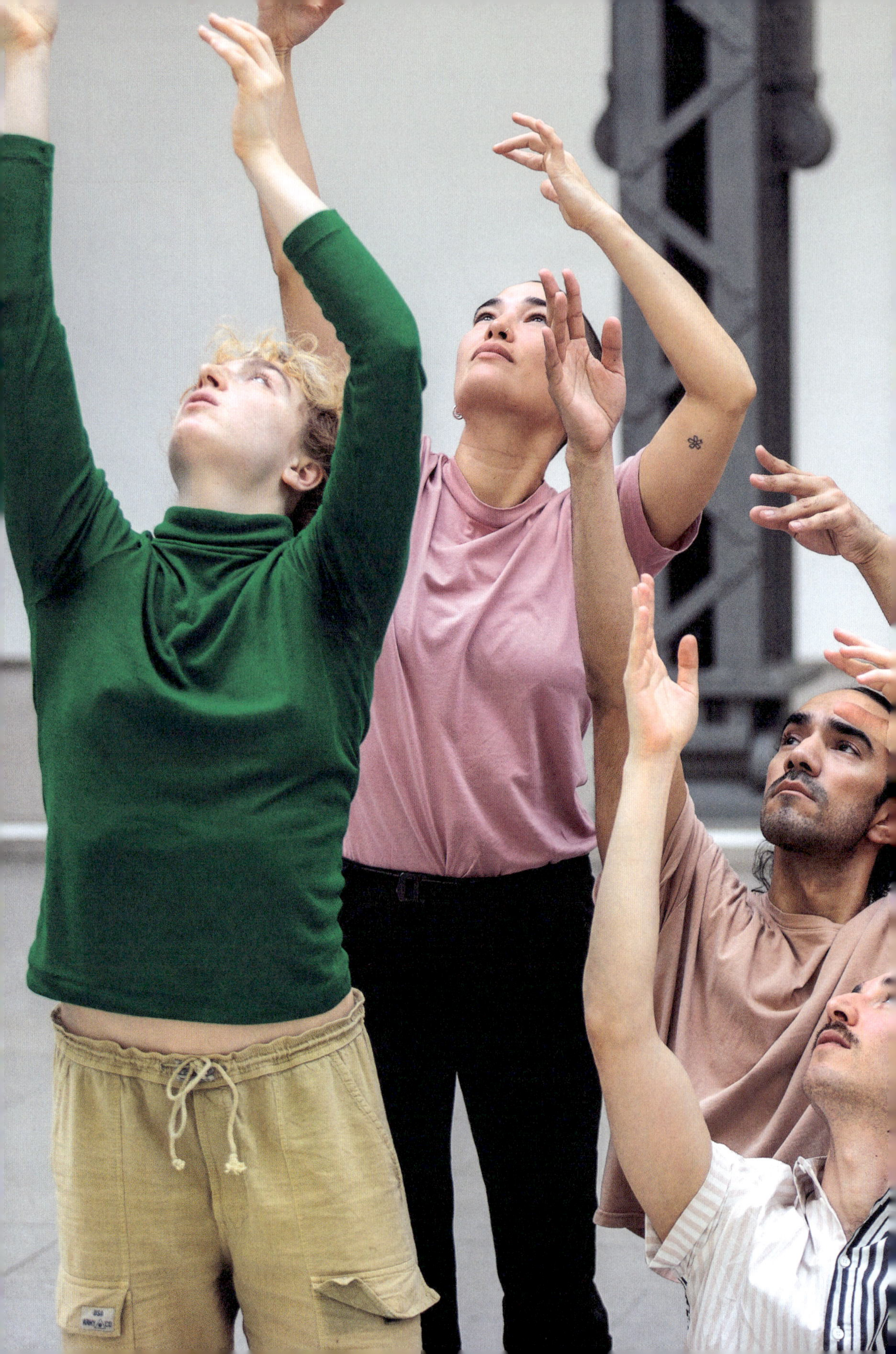

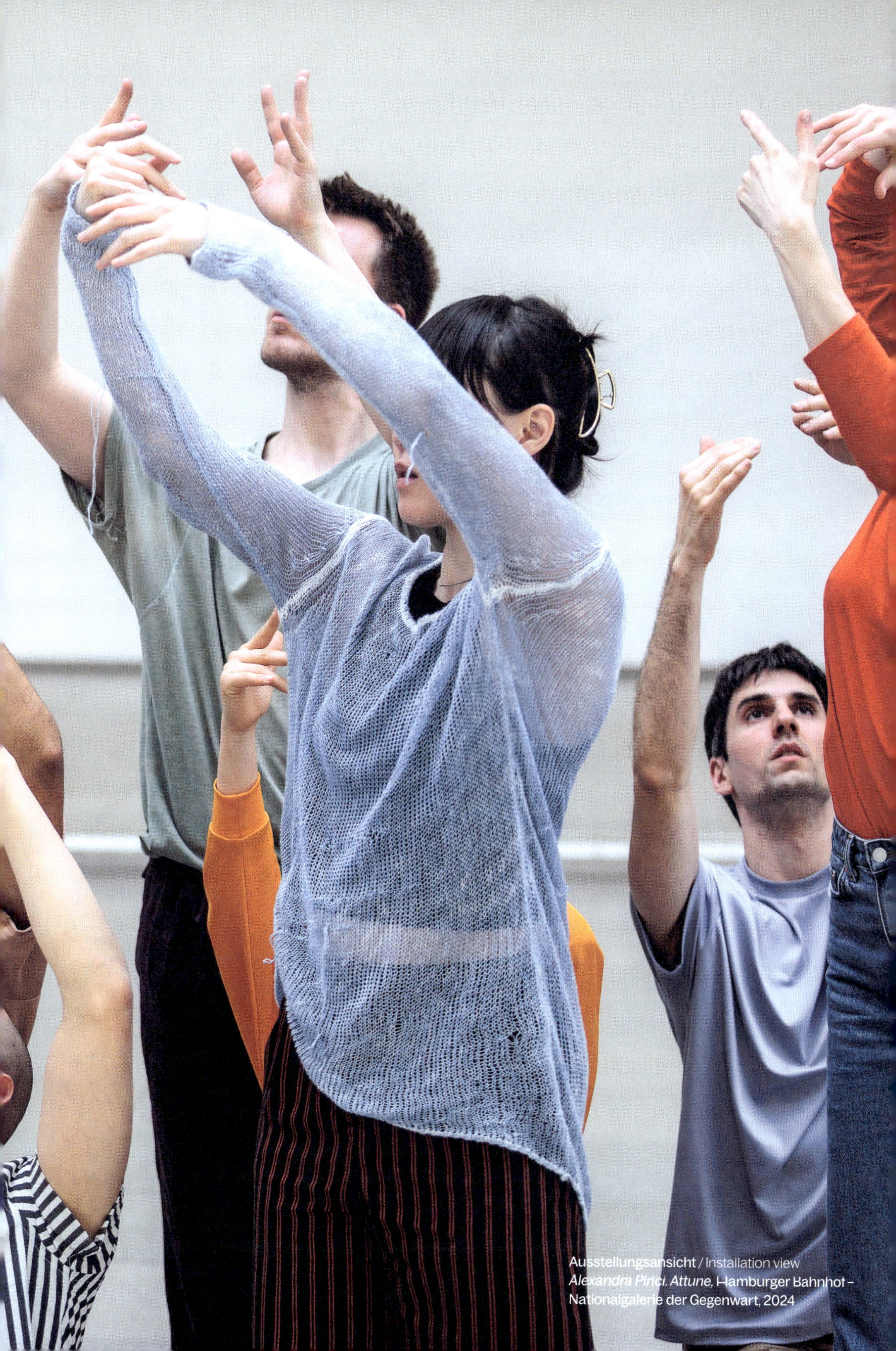

Ausstellungsansicht / Installation view
Alexandra Pirici. Attune, Hamburger Bahnhof –
Nationalgalerie der Gegenwart, 2024

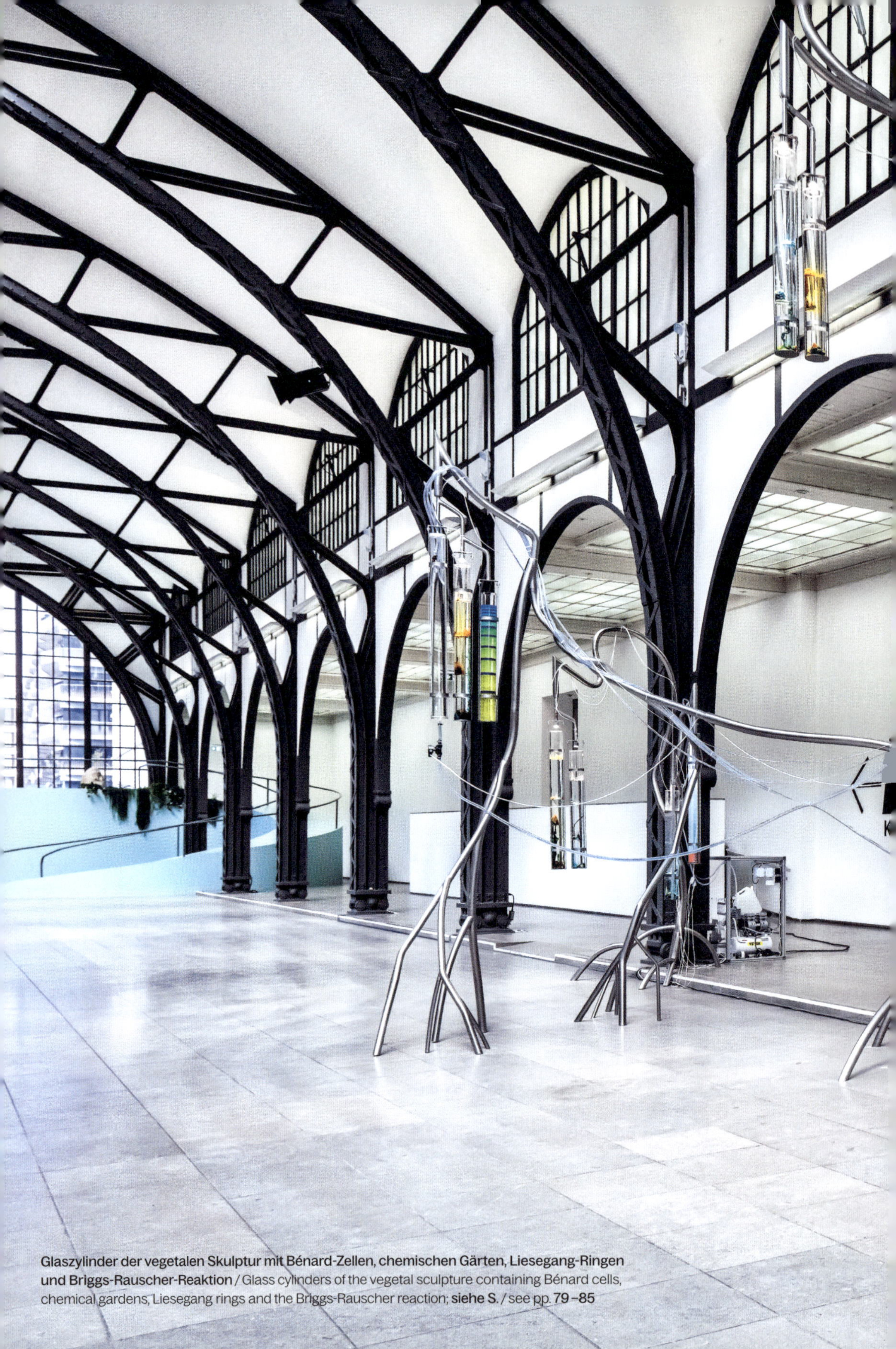

Glaszylinder der vegetalen Skulptur mit Bénard-Zellen, chemischen Gärten, Liesegang-Ringen und Briggs-Rauscher-Reaktion / Glass cylinders of the vegetal sculpture containing Bénard cells, chemical gardens, Liesegang rings and the Briggs-Rauscher reaction; **siehe S.** / see pp. **79–85**

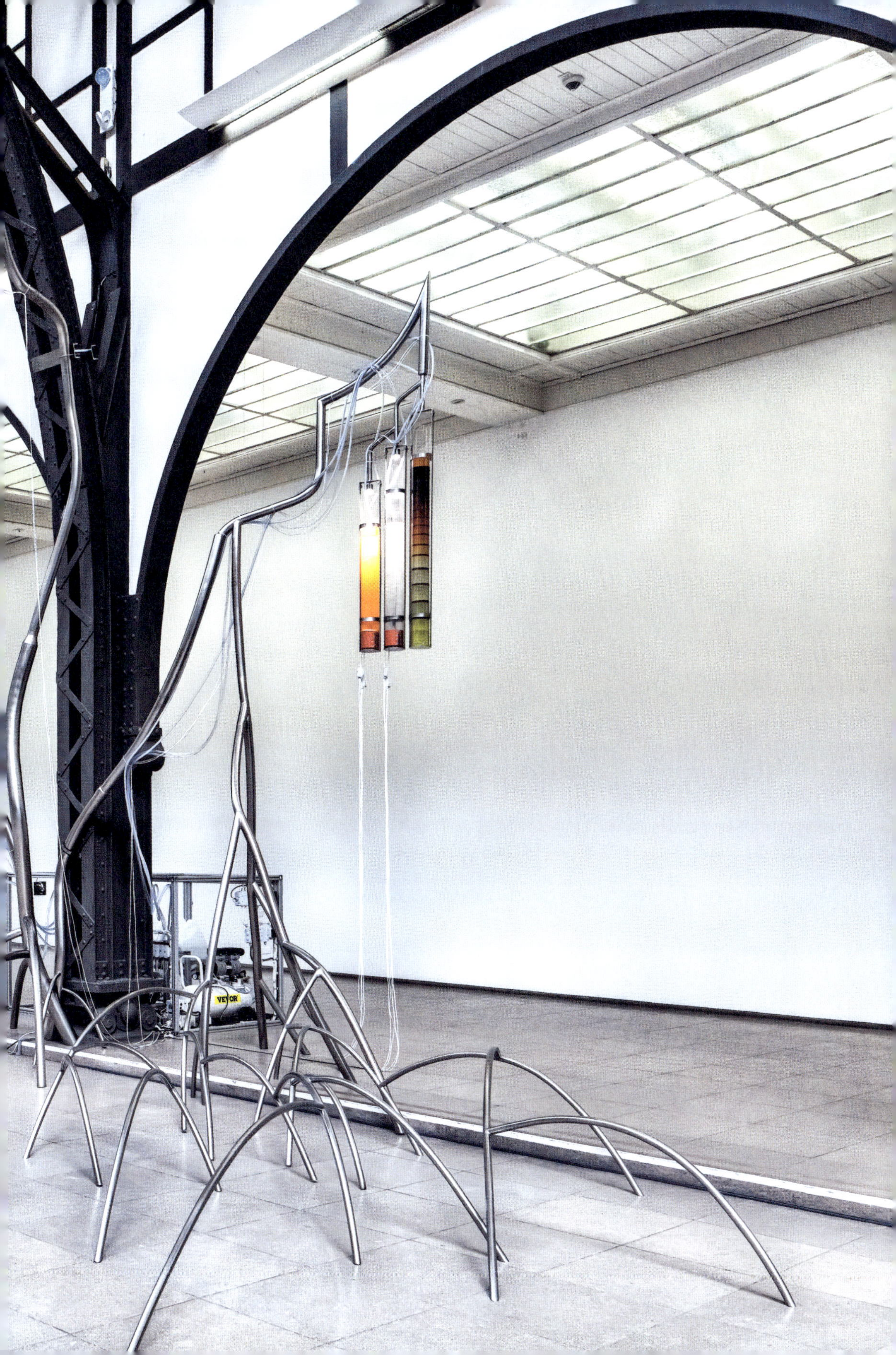

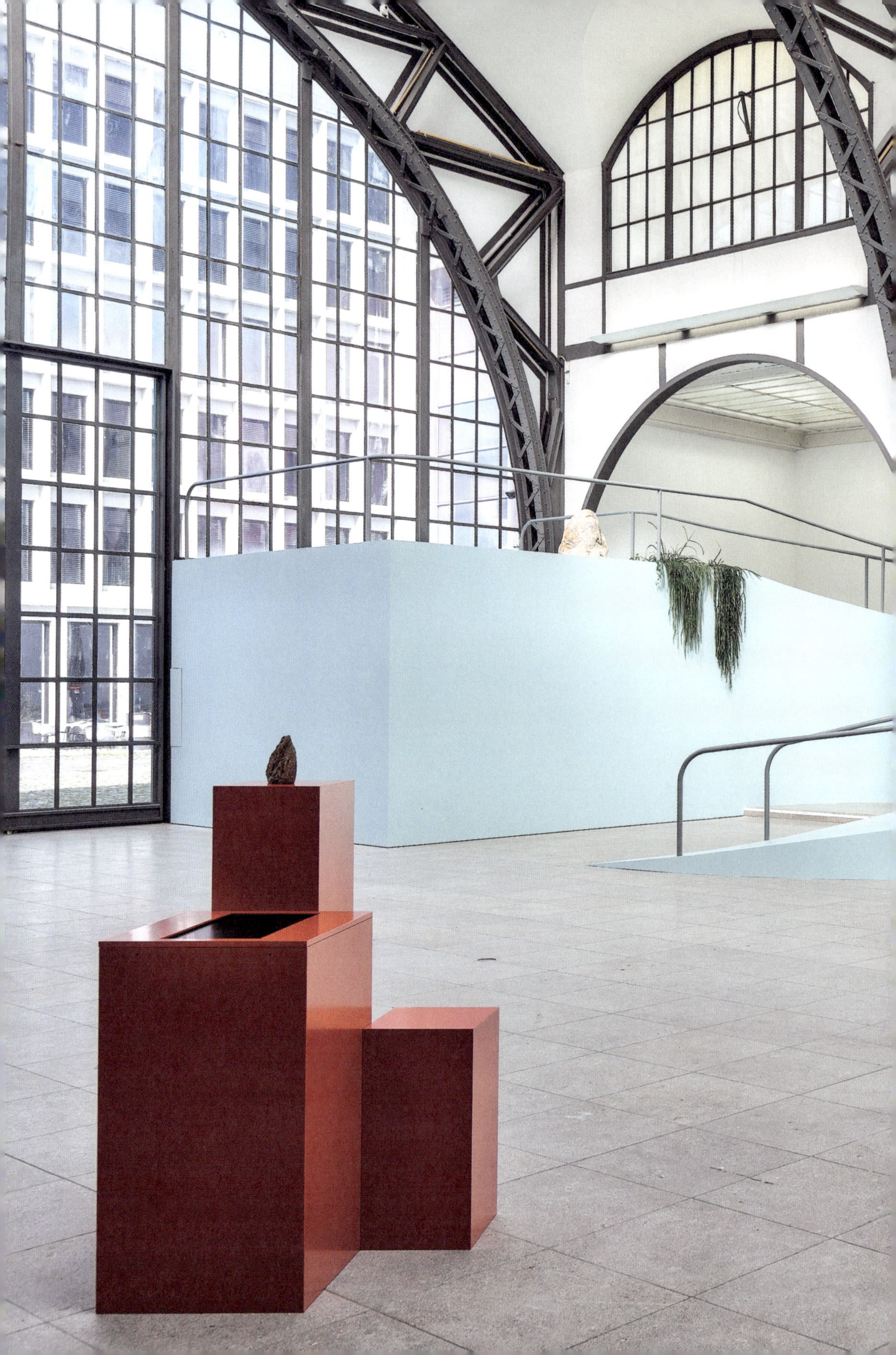

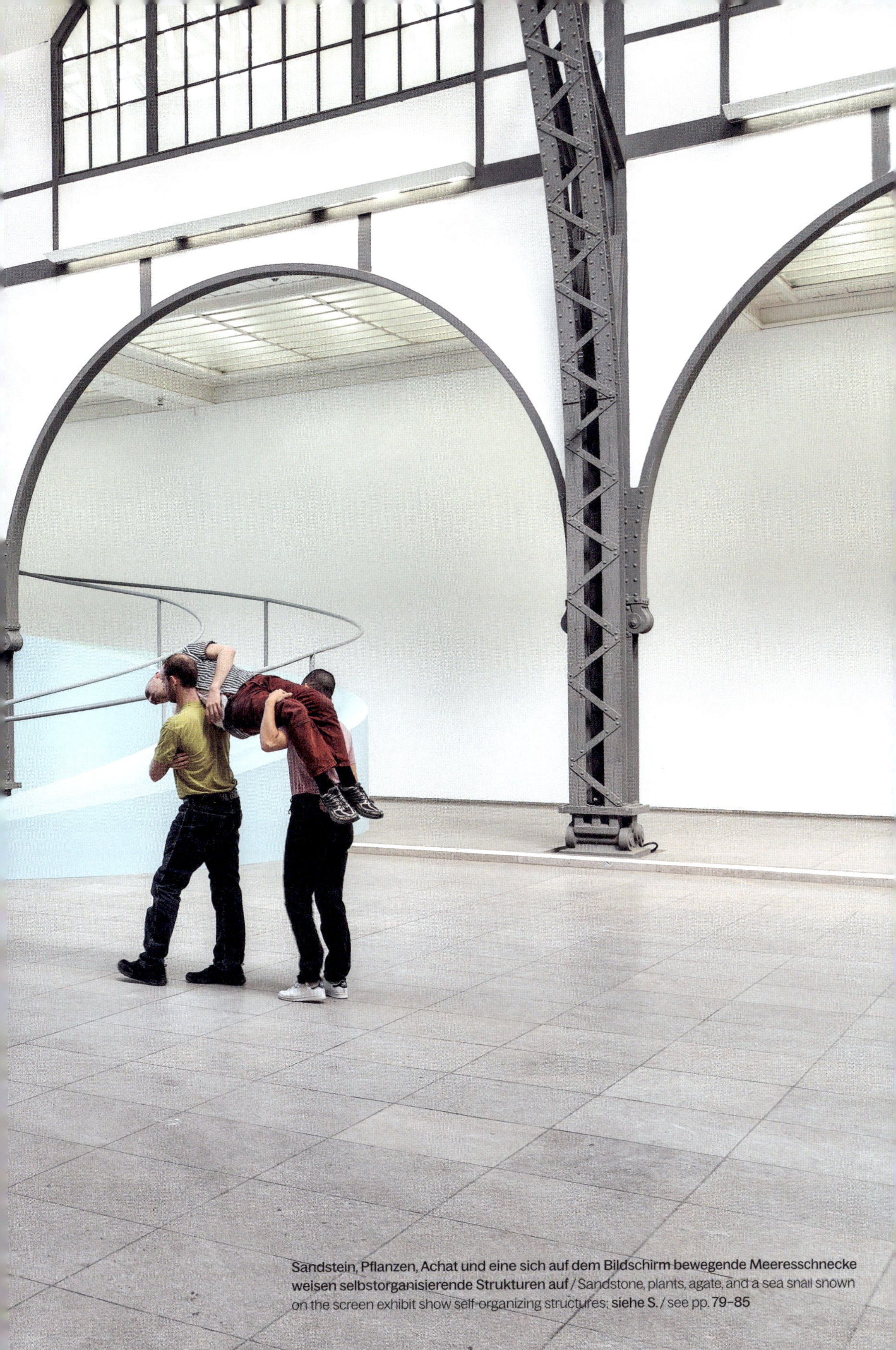

Sandstein, Pflanzen, Achat und eine sich auf dem Bildschirm bewegende Meeresschnecke weisen selbstorganisierende Strukturen auf / Sandstone, plants, agate, and a sea snail shown on the screen exhibit show self-organizing structures; siehe S. / see pp. 79–85

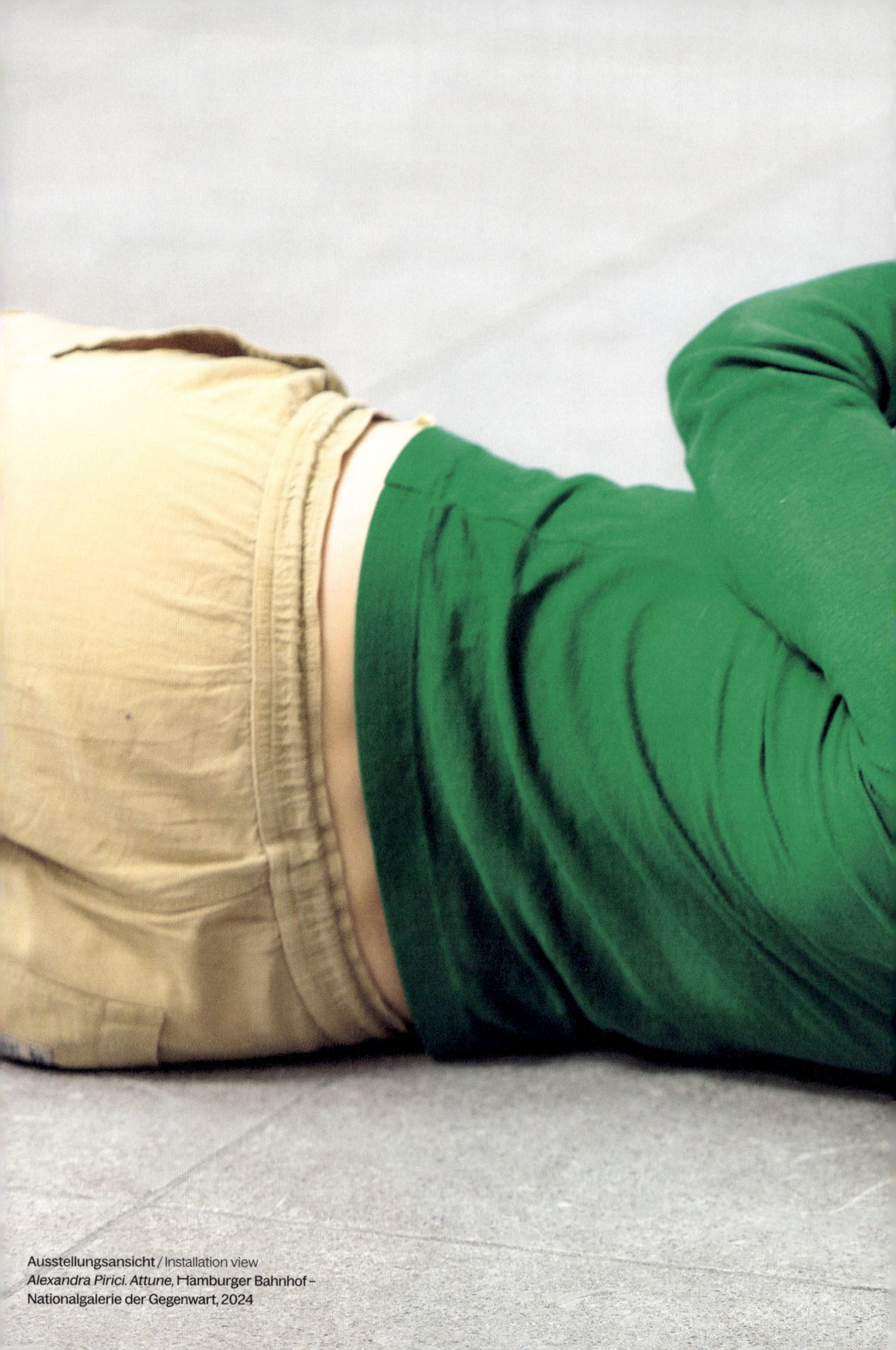

Ausstellungsansicht / Installation view
Alexandra Pirici. Attune, Hamburger Bahnhof –
Nationalgalerie der Gegenwart, 2024

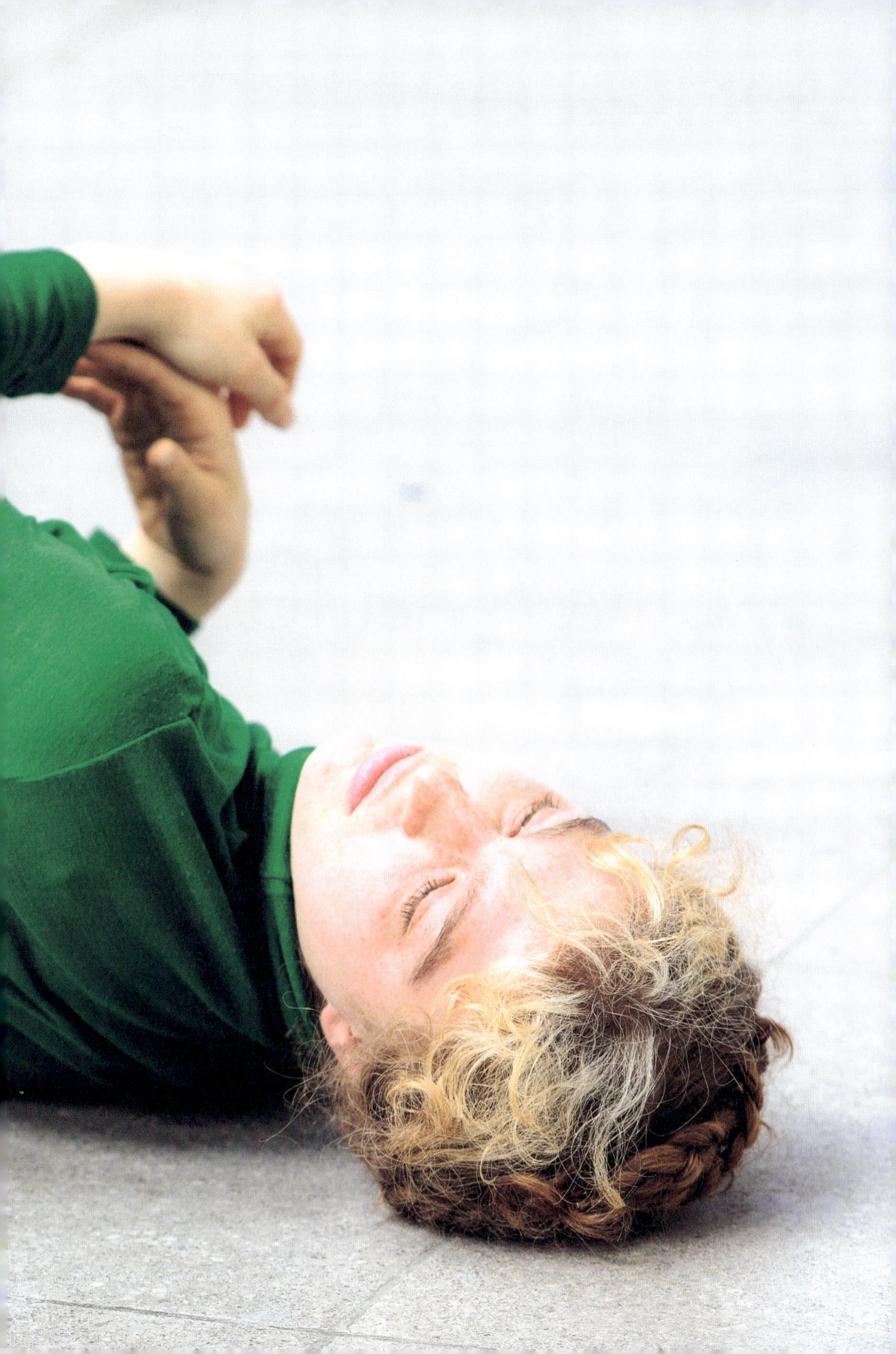

Verkörperlichte Geschichten von aktiver Materie / Embodied Stories of Active Matter

Eine Unterhaltung / A Conversation: **Raluca Voinea mit** / with **Alexandra Pirici**

Raluca Voinea **Beim Betreten deiner Ausstellung *Attune* wird man von Stimmen und Bewegungen, von organischer und anorganischer Materie, von Prozessen und Konstruktionen, von Transformationen und Farben empfangen. Der traditionelle Ausstellungsraum wird infrage gestellt, denn die „Besucher*innen" sehen und hören, bekommen ein immersives Erlebnis geboten und können wissenschaftliche Experimente beobachten, werden sich ihrer Körper bewusst und können erkennen, dass die Bewegungen menschlicher Körper denen anderer nichtmenschlicher und sogar unbelebter Entitäten und Strukturen ähneln. Eine ganze Reihe künstlerischer Interventionen haben sich darüber hinweggesetzt, was eine Ausstellung sein und wie**

Raluca Voinea When entering the exhibition space of *Attune*, one is invited in by voices and movement, organic and inorganic matter, processes and constructions, transformations and colors. The traditional exhibition space is challenged such that the "visitors" not only see but also hear, are not only offered an immersive experience, but are equally challenged to observe scientific experiments, become aware of their bodies while observing how the movements of human bodies resemble that of other, non-human and even non-living entities and structures. There is a history of artistic interventions that have defied the limits of what an exhibition is and how it is meant to be experienced by the public (the exhibition as immersive environment, the exhibition as parliament or as public forum,

sie vom Publikum erfahren werden sollte (die Ausstellung als immersives Environment, die Ausstellung als Parlament oder öffentliches Forum, die Ausstellung als Schule, als archäologisches Areal, als forensisches Labor, als Sozialstation, als Küche oder Café, als Hotel oder Schlafsaal, als Versammlungsplatz für konfrontative Begegnungen, als Raumstation, um nur einige Settings zu nennen). Wie setzt du dich in deiner künstlerischen Praxis mit dieser Geschichte auseinander? Und wie integrierst du andere Lebenswelten in deine Arbeit, zum Beispiel die des wissenschaftlichen Labors, der natürlichen äußeren Umgebung, der performativen Räume oder des Internets?

Alexandra Pirici Momentan sehe ich Ausstellungsräume in erster Linie als Environments, in denen sich andere Welten in jeder Größenordnung, von winzig bis riesig, erträumen lassen – womöglich ist das eine der wenigen Funktionen, die sonstige Räume noch nicht übernommen haben. Und ich finde, dass die Künste und Kunstinstitutionen daran festhalten sollten: einen Raum bereitzustellen für Imagination, Metapher, Spekulation, vielleicht auch für das, was Patricia Reed als nicht-adaptive (Modell-) Welten bezeichnen würde. Wenn wir andere Dynamiken, Formen, Objekte oder Arten der Fortbewegung und Kommunikation erdenken, dann tun wir das nicht unbedingt, weil wir der Realität entfliehen wollen, sondern weil wir sie neu erschaffen wollen. Denn ohne (gute) Poesie und überschüssige Zeit – wie sie Bernard Stiegler in seinem Videovortrag *A quoi sert l'art?* [Wozu überhaupt Kunst?] aus dem Jahr 2003 meint, wenn er beschreibt, wie die ersten Jäger ihre Speere bearbeiteten, schmückten und als ein Objekt markierten, das viel mehr war als nur Jagdgerät: nämlich ein Raum, in den sie ihre symbolische Beziehung zur Welt einschreiben konnten –, kann ich mir echte Emanzipation nicht vorstellen.

In diesem Zusammenhang fallen mir auch die Bücher *Die Parabel des Sämanns* und *Die Parabel der Talente* von Octavia Butler ein. Denn ihre Protagonistin Lauren Olamina

the exhibition as school, as archaeological site, as forensic laboratory, as social care center, as kitchen or café, as hotel or dormitory, as confrontational agora, as open studio, as space station among other settings). How do you engage with this history in your practice and how do you integrate other types of relating to worlds, such as those offered by a scientific laboratory, by natural outdoor environments, by performative spaces, or even by the Internet?

Alexandra Pirici I think at the moment I am mostly interested in the exhibition space as an environment in which worlds other than our own can be dreamt of at whatever scale, small or large – this is perhaps also one of the few functions not already performed by other spaces. And I generally believe the arts and art institutions should hold onto that: providing a space for imagination, metaphor, speculation, maybe for what Patricia Reed would call non-adaptive (model) worlds.

I think affirming and imagining other dynamics, forms, objects, ways of moving or communicating is not about escaping reality but creating it anew.

And without (good) poetry and excess time – of the kind Bernard Stiegler talks about in his 2003 video lecture *A quoi sert l'art?* [What Is Art for?] in which he describes the ancient hunter spending time sculpting his spear, decorating it, marking it as more than a hunting tool: as a space onto which his symbolic relationship with the world can be inscribed – I cannot actually imagine emancipation.

I kind of also like to think of Octavia Butler's books, *Parable of the Sower* and *Parable of the Talents*, and how, in the darkest moments, when whatever we call "civilization" has crumbled, in the poverty, the violence and the dread that envelops much of the world she describes, her lead character, Lauren Olamina, still dreams of space travel. So I am most attracted to this (possible) function of the exhibition space, which surely also involves references to and inspira-

träumt selbst dann noch von der Weltraumfahrt, nachdem das, was wir „Zivilisation" nennen, zusammengebrochen ist und die Welt fast nur noch von Armut, Gewalt und Angst geprägt ist. Diese (mögliche) Funktion des Ausstellungsraums interessiert mich besonders, dazu kommen sicherlich noch Bezüge zur und Anregungen aus Environments aus der echten Welt. Für diese Arbeit habe ich mich mit dem Raum des Laboratoriums beschäftigt und benutze Elemente aus diesem Kontext, nur eben abgewandelt und neu interpretiert. Die Welt der Wissenschaften und Labore ist in eine seltsame Schieflage geraten. Diese Einrichtungen werden gleichzeitig überhöht und niedergemacht, sie erfahren übermäßige Bewunderung und Ablehnung, sind unrealistischen Erwartungen und unfundierter Kritik ausgesetzt.

In den Wissenschaften geht es heute weder darum, Wunder zu bewirken, noch darum, das seit der Aufklärung vorherrschende mechanistisch-reduktionistische Weltbild zu bestätigen. In Büchern wie *Dialog mit der Natur* von Ilya Prigogine und Isabelle Stenger wird herausgestellt, dass die Wissenschaften heute mit einigen der schönsten Metaphern und Geschichten über unsere Welt und unseren Platz darin im Einklang stehen. Mich haben auch Autorinnen wie Robin Wall Kimmerer inspiriert, die poetische und wissenschaftliche Perspektiven, Fiktion und Fakten, strenges Denken und künstlerische Impulse miteinander verbinden.

Was mich außerdem interessiert, ist die Welt da draußen, die „Landschaft", und ich freue mich schon allein wegen der Größe des Raums über die Möglichkeit, in der Historischen Halle des Hamburger Bahnhofs eine Art Landschaft zu erschaffen. Aber es ist mir auch bewusst, dass ich das Unnatürliche des Ausstellungsraums und der dortigen Gegebenheiten zu akzeptieren habe. Deshalb verzichte ich auf das Einbeziehen von Lebensformen, die unter den Bedingungen dort leiden könnten, wie zum Beispiel Insekten, Vögel etc., die manchmal in Ausstellungen integriert werden, ohne dass sie dem zustimmen könnten. Obwohl die Indoor-Landschaft, die ich

tion from other, real-world environments. For this particular work, I have also been interested in the space of the laboratory, so I am using elements from that environment, but they are of course re-interpreted and made into something else. I believe the worlds of the lab and of science are in a strange place today. They are at once too revered and too derided, subject to both excessive admiration and rejection, unreal expectations and easy criticism.

Contemporary science is neither about miracle-making nor about reaffirming the reductionist, mechanistic worldview that has persisted since the Enlightenment. Books like Ilya Prigogine and Isabelle Stengers's *Order out of Chaos*, for example, shed light on how science now seems to harmonize with some of the most beautiful metaphors and stories about our world and our place in it. I am also inspired by authors like Robin Wall Kimmerer, who blend poetic and scientific perspectives, story and fact, rigorous thinking and artistic drift.

Another thing I am interested in is the outdoors, or the "landscape", and the possibility of creating something like a landscape within the historic hall of Hamburger Bahnhof, especially given its scale. At the same time, I think it is important to accept the artificiality of the exhibition space and the conditions of being there. That is why I am not incorporating lifeforms that might suffer from being there, as is often the case when insects, birds, etc. are brought into exhibitions despite being unable to give their consent for being there. The indoor landscape I am trying to create nevertheless suggests a certain kind of "nature", though it is an artificial and constructed one.

This landscape, then, also incorporates a stage-like platform, so a reference to a more traditional theater set-up.

Although I try to stage living and non-living actors throughout the entire space at times, this "stage" is more explicitly such. It has been conceived to show a duet between the living and the non-living, between a stone and a human performer.

erschaffen will, künstlich und konstruiert ist, soll sie auf eine Art „natürlich" wirken. In diese Landschaft wird ein bühnenartiges Podest integriert, als Anspielung auf das traditionelle Theater-Setting. Im gesamten Ausstellungsraum inszeniere ich zu verschiedenen Zeiten lebende und unbelebte Schauspieler*innen, doch ist diese „Bühne" explizit als solche gedacht. Dort soll ein Duett zwischen Belebtem und Unbelebtem stattfinden, zwischen einem Stein und einem oder einer menschlichen Performer*in.

Auch auf die Welt des Internets nehme ich in meiner künstlerischen Praxis oft Bezug. In einigen früheren Arbeiten wie *Signals* oder der *Delicate Instruments*-Serie habe ich mich mit den Dynamiken von Social Media Feeds oder der algorithmischen Generierung von relevantem Content befasst und versucht, diese Räume, Dynamiken und Argumentationsformen im Rahmen der Ausstellung mit verkörperlichtem Denken und Mensch-zu-Mensch-Interaktionen in ein produktives Spannungsverhältnis zu bringen. Außerdem interessiere ich mich für Technologien und technische Geräte, die sich enorm auf unser Leben und Denken auswirken – wie etwa die Google-Suchmaschine oder aktuelle Machine-Learning-Systeme – deren Funktionsweisen und Strategien ich in performative Arbeiten übersetze. Ich hoffe, diese Tradition im Rahmen von *Attune* fortzusetzen.

RV Sowohl bei Octavia Butler als auch bei Robin Wall Kimmerer zieht sich durch das Narrativ der Autorinnen und ihrer Figuren ein roter Faden, der eigentlich in den viel geschmähten Bereich der Spiritualität gehört. Ob er nun wie bei Butlers Hauptfigur Lauren Olamina die Form einer neuen Religion annimmt oder sich als Anrufung der Ahnen, der indigenen Kosmologien und des Glaubens an die Verflochtenheit aller Dinge in den verschiedenen Welten äußert, immer ist es diese Form des Wissens, die Geschichten erzählt und für Verständnis sorgt; das gibt Hoffnung, schafft ein Zusammengehörigkeitsgefühl und gibt der Welt letzten Endes ihren Zau-

When it comes to relating to the world of the web, there are a number of points of reference in my practice. Indeed, in some of my previous works, such as *Signals* or the *Delicate Instruments* series, I reflected on social media feed dynamics or the algorithmic production of relevant content, for example, trying to bring those spaces, dynamics and forms of reasoning into a productive tension with embodied thinking and human-to-human interaction within the exhibition space. Otherwise, I have also been interested in particular technologies or technological objects that seem to have an immense impact on our lives and our thinking – like the Google search engine or current-day machine-learning systems – which I have explored through performative translations of their functions or politics. And I hope there will be a place in *Attune* for continuing that tradition in some way.

RV Both Octavia Butler and Robin Wall Kimmerer accompany their, or their characters', itineraries with a red line that vibrates throughout their narratives, and which is something that belongs to the much-reviled realm of spirituality. Whether it takes the shape of a new religion, as for Lauren Olamina, or it invokes the ancestors, indigenous cosmologies, and beliefs in the interconnectedness of things in the many worlds, this form of knowledge tells stories, opens understandings; it gives hope, creates communities and eventually re-enchants the world. I wanted to comment on the authors you mentioned, not only because they are very dear to me, as we have often discussed, but also because the worlds they imagine or depict seem to be so far from the possibilities that art institutions today, especially those in canonized structures, can create (or perhaps this is my personal disenchantment speaking). I imagine your staging of such complex entanglements and performative references within an exhibition to be a means of turning consumers of art events into active wonderers, a means of reinstating the stimulation of curiosity as an essential task

ber zurück. Ich würde gern auf die von dir erwähnten Autorinnen zurückkommen, nicht nur, weil ich selbst Fan von ihnen bin, sondern weil die von ihnen erdachten Welten so weit entfernt sind von den Möglichkeiten, die Kunstinstitutionen, vor allem solche in kanonisierten Strukturen, heute bieten können (vielleicht spricht hier auch die persönliche Enttäuschung aus mir). Wenn du diese komplexen Verflechtungen und performativen Bezüge in einer Ausstellung in Szene setzt, werden sie zu einem Mittel, um aus Konsument*innen von Kunstevents aktive Fragenstellende zu machen, ein Mittel, um das Wecken von Neugier wieder zu einer der Hauptaufgaben von Kunst zu machen. Da bei deinen Arbeiten ja immer sehr viele Menschen mitwirken, deren Reaktionen, Bewegungen und Kommentare du beobachtest und analysierst, würde ich gern wissen, welche Erwartungen du an die Besucher*innen deiner neuen Arbeit stellst?

AP Zunächst einmal möchte ich anmerken, dass wir der Welt meiner Meinung nach gar nicht ihren Zauber zurückgeben müssen. Vielmehr müssen wir uns erneut darum bemühen, sie überhaupt zu verstehen. Meine Arbeit an *Attune* beruht vor allem auf meiner Überzeugung, dass wir, wenn wir uns nur ernsthaft bemühen, Materie in ihrer wundervollen Komplexität und Schönheit zu verstehen, darauf verzichten können, sie mithilfe von Spiritualität zu verzaubern. In diesem Zusammenhang fallen mir Bücher ein wie *Reinventing the Sacred* von Stuart Kauffman, der darin in eine ähnliche Richtung denkt. In meiner neuen Arbeit nehme ich nur auf zwei Texte konkret Bezug. Beim ersten handelt es sich um ein Gedicht aus Ursula K. Le Guins Roman *Immer nach Hause*. Im Rahmen der Ausstellung soll ein kurzer Auszug daraus fast wortgleich zitiert werden. Lediglich das Wort „Seele" ersetze ich durch „Form". Was mich interessiert, ist eine zutiefst materialistische Weltanschauung und die Erkenntnis, dass erstens, die Materie kein separates Konzept von „Spiritualität" braucht, um Ehrfurcht

of art. As your works are inevitably packed with people, whose reactions, movements and after-comments I know you are always observing and analyzing, I am wondering what kind of expectations you have of the visitors of this new work?

AP I have to start by saying that I do not believe we need a re-enchantment of the world but rather a renewed effort to understand it. For me, the most important reason for working on and making *Attune* has to do with my conviction that if one truly makes the effort to understand matter in all its wondrous complexity and beauty, one does not need spirit to enchant it. When I say that, I am also thinking of books like Stuart Kauffman's *Reinventing the Sacred*, for example, which argue along those lines. Only two explicit references flow into my work, though. One of them is a poem from Ursula K. Le Guin's novel *Always Coming Home*. The short excerpt will be recited almost word for word. The only thing I am changing is the word "soul", which I am replacing with the word "form". I am interested in a deeply materialist worldview and in the acknowledgement that, firstly, matter does not need an outside, separated concept of "spirit" to be awe-inspiring and life-creating, and, secondly, that the specific metaphor of the "soul" might create more problems than solutions in coming to terms with our place in the universe. Perhaps using a concept like "matterspirit" could be a good transitional trick to overcome unproductive dualisms in the lineage of composites such as "natureculture", as introduced by Donna Haraway, or "bodymind", which I often use as it relates to the concept of "embodied cognition". But to me at least (and coming from Romania and an increasingly dogmatic Orthodox context does play a role, perhaps, as does everything else, for that matter), "spirit" seems too platonic and too much connected to an outside, godly force, to be useful at this point.

I am not interested in spirituality as a thing in itself, even though I read, or am inspired by, authors who work with this concept (I might add that Butler's *Xenogenesis* trilogy is much more interested in alien biotech and genetic engineering than religion). My impression is that the

zu wecken und Leben zu erschaffen, und zweitens, die „Seelen"-Metapher eher Probleme schafft als Lösungen anzubieten, wenn wir unseren Platz im Universum begreifen wollen. Vielleicht wäre ein Konzept wie „Materie/Geist" eine gute Übergangslösung, um unfruchtbare Dualismen zu überwinden, etwas, das in der Nachfolge von Donna Haraways Begriffspaar „Natur/Kultur" steht oder auch „Körper/Geist", was ich oft benutze, weil es zum Konzept des „verkörperlichten Denkens" gehört. Für mich jedenfalls (und dabei spielt eine Rolle, dass ich aus Rumänien komme, wo der orthodoxe Dogmatismus immer mehr um sich greift,) klingt der Begriff „Spiritualität" zu platonisch und scheint sich zu sehr auf eine äußere, göttliche Kraft zu beziehen, um uns im Hier und Jetzt weiterzuhelfen.

Für Spiritualität an sich interessiere ich mich nicht, auch wenn ich Autor*innen lese, die mit diesem Konzept arbeiten (obwohl Octavia Butler sich in ihrer *Xenogenesis*-Trilogie mehr mit außerirdischer Biotechnologie und Gentechnik als mit Religion beschäftigt). Ich habe den Eindruck, dass – vor allem im künstlerisch-kulturellen Kontext – nicht „Spiritualität" das am meisten geschmähte Konzept des Tages ist, sondern „Diesseitigkeit" (was bis zu einem gewissen Grad sicherlich auch seine Gründe hat). Ich finde es komisch, dass es in einem der vorherrschenden Diskurse in der Kunstwelt darum geht, die Dichotomie zwischen Körper und Geist, Natur und Kultur infrage zu stellen, während die zwischen Geist und Materie oder Körper und Seele dabei ignoriert wird. In Wirklichkeit gibt es keine grundsätzlichen Unterschiede zwischen dem Organischen und Anorganischen, zwischen belebter und unbelebter Materie, wodurch wir zu einem Teil eines Kontinuums werden, das zwar, um Laura Tripaldi zu paraphrasieren, unterschiedliche materielle Konfigurationen aufweist, aber keine unterschiedlichen „Essenzen". Diese Idee hat mich zu *Attune* inspiriert. In dem Kontext hat es also keinen Sinn, von Materie und Geist zu sprechen.

Wir brauchen Geschichten, aber wir müssen uns aktuelle Geschichten ausdenken, Geschichten, die, ganz gleich von welcher

much-reviled concept of the day is "secularity", not "spirituality", especially in artistic-cultural circles (and maybe for good reasons, to a certain extent). I find it strange that a predominant discourse in the art world seems to be all about challenging dichotomies between body and mind, nature and culture, but not between spirit and matter or body and soul. And the reality is that no fundamental distinction exists between the organic and inorganic, between matter that is alive and matter that is not, and that means that we are part of a continuum – which, to paraphrase Laura Tripaldi, holds differences of material configurations, but not of "essence". This very idea was the inspiration for *Attune*. So it does not really make sense to speak of matter and spirit in this context.

We need stories, indeed, but we need to invent contemporary stories, stories that, whichever older cosmologies they may be inspired by, have to come to terms with the cosmos and our place in it as we know it today – not only after Copernicus but after space telescopes too.

Stories that obscure this reality, no matter how soothing or appealing, will eventually backfire. I should point out that I understand "story" not only as a fictional, linear narration that uses words but also as something less literal and more abstract, as the conveyor of a thought-sensation, which could very well be an artistic experience. I am interested in how we can also tell stories through our bodies and in how performers' bodies can maybe "speak" about, or show, a capacity to become other, to embody the story of shifting, active matter.

And yes, it would be great if the work could make visitors curious to know more (about the physio-chemical processes and self-organizing systems that are referenced or staged in the work) as much as it would be to enable them to enjoy being in its space and experiencing its "world" through movement and song. I believe

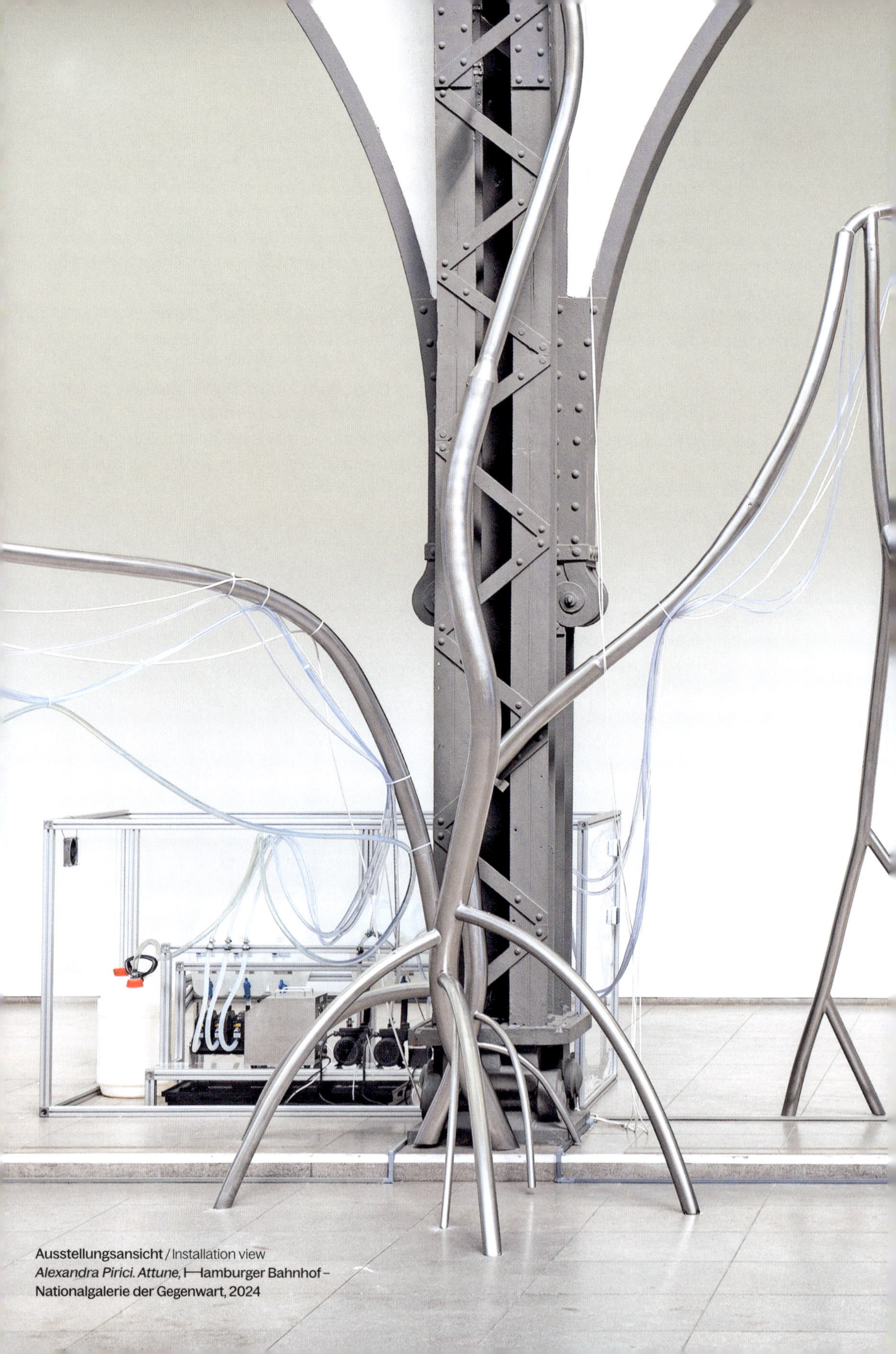

Ausstellungsansicht / Installation view
Alexandra Pirici. Attune, Hamburger Bahnhof –
Nationalgalerie der Gegenwart, 2024

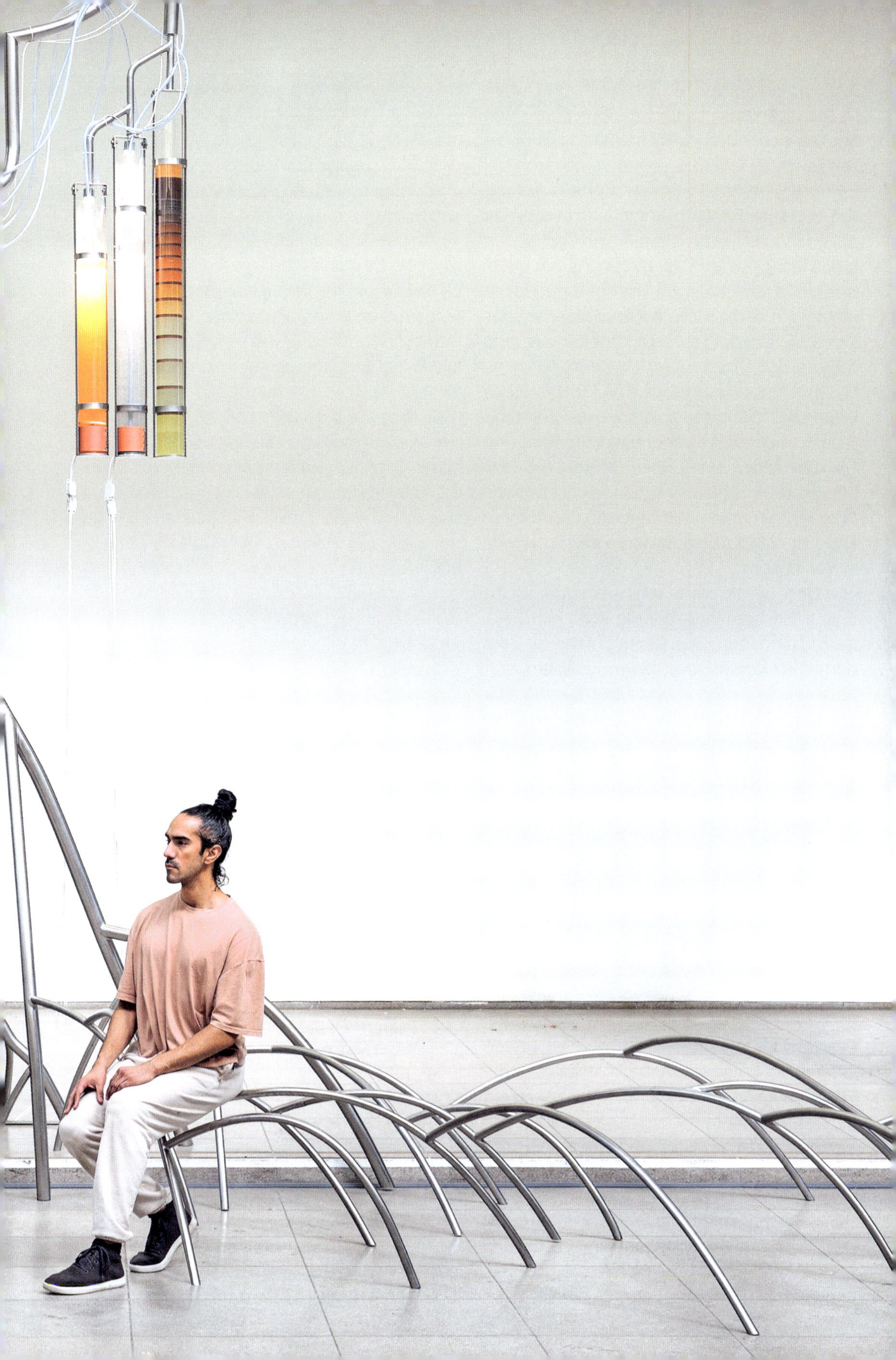

älteren Kosmologie sie inspiriert sind, unseren heutigen Kosmos und unseren Platz darin anerkennen – und damit meine ich nicht die Zeit nach Kopernikus, sondern die nach der Erfindung des Weltraumteleskops. Geschichten, die diese Realität verschleiern, damit sie angenehmer oder tröstender wird, gehen auf lange Sicht immer nach hinten los. Ich muss hier erklären, dass ich unter „Geschichte" nicht nur eine fiktionale, lineare Erzählung aus Wörtern verstehe, sondern eher etwas Abstraktes, den Überbringer eines Gedankens/Gefühls, also zum Beispiel eine künstlerische Erfahrung. Mich interessiert, wie wir Geschichten mit unseren Körper erzählen können und wie die Körper von Performer*innen von der Fähigkeit „erzählen" können, sich in etwas anderes zu verwandeln und die Geschichte einer im Wandel begriffenen, aktiven Materie zu verkörpern.

Und ja, es wäre toll, wenn die Besucher*innen der Ausstellung sich nicht nur gern in dem Raum aufhielten und diese „Welt" mittels Bewegung und Musik erlebten, sondern meine Arbeit sie darüber hinaus neugierig machen würde, mehr zu erfahren (über die physikochemischen Prozesse und selbstorganisierenden Systeme, die ich im Rahmen der Arbeit inszeniere). Ich glaube nämlich, dass sich beides ergänzt. Und vielleicht ist es gerade dieses doppelte Potenzial oder doppelte Bedürfnis, das beim Wecken von Neugier zum Tragen kommt – über komplexe, nicht leicht verständliche Themen zu reden und dafür auf fesselnde Geschichten zurückzugreifen oder packende Erlebnisse zu bieten –, weshalb Kunstinstitutionen am besten für diese Aufgabe geeignet sind. Sie können Orte sein für intellektuelle/Körper-Geist-Reflexionen und zeitgenössische Zeremonien oder Rituale; sie können Besucher*innen dazu einladen, mit Metaphern und wissenschaftlichen Fakten sich zu bewegen und zu denken, also zugleich körperlich und abstrakt vorzugehen. Nur müssen sie dafür natürlich erst einmal die richtigen Bedingungen schaffen, und dazu gehört eben nicht nur, den Leuten eine Show zu bieten. Ich kann deine Enttäuschung von den meisten Kunstinstitutionen durchaus

the two complement each other. And maybe it is precisely because of this double potential, or double need, when it comes to stimulating curiosity – to speak about subjects that are complex and maybe not easy to grasp or discuss, and to do that through interesting and captivating stories or experiences – that art institutions might be best positioned for the task. They can be places for both intellectual/bodymind reflection and contemporary ceremony or ritual; for moving and thinking with metaphor and scientific fact, both through one's entire body and through abstraction. But of course, they also have to create the conditions for this to actually happen and those conditions are not just about offering a show. Your disenchantment with most art institutions today is definitely justified and I share it – there are many exceptions, of course, but many art institutions' bombastic words and mission statements actually go hand in hand with exploitative practices, a total dismantling of any labor standard, or a pioneering of forms for turning art into assets for cunning investors. But again, art institutions are part of the world, and worldly dynamics. Maybe what bothers me more sometimes is the claim that they are not. Also institutions exist through people and maybe people need to change so that institutions change as well. And there are always new initiatives emerging – like the Experimental Station for Research on Art and Life, that you initiated and work on, or the art space/performative sculpture garden (and real garden) my partner and I are hoping to open outdoors, in "nature", which I dream of realizing soon.

But to go back to the work, I would be happy enough if *Attune* – together with many other needed artworks, educational programs, cultural and political initiatives – would enable visitors to come a bit closer to an extended appreciation of the material world and our non-exceptional, albeit important place in it.

nachvollziehen, denn mir geht es genauso – natürlich gibt es jede Menge Ausnahmen, doch bei vielen Kunstinstitutionen gehen die hochtrabenden Ziele, die sie sich auf die Fahnen schreiben, einher mit ausbeuterischen Praktiken, einem Abbau jedweder Arbeitsstandards und einer Vorreiterrolle beim Umwandeln von Kunst in Vermögenswerte für gerissene Anleger*innen. Doch Kunstinstitutionen sind nun mal ein Teil der Welt und ihrer Dynamiken. Vielleicht stört mich eher, dass so oft behauptet wird, sie gehörten nicht dazu. Denn ohne Menschen würden Institutionen nicht existieren, und so müssen sich die Menschen vielleicht ebenso ändern wie die Institutionen. Neue Initiativen gibt es viele – wie die Experimental Station for Research on Art and Life, die du ins Leben gerufen hast und bei der du heute noch mitarbeitest, oder den Art Space/performativen Skulpturengarten (und richtigen Garten), den mein Partner und ich gern bald in der „Natur" eröffnen würden.

Aber zurück zu meiner Arbeit, ich würde mich sehr freuen, wenn *Attune* – zusammen mit anderen Kunstwerken, dringend benötigten Bildungsangeboten sowie kulturellen und politischen Initiativen – es den Besucher*innen ermöglicht, die materielle Welt und unsere zwar nicht einzigartige, aber doch wichtige Rolle darin mehr wertzuschätzen. Wunderbar fände ich, wenn Besucher*innen sich die Ausstellung mindestens ein zweites Mal ansehen würden; ich freue mich immer sehr, wenn mir Performer*innen berichten, dass Zuschauer*innen die Arbeit noch einmal besucht haben – das freut uns alle sehr. Das ist die beste Reaktion, die man sich wünschen kann, vor allem heute. Denn dann haben wir nicht nur Bilder erzeugt, die schnell konsumiert, auf Instagram gepostet und vergessen werden, sondern etwas geschaffen, das man nicht auf den ersten Blick begreift, das man sich erneut anschauen und länger verarbeiten muss. Es geht dann nicht darum, (nur) in diesem einen Moment dabei zu sein oder ein Spektakel zu erleben; die Arbeit entfaltet ihre volle Wirkung erst mit der Zeit und lädt dazu ein, länger über sie nachzudenken.

And, more concretely, I think it is wonderful when visitors come back to an exhibition; I am always very happy when performers tell me that some visitors have come back to see the work again – that is always really nice for all of us. I think it is the best reaction one could hope for, especially today. It might mean that we have not just produced an image, or images, to be rapidly consumed, instagrammed and done with, but rather something that cannot be taken in at a glance, something that needs more thought or revisiting. It is an experience that is not (only) about being there at that one moment or about spectacle, but rather one that invites longer reflection and reveals itself gradually over time.

RV The title of your exhibition resonates first with the sphere of music. One of the structures in the space is a reference to an organ, one of the most complex musical instruments ever created, as you were saying in a conversation we had. The movement of sand in the dune, another sculpture comprising the work, creates sound for an ear more sensitive than the human one, the performers sing alone and in choirs, attuning their voices to the amplitude of a space that is more accustomed to the sound of footsteps and indistinguishable chatter, or of speech amplified by loudspeakers. Would you see these connections to music as a key to reading the entire exhibition's aim of bringing together forms of harmony and showing their interdependence, also in relation to the space?

AP Yes, I definitely do. Although I also hope that *Attune* mobilizes associations beyond music, and the verb functions as general invitation as well: an invitation to recognize and appreciate the wonder and intelligence of self-structuring matter, and the reality of a vibrant, material world, that needs no transcendent plane or imaginary (male) architect to set it in motion or bring it to life. I believe this has very deep implications (our abiotic beginning is only one of them), and it has somehow been the driving force of the entire endeavor. But yes, music is also really important for the work, in its harmonic and

RV Beim Titel deiner Arbeit klingt zunächst einmal die Sphäre der Musik mit. Eine der Strukturen im Raum bezieht sich auf die Orgel, eines der komplexesten Musikinstrumente, die jemals gebaut wurden, wie du mir einmal erzählt hast. Durch die Bewegungen des Sandes der sich ebenfalls im Raum befindlichen Düne entsteht ein Geräusch, das nur ein feineres Gehör als das des Menschen wahrnehmen kann, die Performer*innen singen allein oder im Chor, sie passen ihre Stimmen an die Weite eines Raums an, in dem man sonst eigentlich nur Schritte, Hintergrundgemurmel oder Lautsprecheransagen hören kann. Ist der Bezug zur Musik vielleicht der Schlüssel, um die Intention der Ausstellung zu begreifen, verschiedene Formen von Harmonie zusammenzubringen und ihre gegenseitige Abhängigkeit, auch im Verhältnis zum Raum, aufzuzeigen?

AP Ja, absolut. Obwohl ich hoffe, dass *Attune* noch andere Assoziationen als die zur Musik weckt, und die Aufforderung *attune* [etwa: ein- oder abstimmen] als Einladung verstanden wird, das Wunder und die Intelligenz einer sich selbst strukturierenden Materie wahrzunehmen und die Realität einer dynamischen materiellen Welt zu erkennen, die weder eine transzendente Ebene noch einen imaginären (männlichen) Architekten braucht, um sich in Bewegung zu setzen oder zum Leben zu erwachen. Das alles hat weitreichende Folgen (die abiotischen Faktoren, die für den Beginn unseres Lebens verantwortlich waren, sind nur ein Teil davon) und war beim gesamten Vorhaben die treibende Kraft. Und ja, Musik spielt für die Arbeit ebenfalls eine wichtige Rolle, vor allem in ihrer harmonischen und insbesondere polyfonen Ausprägung. Für die Arbeit habe ich hauptsächlich polyfone Stücke komponiert, weil Polyfonie in unseren heutigen Ohren so seltsam klingt; wir sind es nicht mehr gewohnt, mehreren Melodielinien zuzuhören oder vielen Sänger*innen, die mehrstimmig verschiedene Lieder singen. Sänger*innen mit wenig Erfahrung müssen erst einmal lernen, den

especially polyphonic forms. I have been trying to compose mostly polyphonic pieces for it, because polyphonic music has become such a strange sound to our contemporary ears; we are no longer accustomed to listening to multiple melodic lines at the same time, or multiple voices singing harmonizing but different tunes at the same time. If you are not an experienced singer, it also requires a difficult exercise of listening and literally attuning to the other's voice. It is really about holding your (sonic) ground, and yet you can only do that by listening, always in connection to the other – it is harmony but difficult, an ongoing struggle. Indeed, when I am composing or listening to polyphonic music, I feel an almost physical struggle, alongside any enjoyment. I have also been practicing some improvised polyphonic singing with the students in the class I teach at the Academy of Fine Arts in Munich, and it is always a treat, both for the challenges it poses and the pleasure it affords. And ultimately, what could connect bodies in space or travel better than sound or song in the vast historic hall of Hamburger Bahnhof?

RV In your work, you have brought to the idea of exhibitions human performers, their bodies and voices, as a self-sufficient means of creating strong experiences, which are at the same time intelligent and mesmerizing. Thus you have created, almost like a signature, a minimalism that countered the widespread overloading of performative stagings with sets and props and of exhibition spaces with objects. Gradually you have been (re)turning – I say (re)turning thinking of some of your earlier actions in the spaces more traditionally related to choreography or theater – to a presence of stage design, though very subtle, and sometimes of very present technological devices. I am thinking here, say, of the hologram structure in your 2018 work *Co-natural* at the New Museum in New York. How would you describe the trajectory that brought you to conceive such a complex interplay of materialities for the current show at Hamburger Bahnhof?

anderen genau zuzuhören und sich auf sie einzustimmen. Es geht darum, sich (klanglich) zu behaupten, doch das gelingt nur, indem man den anderen genau zuhört und sich auf sie einlässt – einerseits entsteht Harmonie, andererseits muss man ständig miteinander ringen. Wenn ich polyfone Musikstücke komponiere oder höre, wechseln sich bei mir Genuss und innerer Kampf ab. Mit den Studierenden, die ich an der Akademie der Bildenden Künste in München unterrichte, habe ich improvisierte polyfone Musikstücke geprobt, was immer wieder eine schöne Erfahrung ist, weil es Spaß macht und uns vor unerwartete Herausforderungen stellt. Und was könnte die Menschen in der großen Historischen Halle des Hamburger Bahnhofs besser miteinander verbinden als Klänge und Geräusche?

RV In deinen Arbeiten hast du das Konzept Ausstellung um die Körper und Stimmen menschlicher Performer*innen erweitert; sie werden bei dir zu eigenständigen Mitteln und schaffen so faszinierende wie intellektuell herausfordernde Erlebnisse. Dadurch hast du, fast wie eine Handschrift, einen Minimalismus geschaffen, der sich von anderen mit Requisiten überfrachteten performativen Bühnen und mit Objekten überladenen Ausstellungsräumen stark abhebt. Erst allmählich bist du wieder zu einer stärkeren Bühnengestaltung übergegangen – und ich sage, wieder, weil du für einige frühere Arbeiten ja Räume verwendet hast, wie man sie eher von traditionellen Choreografien und Theaterinszenierungen her kennt – und benutzt als Requisiten zum Teil hochaktuelle Technologien. Ich denke hier beispielsweise an die holografische Projektion, die du in die 2018 im New Museum in New York gezeigte Arbeit *Co-natural* integriert hast. Kannst du beschreiben, welche Überlegungen dich dazu gebracht haben, für die Ausstellung im Hamburger Bahnhof dieses komplexe Zusammenspiel der Materialitäten zu inszenieren?

AP Minimalism is a tradition in its own right, and a signature can sometimes be more of a signal that one is becoming too comfortable with repeating oneself, with reproducing some kind of recipe, whereas I am interested in experimenting. I believe that a work needs what it needs, that there is a co-development of conceptual requirements and material, formal solutions. There is nothing intrinsically wrong or right about particular mediums or fields, and I do not think that one thing is more interesting than another simply because it is a live action and not an object. There are so many other aspects to consider, such as quality, politics, and meaning. I am not looking to carve out a niche for my artistic practice or to mark and defend my territory. I think that can spell the death of pleasure and curiosity, and, to be honest, being able to explore and play and to challenge yourself is what makes being an artist worthwhile. So I do not start out by thinking what I could do with performers alone; I start out by thinking about what is interesting to me, about what I believe is important to communicate at a given moment, and then I think about how that could best be done. And, of course, that is also connected to the people I would like to collaborate with, the things I take pleasure in doing, the skills I believe I have or the ones I would like to develop, and so on.

Another point is that what is radical today, might tomorrow become commonplace and perfectly appropriated by its object of critique; every strategy or choice is, and has to be, contextual, so it has to be constantly changing, as our world also changes at an incredible speed.

Were I to settle for a signature, I would prefer it to be the wide-ranging and ambiguous realm of the "performative"; the biological human body is but one element and does not need to be the only one. In my recent works I have already attempted to come close to, or explore, more-

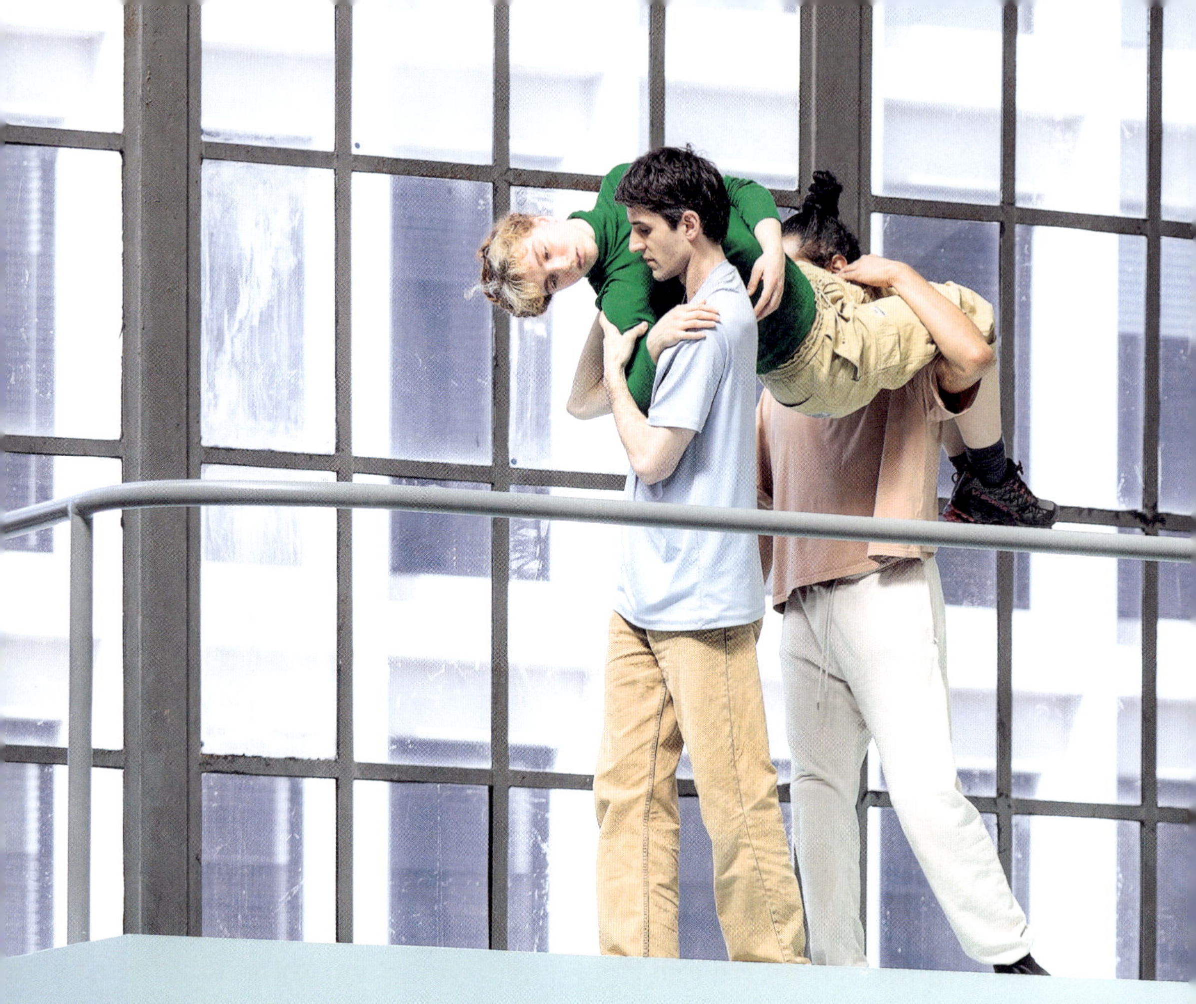

Ausstellungsansicht / Installation view
Alexandra Pirici. Attune, Hamburger Bahnhof –
Nationalgalerie der Gegenwart, 2024

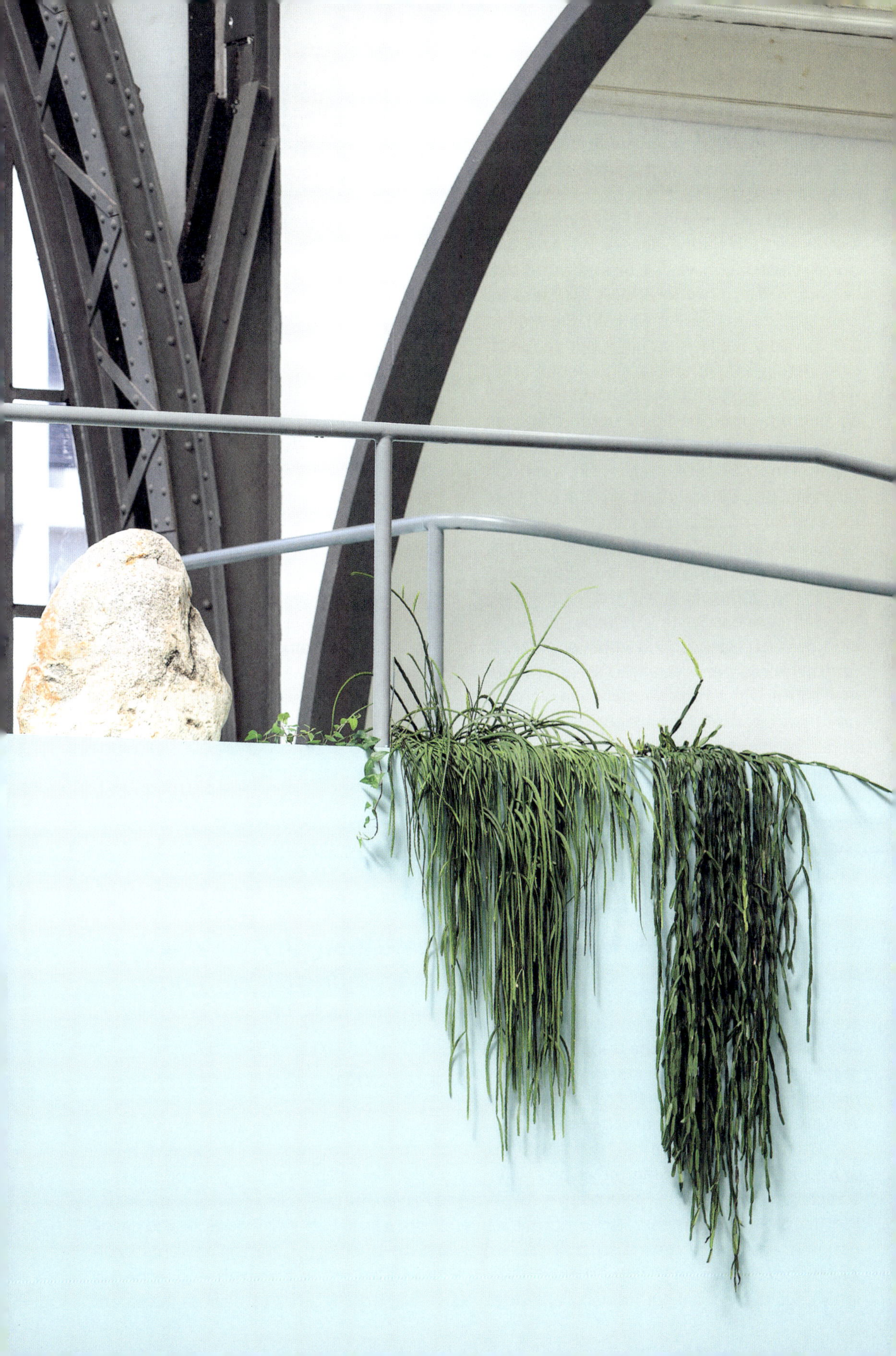

AP Minimalismus hat ja eine ganz eigene Tradition, und eine Handschrift kann auch ein Warnsignal sein, dass man in Bequemlichkeit verfällt und sich nur noch selbst wiederholt oder ein Erfolgsrezept reproduziert, wohingegen mich vor allem das Experimentieren interessiert. Ich glaube, dass sich eine Arbeit quasi selbst sucht, was sie braucht, und sich konzeptionelle Erfordernisse und Materiallösungen zusammen entwickeln. Bestimmte Medien oder Felder sind nicht per se falsch oder richtig, und ich halte eine Arbeit auch nicht automatisch für interessanter, nur weil es sich um eine Live-Performance handelt und nicht um ein Objekt. So viele andere Aspekte müssen bedacht werden, wie Qualität, Politik und Bedeutung. Ich habe nicht vor, mir eine Nische für meine künstlerische Praxis zu schaffen oder mein Territorium zu markieren und zu verteidigen. Im Zweifel bedeutet es den Tod für Begeisterung und Neugier, und für mich ist es das Beste am Dasein als Künstlerin, dass ich spielen, mich selbst erforschen und herausfordern kann. Zu Beginn einer Arbeit überlege ich daher nicht, was ich mit den Performer*innen machen will, sondern denke zuerst darüber nach, was mich interessiert, was ich aktuell für wichtig halte und kommunizieren möchte, und überlege erst dann, wie ich es am besten umsetze. Natürlich hängt es auch von den Leuten ab, mit denen ich zusammenarbeiten möchte, von den Dingen, die ich gerne mache, von den Fähigkeiten, die ich besitze oder die ich mir gern aneignen würde und so weiter. Ein weiterer Punkt ist, dass das, was heute radikal ist, morgen vielleicht schon banal wirkt und von dem Objekt seiner Kritik vollständig appropriiert wurde. Jede Strategie, jede Entscheidung ist kontextabhängig und muss daher ständig angepasst und geändert werden, weil sich ja auch unsere Welt in einem Wahnsinnstempo verändert.

Wollte ich eine Handschrift schaffen, würde ich den breitgefächerten und vielschichtigen Bereich des „Performativen" wählen; der biologische menschliche Körper ist dabei nur ein Element und muss nicht das einzige bleiben. In meinen letzten Arbeiten habe ich versucht, mehr als nur menschliche oder than-human or non-human forms of embodiment, movement, and thinking. At this point in time it felt like a natural development to go a step further and work directly with other material configurations as well, to discover how they behave and perform. Even thinking about what it means to do something "live" gets more complicated if the border between what is and is not alive is porous, not marked by an ontological distinction but simply by configurational and structural difference.

RV What you describe here can be well summarized by defining your practice as "undisciplined". By looking at various disciplines, including art, as ways of relating to the world, each one using their own precise means and methodologies, and by bringing many of them together in the exhibition, I feel you are constructing new perspectives, new shapes, forms and thoughts that can only emerge when the relationality to the world is retotalized, when the artificial boundaries between traditional disciplines are broken and, as you say, the porous reality is allowed to breathe within the work. You have often collaborated with scientists, including for this exhibition. How has this experience been for you and how did the scientists respond to your undertaking? Many artists approach scientists with interest and knowledge, but it does not always work both ways.

AP I have to say that working in inter/transdisciplinary/non-disciplined ways is much easier said than done, especially when it comes to art and science.

This work requires a lot of time and effort: to understand, study, read, learn – at least a bit – from the new discipline you are approaching. And the structure and timeframes of many projects do not allow for that. This work also needs a double opening, a coming towards each other with interest and respect. And respect is earned by making an effort to speak the other's

nicht-menschliche Formen von Verkörperungen, Bewegungen und Denkweisen zu erkunden. Es schien mir eine natürliche Entwicklung, im nächsten Schritt auch mit anderen Materialkonfigurationen zu arbeiten und herauszufinden, wie sie sich verhalten und performen. Es fällt einem schon schwerer, nur darüber nachzudenken, wie man etwas „live" darstellen kann, wenn die Grenze zwischen Belebtem und Unbelebtem durchlässig und nicht durch ontologische, sondern lediglich strukturelle Unterschiede gekennzeichnet ist.

RV Deine Beschreibung lässt sich gut zusammenfassen, indem man deine künstlerische Praxis als im besten Sinne „disziplinlos" bezeichnet. Wenn du verschiedene Disziplinen, also auch die Kunst, als Möglichkeiten betrachtest, sich mithilfe der jeweils eigenen Methodologie mit der Welt in Beziehung zu setzen, und du viele von ihnen in deiner Ausstellung zusammenbringst, konstruierst du damit neue Perspektiven, Formen und Gedanken, die nur entstehen können, wenn die Relationalität der Welt wieder in ein Ganzes überführt wird, wenn die künstlichen Grenzen zwischen den traditionellen Disziplinen eingerissen werden und die, wie du es nennst, durchlässige Realität in der Arbeit atmen darf. Wie bei dieser Ausstellung hast du schon früher mit Wissenschaftler*innen zusammengearbeitet. Welche Erfahrungen hast du dabei gemacht und wie haben die Wissenschaftler*innen auf deine Projekte reagiert? Viele Künstler*innen interessieren sich für die Arbeit von Wissenschaftler*innen und eignen sich dafür zumindest Grundkenntnisse eines bestimmten Fachgebiets an, aber das beruht wohl nicht immer auf Gegenseitigkeit.

AP Nach meiner Erfahrung gestaltet sich die inter-/transdisziplinäre/nicht-disziplinäre Zusammenarbeit als nicht so einfach, vor allem in der Kombination Kunst und Wissenschaft. Eine Zusammenarbeit erfordert Zeit und Einsatz, denn man muss sich – wenigstens

language. It also means that neither the artist nor the scientist should trivialize the other's work and knowledge, and that neither should claim to know what they do not know. Besides, there are different artists and different scientists. It would make a huge difference, say, if you were working on a topic related to evolution and you collaborated with a scientist like Lynn Margulis with her rich world of symbiogenesis, as opposed to someone like Richard Dawkins and his world of the selfish gene; or if a scientist were to work with an artist who made no effort to understand or learn, in a more rigorous manner, about the scientist's field of work – which is actually not an easy task.

We also have to admit that art is not always about precision and rigorous thinking. It might sometimes give the false impression that it is a field where anything goes, where nothing has to be justified and one can make any claim without having to prove it or to come even remotely close to doing so. I have been trying to learn, read, study as much as I can about the scientific topics I am interested in. I have read books that I could not easily understand (and some technical parts I never did). But I have been making the effort, so now, for example, I can quite proficiently discuss some aspects of chemistry with chemists. Sometimes I even have a better overview of certain topics, since chemistry is such a highly specialized field, whereas art affords the luxury of drifting from one discipline or area of research to another, without really having to go into depth until it becomes necessary to acquire expertise. But these are interests that I have been pursuing for several years now. You have to establish common ground. Without it there is no way you can have productive difference or a productive argument, and that is a task in itself. Indeed, it is a task, I admit, that I have not always been willing to take on myself, so I understand that scientists sometimes feel reluctant to engage.

When it comes to *Attune*, it has been really enriching to exchange ideas with two practicing chemists. I began by working with Professor Ulrich Abram from the Institute of Chemistry at Freie Universität Berlin. He is really passionate about chemical demonstrations. He used to make these flamboyant shows for students with

ansatzweise – in die neue Disziplin einlesen und einarbeiten. Das lassen Struktur und Zeitplan vieler Projekte nicht zu. Außerdem erfordert die Zusammenarbeit von beiden Seiten Offenheit, gegenseitiges Interesse und einen respektvollen Umgang miteinander. Respekt verdient man sich, indem man sich bemüht, die Sprache des oder der anderen zu erlernen. Weder die Künstler*innen noch die Wissenschaftler*innen dürfen die Arbeit und das Wissen ihres Gegenübers herunterspielen oder sich ein Wissen anmaßen, das sie eigentlich gar nicht haben. Natürlich sind nicht alle Künstler*innen und Wissenschaftler*innen gleich. Es wäre nämlich etwas völlig anderes, wenn ein*e Künstler*in sich in einer Arbeit mit einem Thema wie Evolution auseinandersetzt und dabei mit einer Wissenschaftlerin wie Lynn Margulis mit ihrer beziehungsreichen Welt der Symbiogenese zusammenarbeitet oder mit jemandem wie Richard Dawkins mit seiner Welt der egoistischen Gene; oder ob Wissenschafler*innen mit Künstler*innen zusammenarbeiten, die sich nicht die Mühe machen, sich tiefer in das Forschungsgebiet des Gegenübers einzulesen – was im Übrigen natürlich gar keine so leichte Aufgabe ist.

Außerdem müssen wir uns eingestehen, dass es in der Kunst nicht immer um Präzision und strenges Denken geht. Manchmal könnte man den falschen Eindruck gewinnen, bei Kunst handele es sich um eine Disziplin, bei der alles erlaubt ist, bei der man nichts rechtfertigen muss und jede Behauptung aufstellen kann, ohne sie auch nur ansatzweise belegen zu müssen. Ich habe immer versucht, mich möglichst intensiv in das Wissenschaftsgebiet, das mich gerade interessiert, einzulesen und einzuarbeiten. Ich habe Bücher gelesen, die für mich nicht einfach zu verstehen waren (einige technische Details habe ich tatsächlich nie verstanden). Trotzdem habe ich mir die Mühe gemacht und kann mich heute, um ein Beispiel zu nennen, mit Chemiker*innen einigermaßen sachkundig über bestimmte Aspekte der Chemie unterhalten. Manchmal habe ich als Außenstehende sogar einen besseren Überblick, weil die Chemie so ein weites Feld ist und Wissenschaftler*innen immer nur

costumes and lights and even music. I remember entering his office on a hot summer's day in Berlin last year, opening up the conversation about the Briggs-Rauscher chemical reaction – an example of self-organization in chemical systems, an oscillating, color-change chemical reaction that I was interested in staging in the exhibition space in an automated manner and at a larger scale than it is usually demonstrated in the lab. I started to explain why I would like to show the reaction, what I think of its implications and was going on and on for a bit when all of a sudden I noticed him smile. He looked off into the distance, waved his hands and said, quite performatively: "Everything is chemistry – or at least that's what we chemists like to say." But by then, the impression had been made and the common ground was there. We did several tests together during the early research phase, but unfortunately, Professor Abram could not continue to help (and has meanwhile retired).

I have nevertheless continued the project with Bogdan Enache, a Bucharest-based chemist, quite young and equally passionate about the beauty of chemistry. Working in the Romanian context means that scientists sometimes have a more "holistic" understanding of processes – it has to do with having fewer resources at your disposal, since some research centers or labs cannot afford specialized departments for every single part of a process. The advantage with having less division of labor is that scientists are encouraged to get involved with more stages of a process and thus acquire a more integrated understanding of it; they can directly trace back problems to the source, and mistakes sometimes become easier to find and correct.

At the time of my writing this, Bodgan and I have just succeeded in reproducing the Briggs-Rauscher reaction at a larger scale with a prototype of an automated system, and we are very hopeful that we will also be able to perform it as part of the exhibition in Berlin.

RV Since we wrote our *Manifesto for the Gynecene* almost ten years ago, the darkness descending upon the world has increased. What we were proposing at that time was already utopian, as the demands

auf bestimmte Teilgebiete spezialisiert sind, ich als Künstlerin dagegen den Luxus genieße, zwischen den Disziplinen oder Forschungsgebieten hin und her zu wechseln, und nur dann in die Tiefe gehen muss, wenn Fachwissen unumgänglich wird. Mit diesen Themen befasse ich mich schon seit ein paar Jahren. Man muss eine gemeinsame Basis schaffen, sonst entstehen keine produktiven Auseinandersetzungen. Das ist eine zusätzliche Aufgabe, und ich muss gestehen, dass ich sie nicht immer gern auf mich genommen habe. Deshalb habe ich auch Verständnis, wenn Wissenschaftler*innen sich nicht auf Anhieb auf eine Zusammenarbeit einlassen wollen.

Bei den Vorbereitungen zu *Attune* hatte ich das Glück, mich mit zwei Chemikern austauschen zu können. Das war wirklich bereichernd. Zuerst habe ich mit Professor Ulrich Abram vom Institut für Chemie an der Freien Universität Berlin zusammengearbeitet. Er kann sich für chemische Vorführungen richtig begeistern. Früher hat er für seine Studierenden extravagante Shows mit Kostümen und Lichteffekten und allem Drum und Dran inszeniert. Ich weiß noch, wie ich im letzten Jahr an einem heißen Sommertag in sein Berliner Büro kam und unser Gespräch gleich zu Beginn auf die Briggs-Rauscher-Reaktion lenkte – dabei handelt es sich um ein Beispiel für Selbstorganisation in chemischen Systemen, eine oszillierende Reaktion mit Farbänderungen, die ich für die Ausstellung automatisieren und dort in einem größeren Maßstab zeigen wollte, als es bei Vorführungen im Labor üblich ist. Ich erklärte ihm, warum ich ausgerechnet diese chemische Reaktion bei meiner Ausstellung zeigen wollte, sprach über ihre tiefere Bedeutung und redete weiter, bis ich plötzlich merkte, wie ein Lächeln über sein Gesicht zog. Als wäre es eine Performance, schweifte sein Blick in die Ferne, er hob die Hände und sagte: „Alles ist Chemie – wenigstens behaupten wir Chemiker das gern." Doch da war unsere gemeinsame Basis bereits geschaffen. Während meiner ersten Recherchen haben wir etliche Tests zusammen durchgeführt, doch leider konnte Professor Abram mich dann nicht weiter unterstützen (und ist inzwischen im Ruhestand).

of any manifesto should be. Yet, as proven by the incredible feedback we received, leading to translations of the manifesto all over the world, there seemed to be a general desire to understand and imagine ways of organizing and being that can counter the hegemonies of oppression. Now this desire is strained by an intensified attack on the forces of life, and 2050, the approximate target that Immanuel Wallerstein posited as the threshold for the change of the current capitalist world-system, seems to be even further away, taking with it all hope and reason. In 2010, he warned that "we cannot expect a better world-system circa 2050 if, in the interim, any of the three pending supercalamities occurs: irrevocable climate change, vast pandemics, and nuclear war." Of these supercalamities, we are already witnessing the effects of the first two, and current wars, even if not yet nuclear, have indefinitely postponed the chance for an overturn of the military complex as the main stimulator of the global economy and regulator of daily lives. What is your perception of the current cataclysmic reality, and if you were to write the *Manifesto for the Gynecene* today, what would be your main demand?

AP To be honest, I am a bit tired of making demands, or at least of making them loudly. I am not sure spoken or written demands are the most effective means of achieving real change today.

I work quietly for the political goals and concrete tasks that depend on me and my direct interaction with other human and non-human actors in a more straightforward way. I mostly try to speak and write through my work. And besides art, I also spend time gardening, doing some construction work at my grandmother's place, and learning more about chemistry. I think surviving what lies ahead will require knowing, or remembering, not only how to sing, dance, and think

Das Projekt habe ich trotzdem fortgesetzt, nun mit dem in Bukarest forschenden Chemiker Bogdan Enache. Er ist noch recht jung und ebenfalls begeistert von der Schönheit der Chemie. Einige Wissenschaftler*innen aus Rumänien haben ein eher „holistisches" Verständnis von Prozessen – das liegt daran, dass ihnen weniger Mittel zur Verfügung stehen, weil einige Forschungszentren oder Laboratorien sich keine Spezialabteilungen für jeden einzelnen Schritt des Prozesses leisten können. Eine geringere Arbeitsteilung hat den Vorteil, dass Wissenschaftler*innen Prozesse über mehrere Stadien begleiten und so ein umfassenderes Verständnis davon entwickeln können; Ursachen von Problemen können so leichter zurückverfolgt, Fehler frühzeitig entdeckt und korrigiert werden.

Vor Kurzem erst ist es Bogdan und mir gelungen, die Briggs-Rauscher-Reaktion in größerem Maßstab zu reproduzieren, außerdem haben wir den Prototyp eines automatisierten Systems entwickelt, den wir höchstwahrscheinlich im Rahmen der Berliner Ausstellung vorführen können.

RV Seit wir vor fast zehn Jahren gemeinsam das *Manifest für das Gynozän* verfasst haben, ist die Welt noch finsterer geworden. Unsere Forderungen damals waren utopisch, es handelte sich ja auch um ein Manifest. Das unglaubliche Feedback, das uns erreicht und dazu geführt hat, dass das Manifest in etliche Sprachen übersetzt wurde, ließ vermuten, dass sich viele Menschen neue Formen des Organisierens wünschen, als Gegenmittel gegen hegemoniale Strukturen und Unterdrückung. Heute setzen die verstärkten Angriffe auf die Kräfte des Lebens diesem Wunsch stark zu, und das Jahr 2050, ab dem laut Immanuel Wallerstein das kapitalistische Weltsystem hätte zu kippen beginnen sollen, scheint in weite Ferne gerückt zu sein. 2010 warnte Wallerstein, dass „wir ab ca. 2050 kein besseres Weltsystem erwarten dürfen, sofern bis dahin eine der folgenden Superkatastrophen eintrifft: unumkehr-

abstractly but also how to wire an electrical circuit, build a toolshed, and other, hands-on work – a lot of work. I try to be neither paralyzed by complexity and the scale of the trouble we are in, nor overly excited by political actions that might be largely symbolic, merely simulating impact within or without social media.

It also seems to me that there is a fine line between utopian thinking and a kind of attitude like "be realistic, demand the impossible", a kind of refusal to settle for anything less than what is ultimately impossible to achieve, a kind of rigid commitment to only fight for that which cannot be obtained – in other words, a glorification of defeat.

Impossible goals, that are never meant to – or cannot – be realized, might well offer the gratification of being right, and also exonerate one from having to measure anything against reality, having to measure the actual impact of one's actions, what they actually achieve – almost as though it were enough to be right and state it, or merely make a demand. But I just do not think that is enough anymore. So maybe I have become quieter (people who interact with me might disagree), or maybe more strategic; or maybe just older. Within the life of the planet, our current era is less than an instant. That does not mean we should not care about what happens, but I believe we do need to consider our own insignificance or, to use the kinder term, non-exceptionalism. Only from this position of humility and distancing might we be able to mitigate ever-increasing conflicts. In response to your question about our manifesto, I would not write a manifesto today. However, I still stand by what we wrote back then, especially the ending, which talks about "recognizing each other as individual instants in a collective, fragile, subjective time, facing the vastness of our cosmic surroundings" and about "this togetherness, in its

barer Klimawandel, weltweite Pandemien oder atomarer Krieg". Die Folgen der ersten beiden Superkatastrophen haben wir bereits erlebt, und die derzeitigen Kriege, obwohl sie noch nicht nuklear geführt werden, haben die Chance, den militärischen Komplex als wichtigste Antriebskraft der Weltwirtschaft zu überwinden, auf unbestimmte Zeit verschoben. Wie siehst du die dramatische Weltenlage und welche Hauptforderung würdest du heute stellen, wenn du das *Manifest für das Gynozän* noch einmal schreiben würdest?

AP Ganz ehrlich? Ich bin es langsam müde, Forderungen zu stellen oder mich zumindest öffentlich dafür stark zu machen. Ob schriftliche oder mündliche Forderungen heute noch das effektivste Mittel sind, um echten Wandel zu bewirken, weiß ich nicht. Lieber arbeite ich im Stillen für politische Ziele und widme mich konkreten Aufgaben, indem ich direkt mit anderen menschlichen und nichtmenschlichen Performer*innen interagiere. Meistens drücke ich mich durch meine Arbeit aus. Abgesehen von der Kunst befasse ich mich mit Gartenarbeit, baue das Haus meiner Großmutter um und beschäftige mich intensiv mit Chemie. Wenn wir auch in Zukunft überleben wollen, müssen wir Wissen anhäufen und uns nicht nur einprägen, wie man singt, tanzt und abstrakt denkt, sondern auch, wie man einen Stromkreis herstellt, einen Geräteschuppen baut und andere praktische Dinge verrichtet – also vor allem handwerkliche Arbeiten. Ich versuche, mich von der Komplexität und Größenordnung unserer Probleme nicht lähmen zu lassen und mich auch nicht zu sehr für politische Aktionen zu begeistern, die lediglich symbolischen Wert haben und sich in erster Linie in den sozialen Medien auswirken. Meiner Meinung nach verläuft nur eine sehr schmale Grenze zwischen dem utopischen Denken und der „Sei realistisch, verlange das Unmögliche"-Haltung, also dieser Weigerung, sich mit weniger zufrieden zu geben als mit dem, was letzten Endes immer unerreichbar bleiben wird, die-

most abstract form, that should be capable of creating a sense of unity across our seemingly incompatible histories [...]."

Maybe some of that abstract togetherness can also become concrete through *Attune*: through spending time with song and movement, with each other or with a pool of liquid that organizes itself – by means of a process similar to how we ourselves acquire form through morphogenesis – into a structure of beautiful, changing patterns, simply when traversed by a temperature gradient.

ses starre Festhalten an einem Kampf, den man nie
gewinnen kann – mit anderen Worten, die Glorifizie-
rung der Niederlage.

Setzt man sich Ziele, die niemals verwirklicht
werden können, verschafft einem das am Ende vielleicht die Genugtuung, Recht behalten zu haben,
und es entbindet einen von der Pflicht, die Auswir-
kungen der eigenen Handlungen an der Realität
messen zu müssen – als würde es schon genügen,
wenn man behauptet, Recht zu haben, oder wenn
man einfach nur eine Forderung stellt und nicht auf
ihre Verwirklichung hinarbeitet. Ich glaube nicht,
dass das heute noch genügt. Mag sein, dass ich
ruhiger geworden bin (auch wenn Menschen, die
mit mir interagieren, das vielleicht anders sehen)
oder besonnener oder einfach nur älter. Denken wir
an die Lebensdauer unseres Planeten, dann stellt
unser Zeitalter nur einen winzigen Abschnitt dar.
Das bedeutet allerdings nicht, dass uns egal sein
sollte, was um uns herum geschieht; aber wir müssen uns eben auch damit auseinandersetzen, dass
wir unbedeutend sind oder, um es freundlicher zu
formulieren, nicht außergewöhnlich. Nur aus einer
demütigen, bescheidenen Position heraus wird es
uns gelingen, die sich immer weiter hochschaukeln-
den Konflikte abzuschwächen und zu lösen. Aber
zurück zu deiner Frage nach unserem Manifest –
heute würde ich keins mehr verfassen. Trotzdem
stehe ich immer noch hinter dem, was wir damals
geschrieben haben, vor allem hinter dem Schluss,
wo es heißt: „Wir glauben, dass die endlose Suche
nach Bedeutung vorübergehend dadurch befrie-
digt werden kann, dass wir einander erkennen als
verschiedene Momente in einer kollektiven, fragi-
len, subjektiven Zeit, die der Weite unserer kosmi-
schen Umgebung begegnen. … Es ist diese Gemein-
samkeit in ihrer abstraktesten Form, die dazu in der
Lage sein sollte, über unsere scheinbar inkompatib-
len Geschichten hinweg ein Gefühl der Einigkeit zu
schaffen…“.

Vielleicht kann *Attune* ja dieses abstrakte Miteinander ein wenig konkretisieren: indem wir uns
Zeit nehmen für Musik und Bewegungen, Zeit fürei-
nander oder für eine Flüssigkeit, die sich selbst orga-
nisiert – indem sie einen Prozess durchläuft ähnlich
wie die Morphogenese, durch die wir unsere Form
erhalten – und zu einer Struktur aus schönen, chan-
gierenden Mustern wird, die nur entstehen, weil ein
Temperaturgradient sie kreuzt.

Ausstellungsansicht / Installation view
Alexandra Pirici. Attune, Hamburger Bahnhof –
Nationalgalerie der Gegenwart, 2024

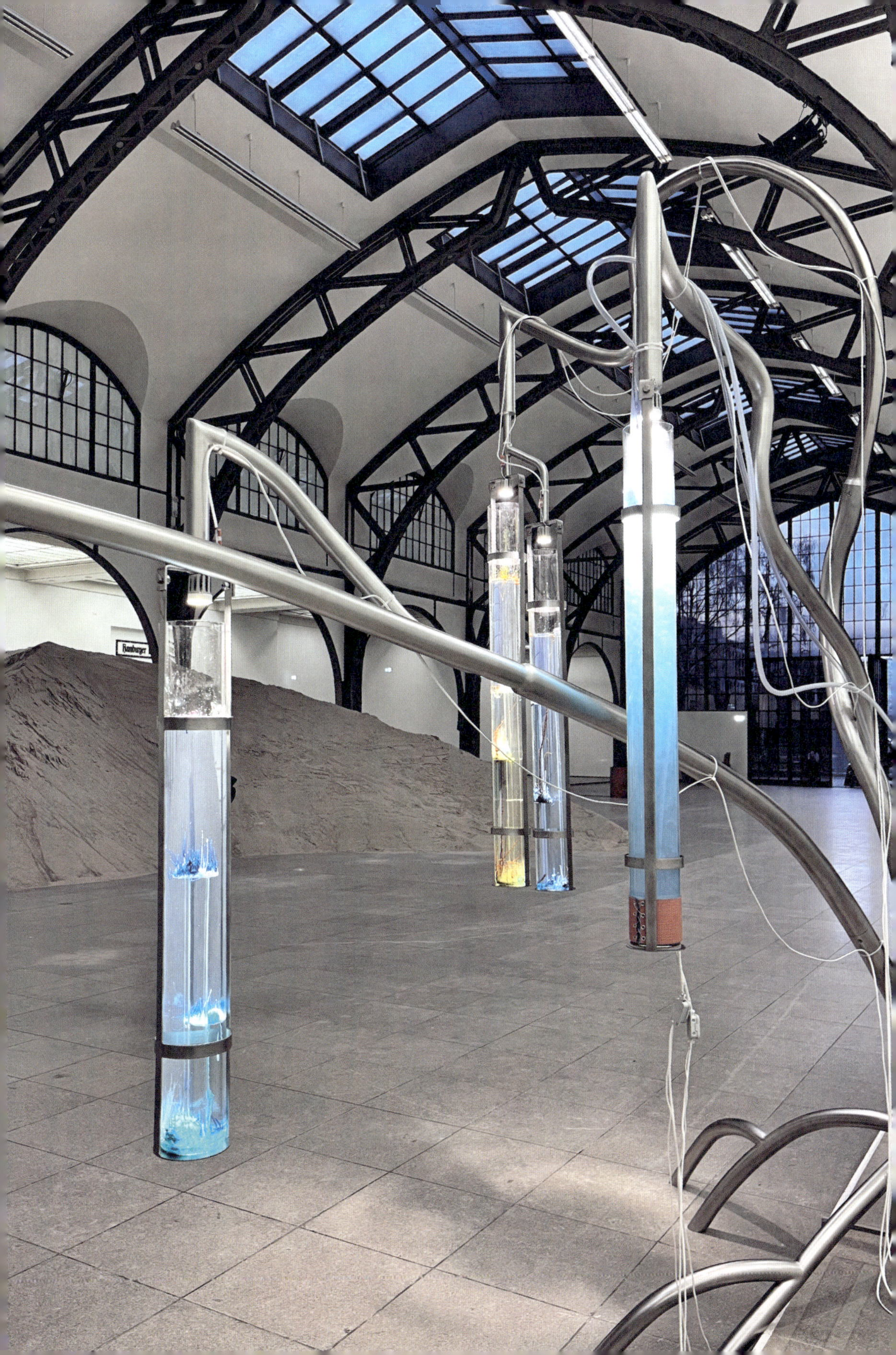

Eine endlose Reihe von Gesten / An Endless Series of Gestures

Cecilia Alemani

Die Geschichte der Kunst ist eine Geschichte von Körpern. Werden der symbolische Gehalt sowie Fragen der Ikonologie und des Stils einmal außer Acht gelassen, stellt sich die Kunstgeschichte – zumindest die der figürlichen Kunst – als eine endlose Reihe von Gesten dar: eine Abfolge von Körpern, die sich, den figürlichen Darstellungen in einer uralten Schriftrolle gleich, zu einem langen Band ausrollen lassen und die Entwicklungen über die Jahrhunderte hinweg aufzeigen. Wenn ich durch Kataloge blättere oder mir Abbildungen in Kunstbüchern anschaue, finde ich es jedes Mal spannend, der Kontinuität bestimmter Gesten nachzuspüren: die Hand, die auf dem Bauch der schwangeren Madonna ruht, die an- oder wehklagend zum Himmel emporgereckten Arme, die auf dem Bett ausgestreckte, geöffnete Hand als Zeichen der Hingabe, der nach einer Niederlage gesenkte Kopf...

Art history is a history of bodies. When stripped of symbolism, iconology, and questions of style, the history of art – of figurative art, at least – begins to look like an endless series of gestures: a choreography of bodies reeling out in a long ribbon, like the sculpted figures of an ancient column that unspools over the centuries. As I leaf through catalogs and illustrated books, I have always enjoyed tracing the continuity of certain gestures: the hand resting on the Madonna's pregnant belly, the arms raised to the sky in grief or lamentation, the upturned palm flung out on the bed to express abandon, the head bowed in defeat...

At least since the publication of Marcel Mauss's essay "Techniques of the Body", it has been generally accepted that gestures themselves are a product of culture. However natural they may seem when performed by our bodies, gestures are tied to the complex process of

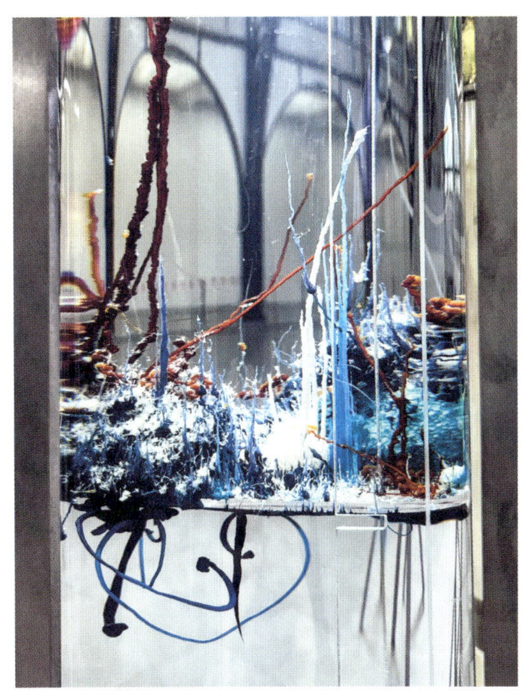

Alexandra Pirici. Attune, 2024, Detail eines chemischen Gartens / detail of a chemical garden; siehe S. / see p. 82

Spätestens seit dem Erscheinen von Marcel Mauss' Essay „Techniken des Körpers" ist allgemein akzeptiert, dass Gesten kulturelle Produkte sind. Wie natürlich sie auch immer erscheinen mögen, wenn unser Körper sie ausführt, so sind Gesten doch stets mit einem komplexen Lernprozess verbunden, und indem wir sie nachahmen oder sie uns antrainiert werden, weist uns ihr Gebrauch als einer bestimmten Gesellschaft, Gruppe oder Gemeinschaft zugehörig aus.

Ungeachtet ihrer kulturellen Ursprünge werden Gesten häufig als unvermittelte emotionale Reaktionen gesehen und führen demzufolge zu Annahmen: Von Gesten erwarten wir, dass sie die Wahrheit ausdrücken oder zumindest einen ehrlicheren, unverstellten Zugang zur Welt unserer Gefühle bieten. Gesten werden oftmals als etwas erachtet, das unsere ehrlichsten und intimsten Reaktionen und Einstellungen wiedergibt: Vergleichbar mit gutturalen Lauten haben sie etwas Vorsprachliches an sich, sodass wir sie mit Tiefe und Urinstinkten assoziieren. Noch die affektierteste, kryptischste Geste scheint die wahre Natur einer Person mehr zu offenbaren als es ihre Worte

learning, by imitation or inculcation, that defines us as members of a certain society, group, or community.

Despite their cultural origin, gestures are often thought of as an unmediated expression of emotion, so they always come laden with assumptions; we expect gestures to express the truth, or at least to offer a more honest, immediate window onto the universe of feelings. Gestures are often interpreted as emanating directly from our most sincere and intimate responses and opinions: like guttural exclamations, they have something pre-linguistic about them, and are therefore considered deep and primal. Even the most affected, codified gestures seem to reveal a person's true nature more than their words and ideas do. That is why gestures are closely linked to the notion of decency. One need only think of the almost primitive brutality of certain obscene gestures, or, by contrast, the supposedly innocent, exquisite sophistication of other poses.

Alexandra Pirici's art is an art of gestures, and dwells in the paradox of being both hyper-cultural and direct, intellectual and physical, sophisticated and raw. Pirici's performative

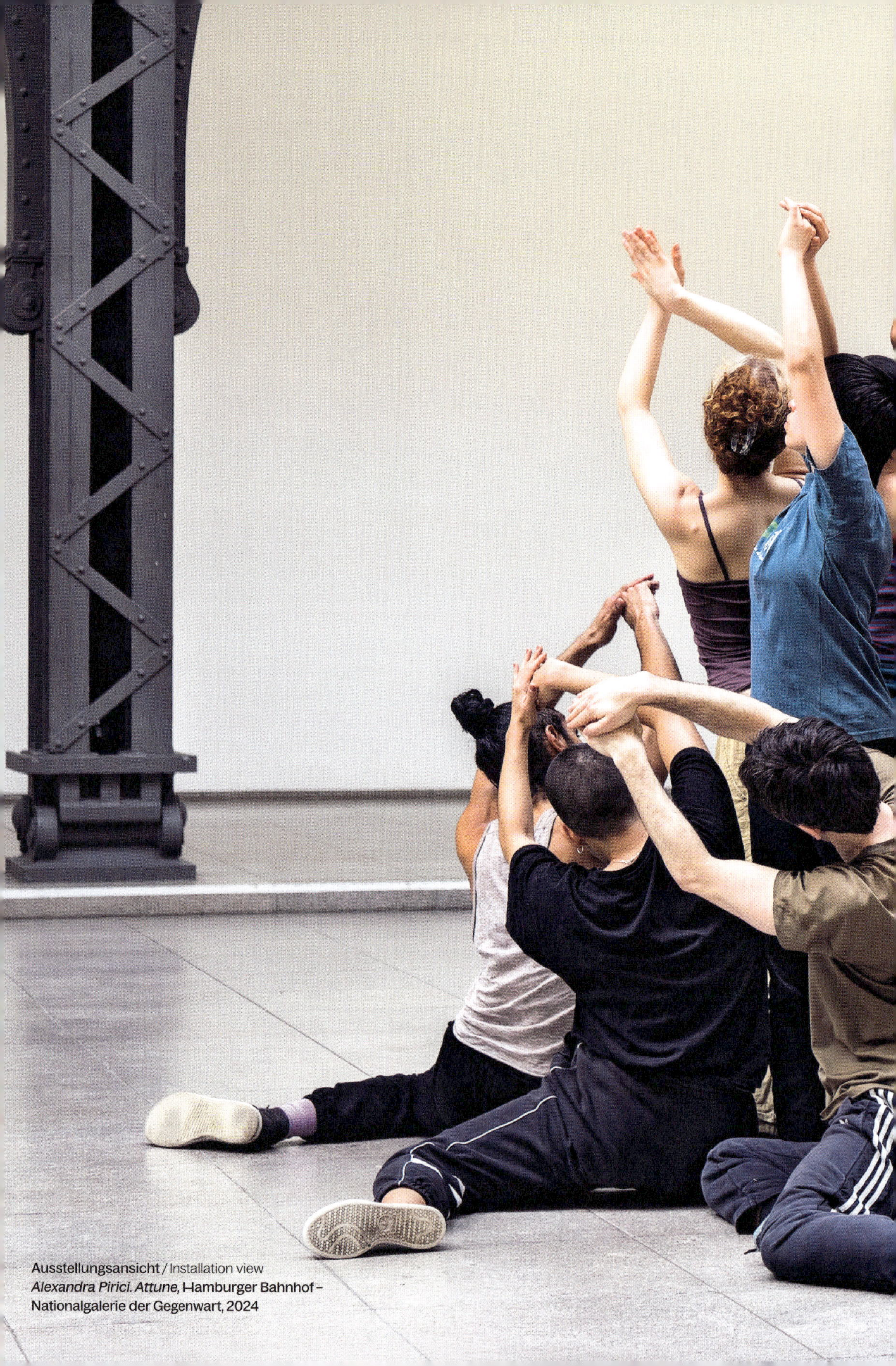

Ausstellungsansicht / Installation view
Alexandra Pirici. Attune, Hamburger Bahnhof –
Nationalgalerie der Gegenwart, 2024

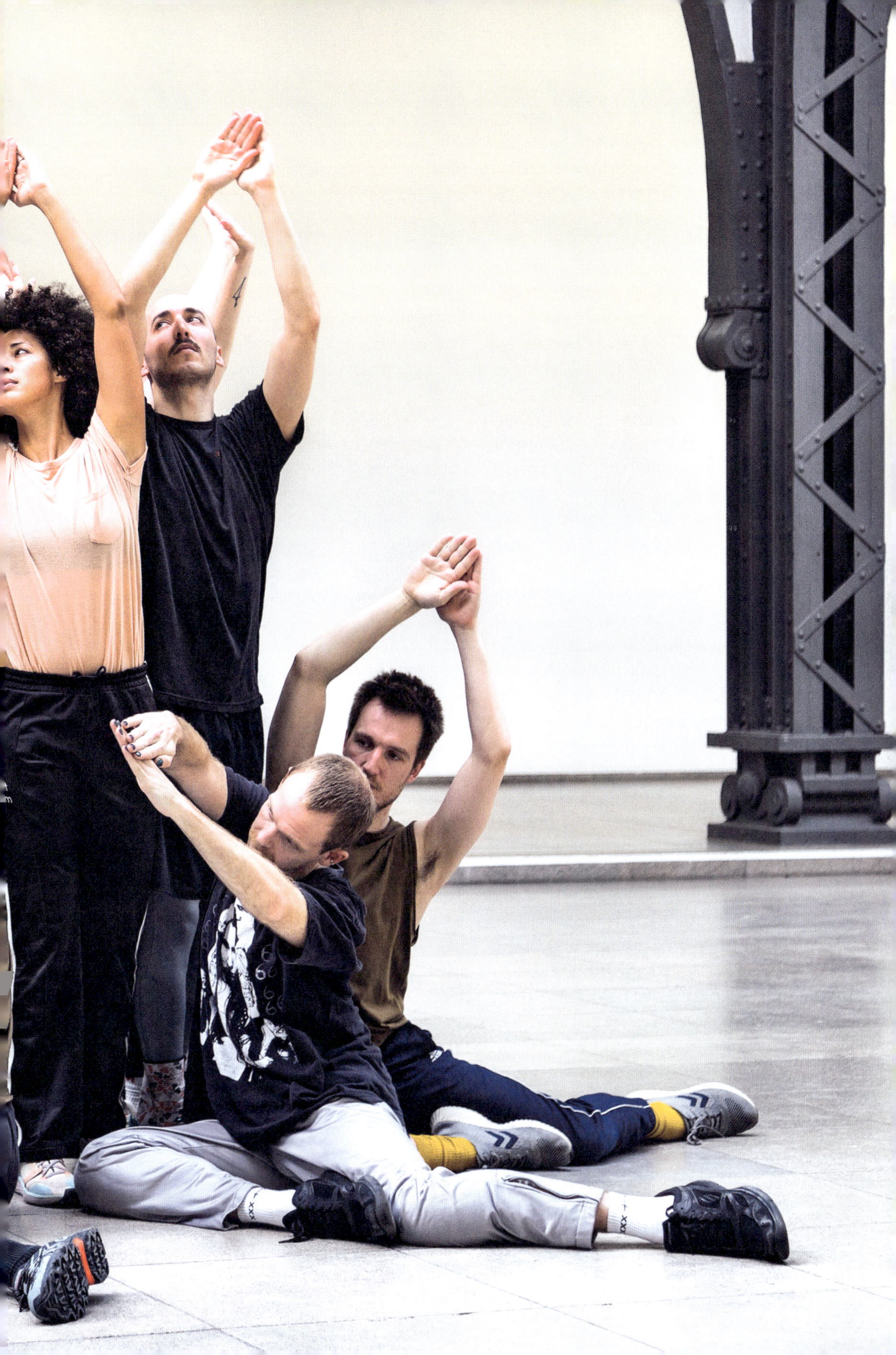

oder Ideen zu tun vermögen. Das ist auch der Grund, warum Gesten eng mit der Vorstellung von Schicklichkeit verknüpft sind; man führe sich nur die geradezu primitive Brutalität gewisser obszöner Gesten vor Augen oder – als Kontrast dazu – die vermeintlich unschuldige, exquisite Raffinesse anderer Posen.

Alexandra Piricis Kunst ist eine Kunst der Gesten. Ihre Praxis zeichnet sich durch das Paradoxon aus, zugleich hyperkulturell und direkt, intellektuell und physisch, hochentwickelt und ungeschliffen roh zu sein. Piricis performative Aktionen wirken nicht natürlich; sie scheinen vielmehr minutiös choreografiert und von diversen Schichten – Erzählungen, Andeutungen, Anspielungen und Querverweisen – überlagert oder gar überkrustet zu sein. Zur selben Zeit jedoch ist dies eine Kunst, die mit Anstrengung verbunden ist, mit Körpern und Schweiß.

Pirici spricht von ihrer Praxis häufig als körperlicher Arbeit und setzt sie somit direkt oder indirekt in eine Beziehung zu einer spezifischen Tradition der avantgardistischen Performance. Im frühen 20. Jahrhundert begannen Tänzer*innen, sich mit den formalen Qualitäten der Geste auseinanderzusetzen, wobei die unverbundenen, quantifizierbaren, stakkatoartigen Bewegungen, die im Tanz nunmehr zu sehen waren, auf eine Art den Abläufen in Fabriken ähnelten, nachdem die industriellen Produktionsprozesse durch Einführung des Taylorismus allseits standardisiert und optimiert worden waren.

Ungeachtet ihrer vergänglichen Natur ist Piricis Kunst mit ihren historischen Vorläufern bestens vertraut. Es ist kein Zufall, dass eine ihrer ersten öffentlichen Präsentationen – ihr Konzept für den rumänischen Pavillon auf der Biennale zu Venedig 2013 – eine Art visuelle Enzyklopädie berühmter Kunstwerke war, die sie als *Tableaux vivants* oder performative Aktionen neu inszenierte. Mit anderen Worten hatte man hier ein hyper-historisiertes Werk, das sich seiner Position im Fluss der Geschichte höchst bewusst war. Einige Jahre später konzipierte Pirici – für die Skulptur Projekte Münster 2017 – eine andere Arbeit, die ihr tiefes Unbehagen über Formen der Einfluss-

actions do not seem natural, but carefully choreographed and layered – even encrusted – with narratives, intimations, allusions, and cross-references. At the same time, however, this is an art of effort, of bodies and sweat.

Pirici often speaks of her work in terms of labor, implicitly or explicitly connecting it to an entire tradition of avant-garde performance. In the early 20th century, dance began to adopt an economy of gesture – discrete, quantifiable, staccato movements – not unlike the one that characterized factory life at the time, with the introduction of the new science of Taylorism.

And despite its ephemeral nature, Pirici's art is extremely conscious of its historical precedents. It is no coincidence then that one of her first public works – for the Romanian Pavilion at the Venice Biennale in 2013 – was a sort of visual encyclopedia of famous artworks, recreated as *tableaux vivants* or performative actions: in other words, a hyper-historicized work, keenly aware of its position in the flow of history. A few years later – in 2017, for Skulptur Projekte Münster – Pirici presented another piece that was in its own way affected by a deep anxiety of influence: *Leaking Territories* was a choreography that worked like a human search engine, with performers taking on the futile, at the same time heroic task of standing in for the vast sea of instant information we have become accustomed to finding online. More recently, Pirici's actions have become even more complex, though they are still primarily concerned with the transmission of knowledge through gestures, sounds, and language. Her pieces are veritable "encyclopedias of relations", to borrow the title she used to describe her work for the 59th Venice Biennale. These ongoing actions are "aggregates" – again, Pirici's own description of a work that debuted in Berlin in 2017, moved to Buenos Aires the following year, and culminated in Basel in 2019 – of knowledge and actions, where nature and culture intertwine in complex forms of embodiment.

Among the historic precursors of Pirici's actions, one must inevitably consider the vast universe of performance art in the 1960s and 70s. Compared to these antecedents, the actions by Pirici and other contemporaries – who include very different figures, such as Alexandra

nahme auf eine ganz eigene Art vorbrachte: *Leaking Territories* war eine Choreografie, die wie eine menschliche Suchmaschine funktionierte. Hier waren Performende mit der so aussichtslosen wie heroischen Mission betraut, stellvertretend für die gigantische Informationsflut einzustehen, an deren sofortige Online-Abrufbarkeit wir uns mittlerweile gewöhnt haben. In jüngster Zeit haben Piricis Aktionen sogar noch an Komplexität gewonnen, obgleich sie noch immer primär mit der Übermittlung von Wissen mithilfe von Gesten, Sound und Sprache befasst sind. In Anlehnung an den Titel, den sie für ihr Projekt für die 59. Biennale in Venedig wählte *(Encyclopedia of Relations)*, lassen sich ihre Arbeiten in der Tat als regelrechte „Enzyklopädien der Beziehungen" beschreiben. Diese fortlaufenden Aktionen sind „Aggregate" – auch dies wiederum Piricis eigene Worte und der Titel einer weiteren Arbeit, die erstmals 2017 in Berlin zu sehen war, im darauffolgenden Jahr dann nach Buenos Aires reiste und 2019 schließlich in Basel gezeigt wurde. Und zwar sind es Aggregate aus Wissen und Aktionen, komplexe personifizierte Darstellungen, in denen Natur und Kultur miteinander verschmelzen.

Betrachtet man die historischen Vorgänger*innen von Piricis Aktionen, ist die Performanceszene der 1960er- und 70er-Jahre zweifelsohne von besonderer Bedeutung. Im Gegensatz zu diesen Vorformen gilt für Pirici und andere Künstler*innen ihrer Generation – zu denen höchst unterschiedliche Positionen wie Alexandra Bachzetsis, Maria Hassabi, Anne Imhof, Ragnar Kjartansson oder Tino Sehgal zu zählen sind – dass sie in ihren Aktionen weder auf besondere Höhepunkte hinarbeiten, noch auf Spontaneität setzen. Ihre Art der Performancekunst, wie sie sich in den ersten Jahrzehnten des 21. Jahrhunderts herauskristallisiert hat, setzt vielmehr auf Kreisläufe und Wiederholungen: Es ist eine Kunst, die das Spektakel zu verlängern – und zu subvertieren – sucht durch choreografierte Bewegungsabläufe, die bis ins Detail geprobt und kontrolliert und auf nahezu identische Art und Weise wiederholt werden, und zwar potenziell *ad infinitum.* Diese Kunst wird häufig als lebende

Bachzetsis, Maria Hassabi, Anne Imhof, Ragnar Kjartansson, and Tino Sehgal – reject the idea of climax and spontaneity. The performance art that has emerged in the first decades of the 21st century is based on loops and repetition: it is an art that prolongs – and tries to subvert – the spectacle through a choreography of carefully rehearsed and controlled movements, repeated in an almost identical way, potentially ad infinitum. They have been described as living sculptures. There are no grand finales or moments of catharsis in these works, but rather a succession of individual, minute gestures, or collective, choral ones; they may reach sudden emotional peaks, but they also move through vast zones of silence and quiet, and almost never conclude with a striking theatrical ending.

To borrow an apt expression coined in the 1980s by the Italian art historian and curator Francesca Alinovi, the works created by Pirici and many of her generation are *performance vestite*, "clothed performances". In other words, they reject the supposed regression to a primal state on which quite a bit of performance art of the 1960s and 70s was essentially based – Marina Abramovic being a prime example. These performances are "clothed" in a literal sense: the performers are rarely naked. They are often dressed in ordinary, everyday garments – like those worn by Alexandra Pirici's performers that seem to belong to a sort of radical underground look – or sometimes in extravagant, over-the-top costumes, like the ones used by Hassabi, Bachzetsis, or Kjartasson. Many of these performances actually celebrate the artifice and sex appeal of the inorganic realm:

"clothing" also becomes a metaphor that envisions performance and dance as the manifestation of a society deeply embroiled in a system of advanced capitalism, or even emotional capitalism.

There is no way to break out of the economy of spectacle: there is no regression to a mythical state of nature – and Eden-like innocence – as in

Skulptur bezeichnet. Es gibt in diesen Arbeiten keine großen Finale oder kathartische Momente; es sind vielmehr Abfolgen minuziöser Gesten, die von einzelnen Personen, mitunter aber auch im Kollektiv, quasi im Chor, performt werden. Gelegentlich sind Momente der plötzlichen emotionalen Zuspitzung zu beobachten, die alsdann jedoch wieder langen Strecken der Ruhe und Stille weichen, und am Ende wird so gut wie nie ein unerwarteter dramatischer Schlusspunkt gesetzt.

Um einen treffenden Ausdruck zu gebrauchen, den die italienische Kunsthistorikerin und Kuratorin Francesca Alinovi bereits in den 1980er-Jahren prägte: Die von Pirici und vielen anderen Künstler*innen ihrer Generation produzierten Arbeiten gehören zu einer Art *performance vestite*, sie sind „bekleidete Performances". Mit anderen Worten lehnen sie den vermeintlichen Rückfall in jenen ursprünglichen Körperzustand ab, der aus den Performances der 1960er- und 70er-Jahre nicht wegzudenken ist – wobei Marina Abramovic sicherlich als das Paradebeispiel anzuführen wäre. Diese Performances sind im wortwörtlichen Sinn „bekleidet", das heißt die Performenden sind in den seltensten Fällen nackt. Wie Alexandra Piricis Performer*innen, in deren Outfits sich ein radikaler Underground-Look manifestiert, treten sie oftmals in gewöhnlicher Alltagskleidung auf, gelegentlich aber auch in extravaganter, übertriebener Kostümierung, wie bei Hassabi, Bachzetsis oder Kjartasson. Tatsächlich wird in vielen dieser Performances die Künstlichkeit und Anziehungskraft dieses anorganischen Elements zelebriert, wobei „Bekleidung" zur Metapher mutiert und Performance und Tanz zum visuellen Ausdruck einer Gesellschaft werden, die unauflöslich mit dem System des fortgeschrittenen oder, zutreffender, des emotionalen Kapitalismus verbunden ist. Es ist gänzlich unmöglich, dem Wirkungskreis des Spektakels zu entkommen: Es führt kein Weg zurück zum Mythos Natur – dem Zustand paradiesischer Unschuld, wie sie in vielen Performances der 1970er-Jahre heraufbeschworen wurde. Im Gegenteil, die Vorstellung von Körpern, Bekleidung und Gesten geht nun-

much performance art of the 1970s. On the contrary, there is a conception of the body, of clothing, and of gesture as directly caught up in a system of signs, values, and images, which in turn is immediately propagated through an infinite chain of smartphones and Instagram posts.

It is no coincidence that the poses of Pirici's performers have the incisive precision of certain fashion shots; the hands, arms, and intertwined bodies strike a perfect balance between sophistication and ease.

In the end they are much like Wolfgang Tillmans' photos, with the blend of nonchalance, coolness, and extreme formalism that marks the twilight years of a certain kind of Western culture, a tired, listless dandyism. Frozen on an iPhone screen, these choreographies are a perfect, perverse combination of glamour and labor – the coded image of a precarious creative class, which translates effort into image.

The very fact that the pieces created by Pirici and many of her generation are themselves delegated to others – to performers and dancers who may be professionals or may be enthusiastic amateurs – underscores how these works are bound up in a complex system of emotion and action, where intimacy and alienation are seamlessly interlaced.

In the first decades of the 21st century, performance is not confessional or visceral, not first-person; instead, it is a performance of multitudes – and solitudes – that are interconnected and interchangeable. For this reason, Pirici's clusters sometimes look like utopian models of future communities, built around deep ties of neighborliness and care. At other times, however, they remind of beehives regulated by strict military discipline, so obsessive that it verges on madness.

mehr mit einem System aus Zeichen, Werten und Bildern konform, das mithilfe einer endlosen Kette von Smartphones und Instagram-Posts eifrig verbreitet wird.

Es ist kein Zufall, dass den Posen von Piricis Performer*innen die unverkennbare Präzision mancher Modefotografien zu eigen ist; die Hände, Arme und ineinander verschlungenen Körper erzielen eine perfekte Balance zwischen Raffinesse und Leichtigkeit. Am Ende sind sie wie die Fotos von Wolfgang Tillmans, eine Mischung aus Lässigkeit, Kalkül und einem extremen Formalismus, eine Erscheinungsform in der westlichen Kultur, die nun ihrem Ende entgegenblickt, ein erschöpfter, lustlos gewordener Dandyismus. Auf das Display eines iPhones gebannt, sind diese Choreografien eine so perfekte wie perverse Kombination aus Glamour und körperlicher Arbeit – die chiffrierten Bilder einer unter prekären Bedingungen arbeitenden kreativen Klasse, die Kraftanstrengung in Bilder übersetzt.

Dass Pirici und viele andere Künstler*innen ihrer Generation die von ihnen konzipierten Aufführungen an andere delegieren – sei es an professionelle Performer*innen und Tänzer*innen oder enthusiastische Amateur*innen – betont einmal mehr, dass diese Arbeiten komplexe Gefüge aus Emotionen und Aktionen sind, in denen Intimität und Entfremdung nahtlos ineinander übergehen.

In den ersten Jahrzehnten des 21. Jahrhunderts ist Performancekunst weder bekenntnishaft noch fleischlich, auch ist sie nicht in der Ichform konzipiert; stattdessen haben wir es mit einer Performance der vielen Gestalten – und der gesonderten Momente – zu tun, einer, in der alles mit allem in Verbindung steht und substituierbar ist. Aus diesem Grunde treten Piricis Konstellationen mitunter wie utopische Modelle zukünftiger Gemeinschaften hervor, gegründet auf vertrauensvolle Nachbarschaft und Fürsorglichkeit. Zu anderen Zeiten wiederum erinnern sie eher an Bienenstöcke, die von strikter militärischer Disziplin geleitet werden und zwar so obsessiv, dass es beinahe an Wahnsinn grenzt

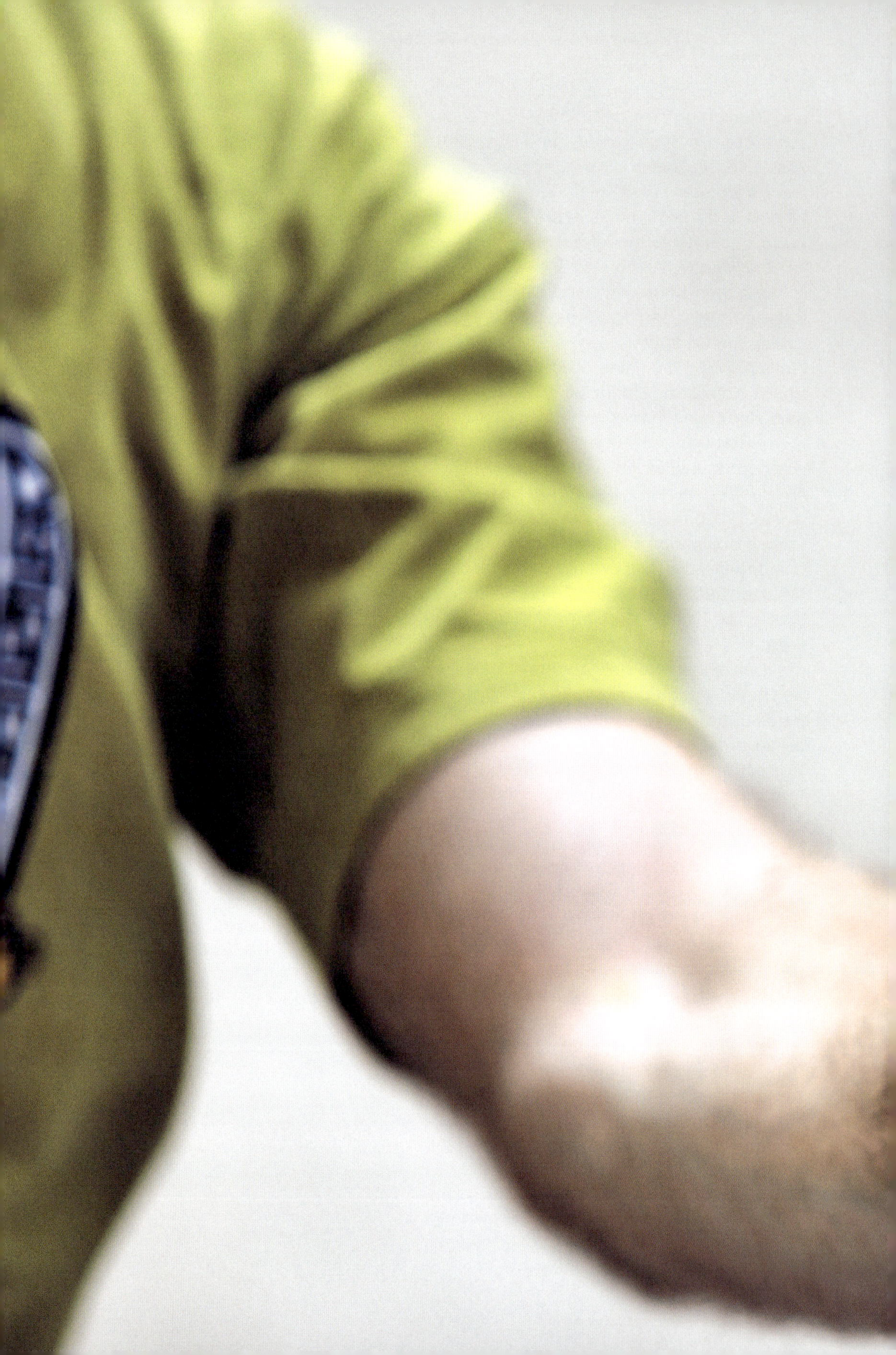

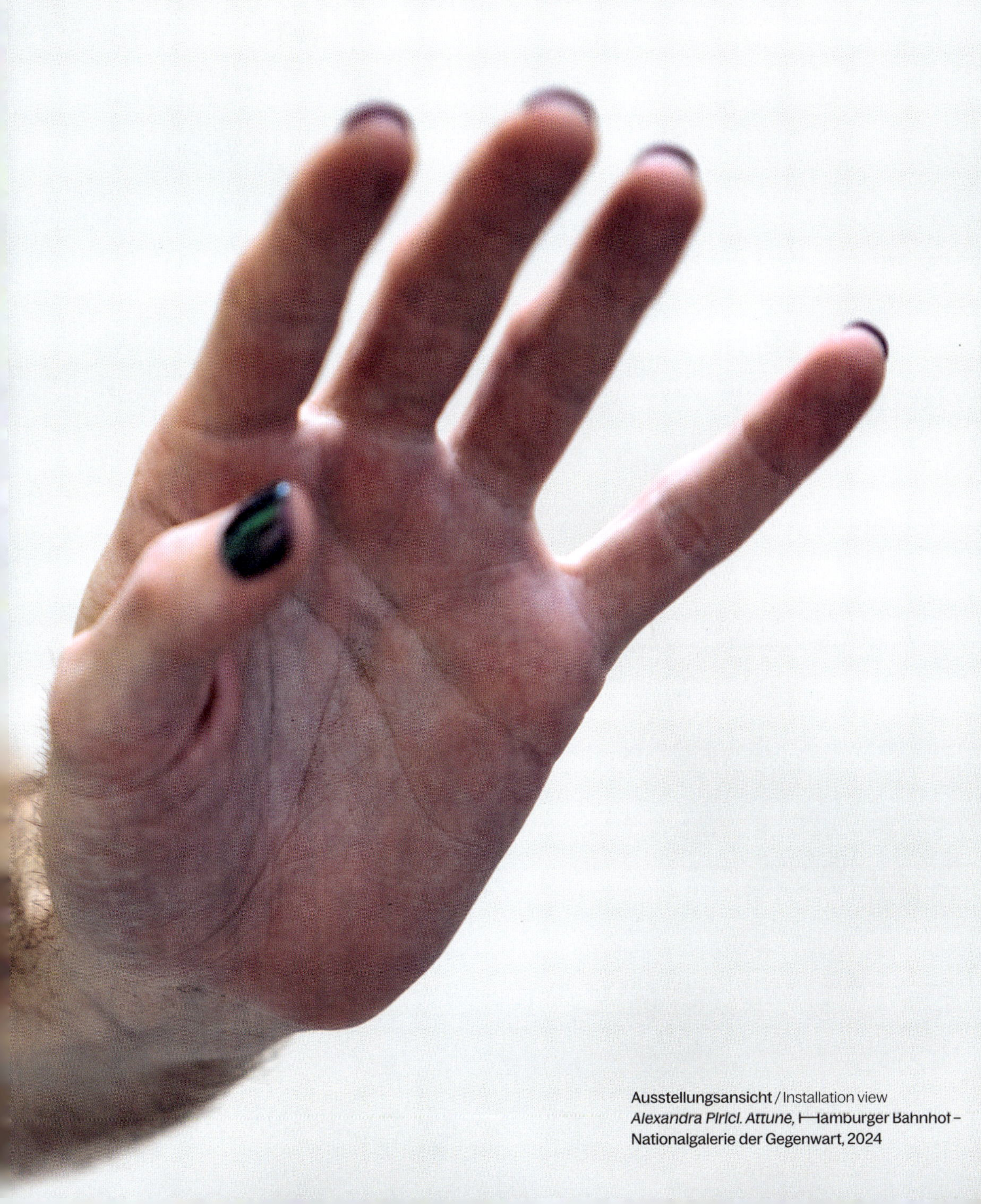

Ausstellungsansicht / Installation view
Alexandra Pirici. Attune, Hamburger Bahnhof –
Nationalgalerie der Gegenwart, 2024

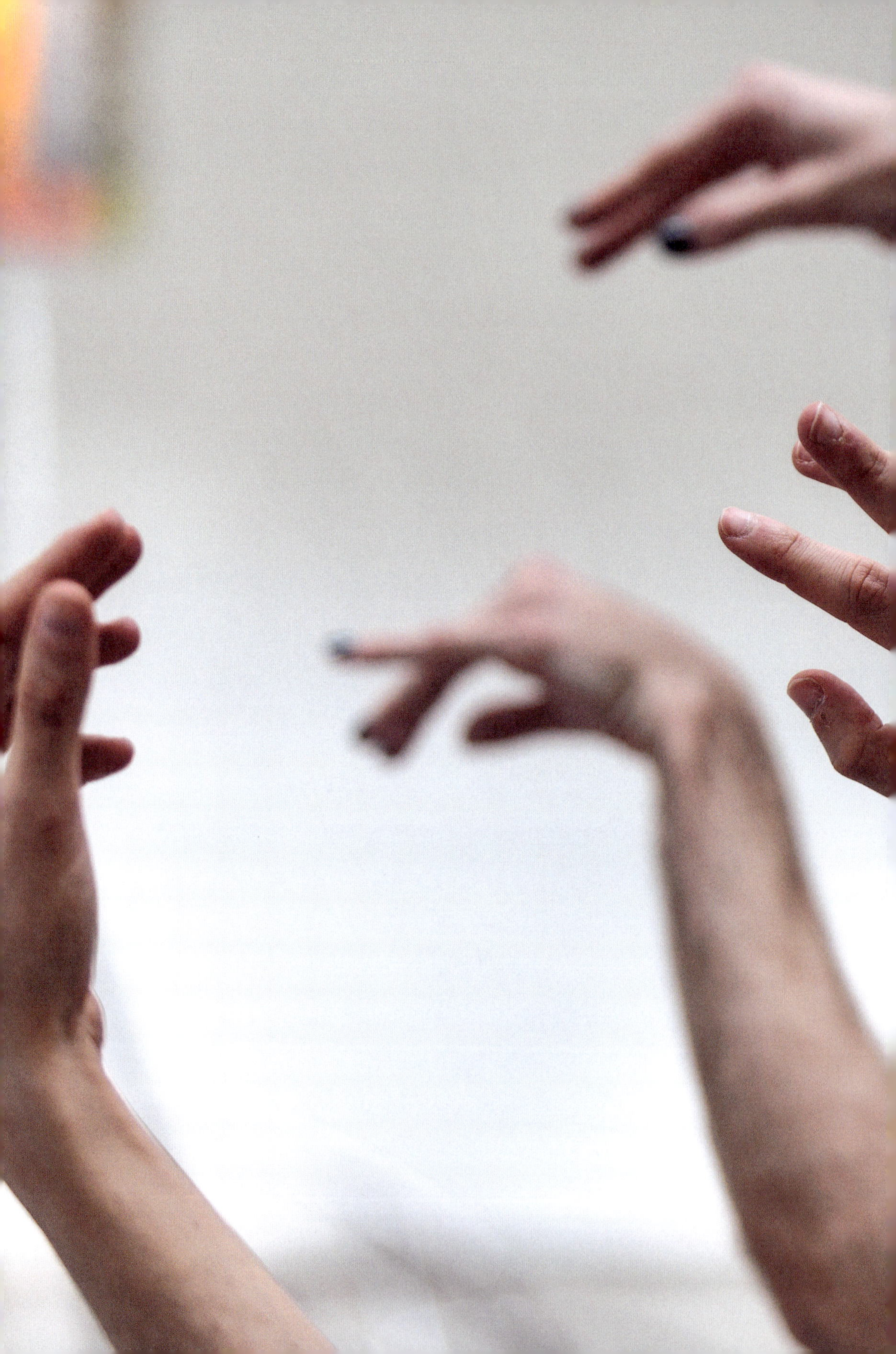

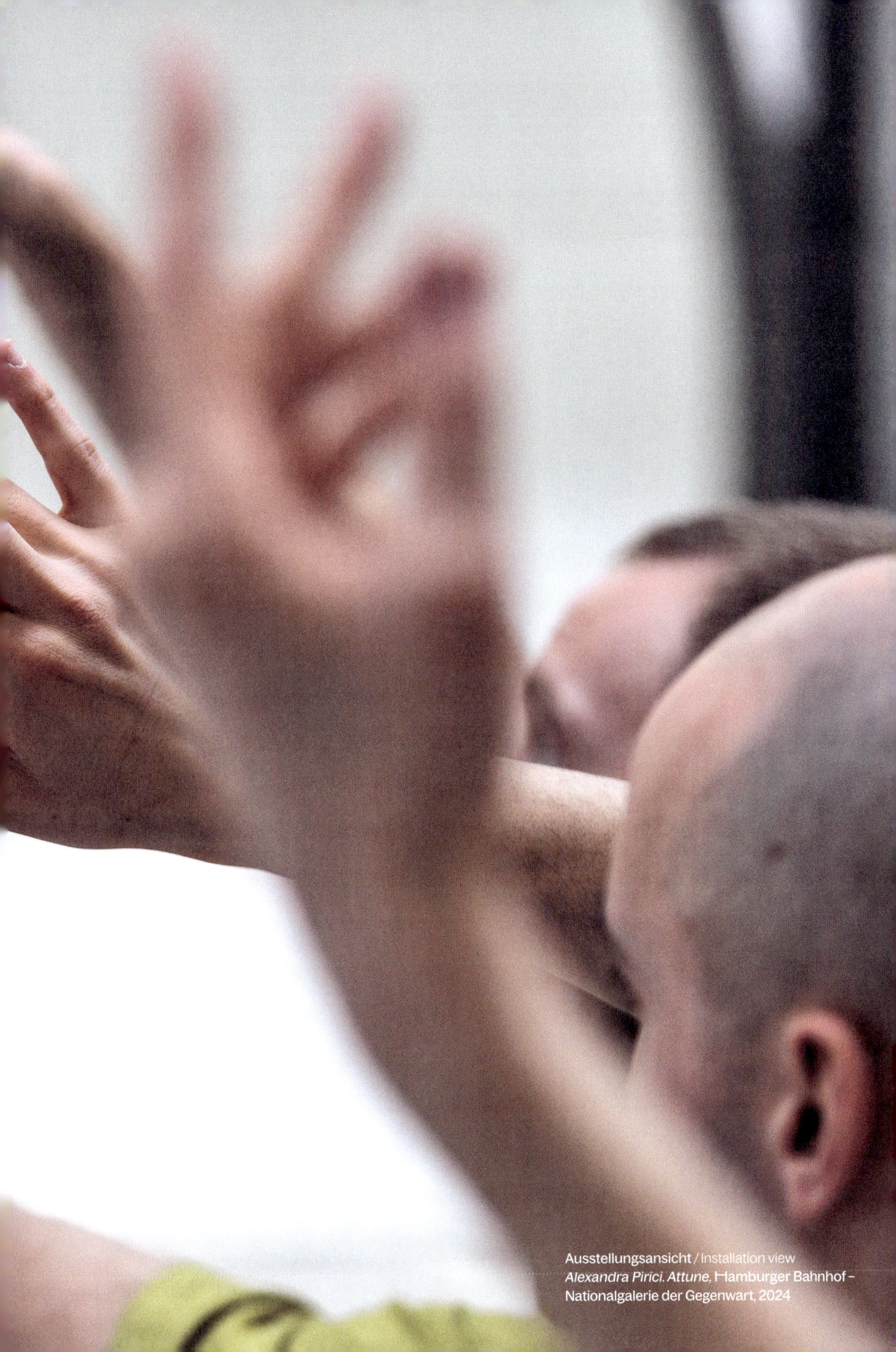

Ausstellungsansicht / Installation view
Alexandra Pirici. Attune, Hamburger Bahnhof –
Nationalgalerie der Gegenwart, 2024

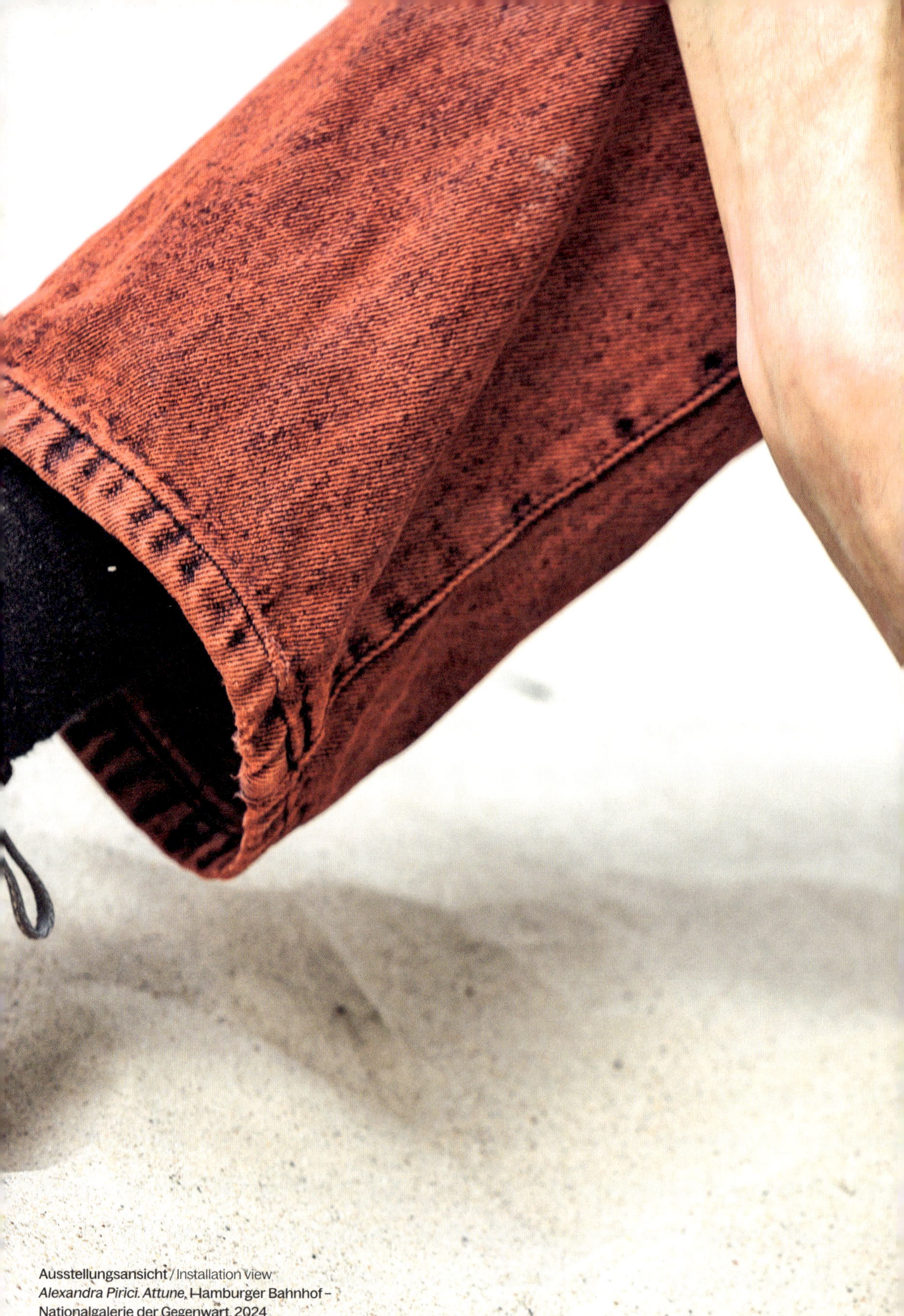

Ausstellungsansicht / Installation view
Alexandra Pirici. Attune, Hamburger Bahnhof –
Nationalgalerie der Gegenwart, 2024

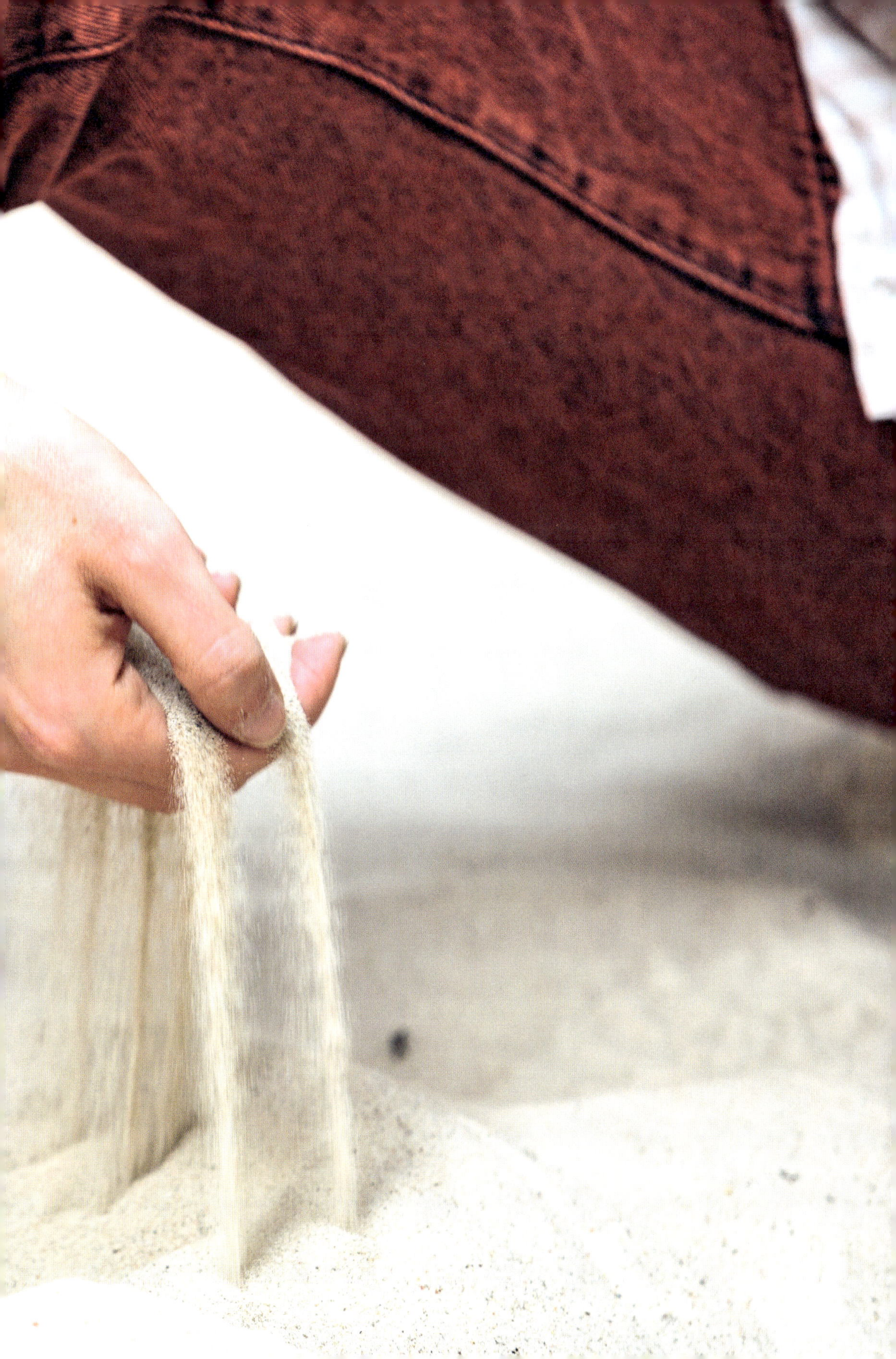

Ein Glossar /
A Glossary

von / by
Catherine Nichols

Dieses Glossar bietet einen kurzen Einblick in die selbstorganisierenden Prozesse, die Alexandra Pirici in ihrem Werk *Attune* [Einstimmen] erkundet. Gemeinsam veranschaulichen sie, wie aus einem zufälligen Grundrauschen von Atomen, Molekülen und Zellen stabile Strukturen in belebter wie unbelebter Materie entstehen.

This glossary offers a brief insight into the self-organizing processes explored by Alexandra Pirici in *Attune*. Together they illustrate how stable structures in both animate and inanimate matter emerge from the random behaviors of atoms, molecules, and cells.

Bénard-Zellen

Jedes Mal, wenn man Öl in einer Pfanne erhitzt, entstehen filigrane selbstorganisierende Strukturen, ohne dass man sie wahrnimmt. Fügt man ein wenig Glimmer hinzu – ein Mineral, das häufig in Farben und Kosmetika verwendet wird –, tritt ein geordnetes Muster sechseckiger Zellen zum Vorschein. Die Zellen entstehen durch Konvektion: Wenn das Öl am Boden der Pfanne warm wird, verliert es an Dichte, gewinnt Auftrieb und steigt an die Oberfläche. Dort kühlt es ab, gewinnt wieder an Dichte und sinkt zurück zum Boden, wo der Prozess von neuem beginnt. Dieses einfache Experiment wurde erstmals im Jahr 1900 von dem französischen Physiker Henri Bénard beschrieben, dem die Konvektionszellen ihren Namen verdanken. Wie Alexandra Pirici in *Attune* zeigt, erweisen sich solche Systeme als sehr widerstandsfähig: Selbst wenn man das Muster durch Umrühren der Flüssigkeit stört, stellt sich die Ordnung bald wieder ein.

Bénard Cells

Every time you heat oil in a frying pan you create intricate self-organizing structures without realizing it. Yet if you add mica – a common mineral used in paints and cosmetics – you can clearly observe the emergence of a highly ordered pattern of hexagonal cells. The cells are formed through convection: as the oil at the bottom of the pan grows warm it becomes less dense, thus more buoyant and floats to the surface. There it cools, increases in density, and sinks back down to the bottom where the process starts all over again. This simple experiment was first described in 1900 by the French physicist Henri Bénard, to whom the convection cells owe their name. As Alexandra Pirici shows in *Attune*, such systems are remarkably robust: even if you disrupt the pattern by stirring the liquid, order soon reemerges.

Briggs-Rauscher-Reaktion

Drei klare Flüssigkeiten strömen in ein Reagenzglas. Kurz darauf färbt sich die Mischung goldgelb, bevor sie ein tiefes Violettblau annimmt. Sekunden später wird sie wieder gelb und bald darauf wieder blau. Immer wieder wechselt die Lösung zwischen den beiden Zuständen, bevor die Reaktion schließlich zu einem Ende kommt. Diese sogenannte Briggs-Rauscher-Reaktion, benannt nach zwei High-

Briggs-Rauscher Reaction

Three clear liquids gush into a glass cylinder. A moment later the mixture turns a deep shade of yellow, before shifting to a deep purplish blue. Seconds later it reverts to yellow, and then back to blue. Over and over again the solution shifts between the two states before the reaction finally comes to an end. Named after the two high school science teachers from San Francisco who developed it in the 1970s, the Briggs-Rauscher

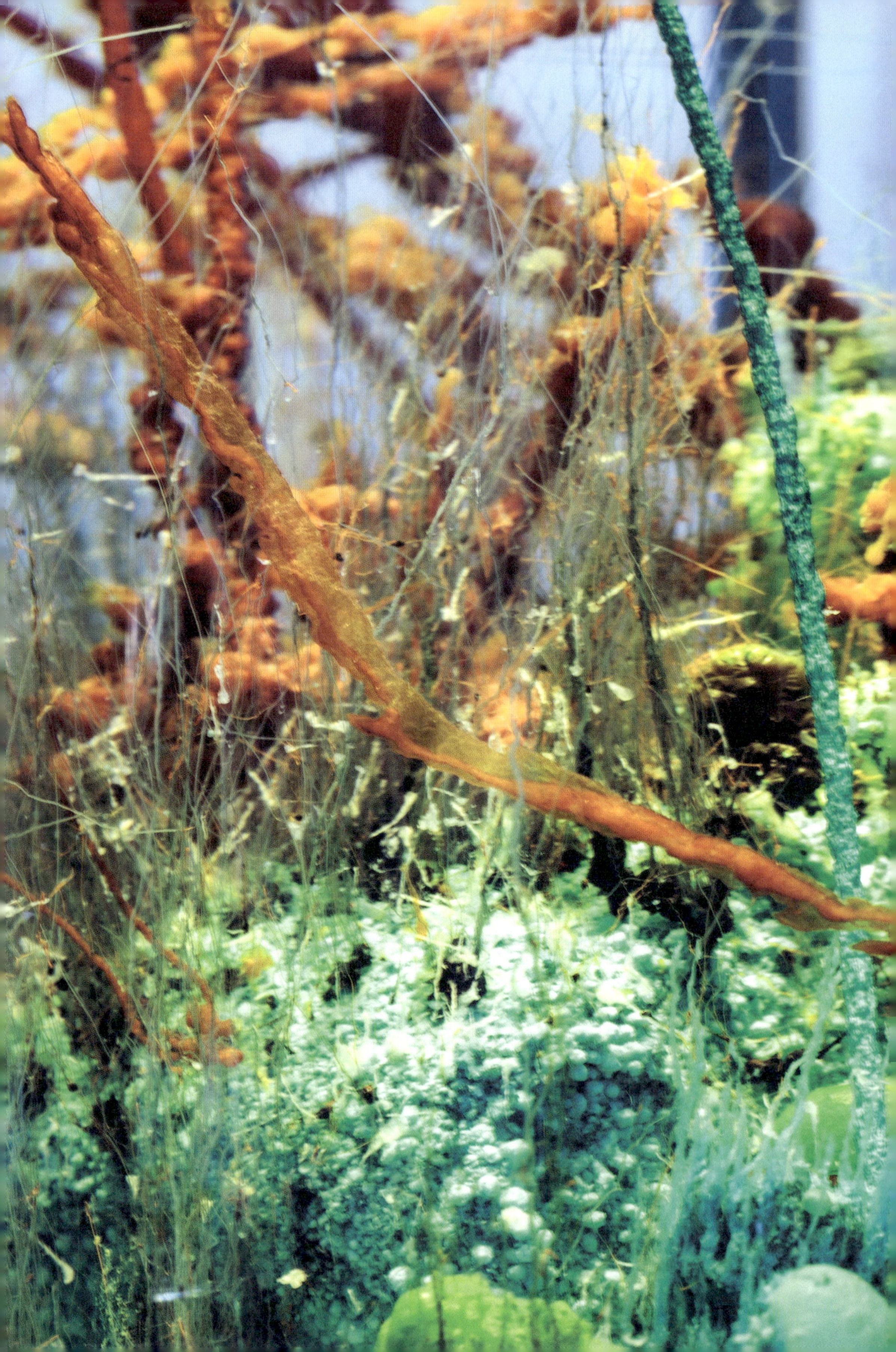

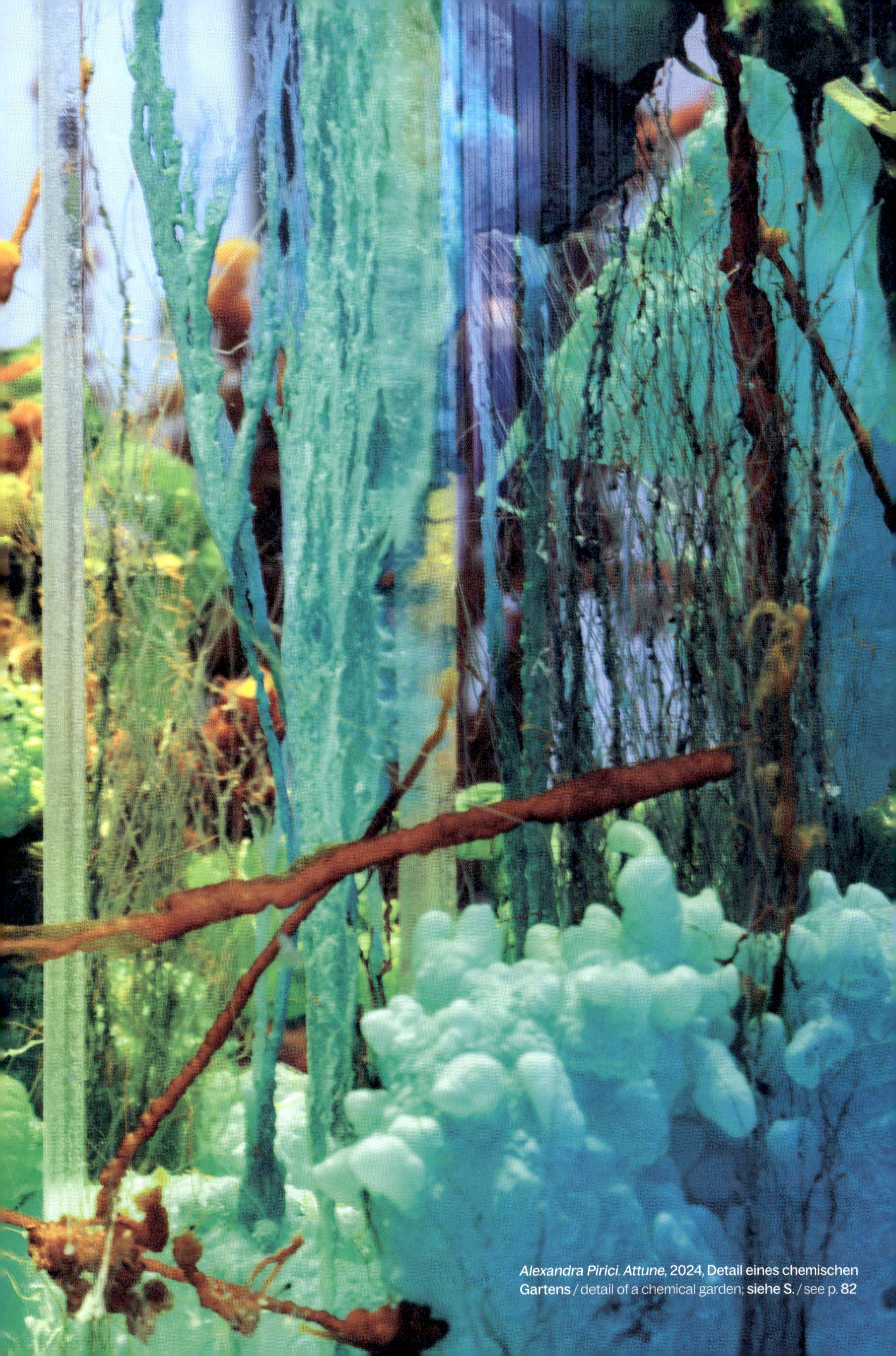

Alexandra Pirici. Attune, 2024, Detail eines chemischen Gartens / detail of a chemical garden; siehe S. / see p. **82**

School Lehrern aus San Francisco, die sie in den 1970er-Jahren entwickelten, ist ein Beispiel für eine oszillierende chemische Reaktion. Wie ihre russische Vorläuferin – die Belousov-Zhabotinsky-Reaktion – wird sie häufig zur Demonstration selbstorganisierender Muster in der Chemie verwendet. Viele Wissenschaftler*innen sehen in der Reaktion, die noch lange nicht in allen Facetten verstanden wird, ein mögliches Modell für die Entstehung von Leben in biochemischen Systemen. Für *Attune* hat Alexandra Pirici mit Chemikern und Ingenieuren zusammengearbeitet, um die Reaktion im Maßstab zu vergrößern und erstmals vollständig zu automatisieren. Im Rahmen der Ausstellung wird sie mehrfach vorgeführt.

reaction is a frequently cited example of an oscillating chemical reaction. Like its Russian predecessor, the Belousov-Zhabotinsky reaction, it is often used to demonstrate self-organizing patterns in chemistry. Many scientists regard the reaction, which is not yet well understood, as a potential model for the emergence of life in biochemical systems. For *Attune*, Alexandra Pirici has collaborated with chemists and engineers to significantly scale up and, for the first time, to fully automate the reaction. It will be performed several times in the course of the exhibition.

Chemische Gärten

Chemical Gardens

Von der pflanzenartigen Skulptur Alexandra Piricis hängen mehrere chemische Gärten in Glaszylindern hinab. Sie ähneln lebenden Organismen wie Korallen, Pflanzen oder Pilzen. Dabei sind sie völlig unbelebt. Solche Gärten entstehen durch das Auflösen verschiedener Metallsalze in einer wässrigen Natriumsilikatlösung. Innerhalb weniger Minuten beginnen selbstorganisierende Strukturen zu wachsen, die rasch an Größe und Komplexität zunehmen. Bereits nach wenigen Tagen sind sie voll ausgewachsen. Die Farben der Gewächse hängen von den Chemikalien ab. Chemische Gärten sind seit Mitte des 17. Jahrhunderts bekannt und gehören zu den ältesten Forschungsgegenständen der Chemie. Da sie biologisches Wachstum und seine Formen nachzuahmen scheinen, sind sie von großem Interesse für die Evolutionsforschung und die theoretische Biologie.

Dangling in glass cylinders from Alexandra Pirici's vegetal sculpture are several chemical gardens. They resemble living organisms such as coral, plants, and fungi. Yet their vibrant tubular forms are completely inanimate. Formed by dissolving various metal salts in an aqueous solution of sodium silicate, the gardens begin to grow in size and complexity in a matter of minutes. Within a day or two they tend to be fully grown. Gardens can range in color depending on the chemicals used. Chemical gardens have been known since the mid-17th century and are one of the oldest subjects in chemistry. As they appear to mimic biological growth and its forms, they are of great interest for evolutionary research and theoretical biology.

Liesegangsche Ringe

Liesegang Rings

Ausgeprägte konzentrische Bänder, die als Liesegang-Ringe bekannt sind, treten sowohl bei chemischen Reaktionen als auch bei geologischen Formationen auf. Die nach dem deutschen Chemiker Raphael Eduard

Distinctive concentric bands known as Liesegang Rings appear in both chemical reactions and geological formations. Named after the German chemist Raphael Eduard Liesegang, the rings are easy to recognize in sedimentary rocks

Liesegang benannten Ringe sind in Sedimentgesteinen wie Kalkstein und Sandstein leicht zu erkennen. Liesegang entdeckte sie Ende des 19. Jahrhunderts, als er das Wachstum von Kristallen untersuchte. Als er eine Silbernitratlösung auf eine Gelatineschicht tropfte, zeigten sich konzentrische Ringe anstelle der gleichmäßigen Lösung, die er erwartet hätte. Später stellte Liesegang ein ähnlich rhythmisches Muster von Ringen in Mineralien fest, darunter auch Achat. Neuerdings werden solche Ringe als lehrreiche Modelle der Selbstorganisation betrachtet und untersucht, obwohl ihre Entstehung noch nicht vollständig verstanden wird. In Alexandra Piricis Werk finden sich Beispiele für periodische Schichtungsmuster sowohl in Reagenzgläsern als auch in den Mineralformationen einer tiefblauen Achatscheibe und eines imposanten Sandsteinfindlings.

such as limestone and sandstone. Liesegang discovered them at the end of the 19th century while studying the growth of crystals. When he dripped a silver nitrate solution onto a layer of gelatin, concentric rings formed instead of the uniform precipitate he would have expected. Liesegang later observed a similarly rhythmic pattern of rings in minerals, among them agate. In recent decades the rings have come to be regarded and studied as instructive models of self-organization, although their formation has yet to be fully understood. In Alexandra Pirici's work, examples of such periodic stratification patterns appear both in test tubes and in mineral formations, such as a deep-blue slice of agate and an imposing sandstone boulder.

Pflanzenwachstum

Pflanzen wachsen grundlegend anders als Tiere. Während die Gestalt von Tieren bereits im Embryonalstadium weitgehend festgelegt ist, ist die Form von Pflanzen offen und unbestimmt. Pflanzen produzieren durch die ständige Wiederholung von Prozessen immer wieder neue Organe wie Blätter, Knospen, Früchte und Blüten. Diese haben sich dank mathematischer Modellierungen als auf molekularer Ebene selbstorganisierend erwiesen. Scheinbar zufällige Vorgänge führen zu hochgradig geordneten Mustern, darunter die kreisende Anordnung von Blütenblättern, die Stellung der Blätter entlang eines Stängels oder das Austreiben von Wurzeln, Sprossen oder Zweigen. Solche Muster verleihen Pflanzen nicht nur ihre individuelle Erscheinungsform, sondern ermöglichen ihnen auch, die Lichtaufnahme zu maximieren. Diese hilft ihnen wiederum, Sauerstoff und Wasser in Energie umzuwandeln, um nach eben diesen selbstorganisierenden Prinzipien weiter zu wachsen.

Plant Growth

Plants grow in a fundamentally different way from animals. Whereas the form of animals is largely determined during the embryonic stage, the form of plants remains indeterminate. Plants keep producing new organs such as leaves, buds, fruit and flowers, through the constant repetition of processes. Mathematical modelling has shown these to be self-organizing on a molecular level. An apparent randomness gives rise to highly ordered patterns such as the arrangement of petals, the spacing of leaves along a stem, or the sprouting of roots, shoots or branches. These patterns not only give plants their distinctive appearance but also enable them to maximize their exposure to light. This in turn helps them to convert oxygen and water into energy and thus to continue to grow according to the same self-organizing principles.

Sanddünenbildung

Sandrippel und Dünen zählen zu den bekanntesten Beispielen für dynamische, sich selbst organisierende Muster in der Natur. Sie entstehen durch die chaotische Interaktion ihrer unzähligen winzigen Partikel miteinander wie mit dem Wind. Wenn der Wind Sandpartikel über die Erdoberfläche treibt, sammeln sie sich überall dort, wo sie durch ein Hindernis wie einen Felsen, eine Pflanze oder zufällige Ansammlungen von weiteren Sandkörnern aufgehalten werden. Der Sand häuft sich auf der windzugewandten Seite des Hindernisses. Der Wind wird beschleunigt, wenn er über ein Hindernis strömt. So landet jener Sand, der es über die Spitze schafft, in größerer Entfernung und bildet dort die nächste Erhebung der Reihe. Das Muster wiederholt sich. Die sich so herausbildende, stets im Wandel begriffene Form richtet sich ebenso nach Größe und Gewicht der Sandkörner wie nach der Stärke des Winds.

Symbiogenese

Die Symbiogenese ist ein relativ neues Verständnis von der Entstehung komplexen Lebens. Sie sieht wechselseitige, abhängige Beziehungen zwischen Organismen als eine treibende Kraft der Evolution – und nicht mehr allein die von Charles Darwin vorgeschlagene Kombination aus natürlicher Selektion und zufälliger Mutation. Dieses neue Evolutionsmodell wurde zu Beginn des 20. Jahrhunderts von dem russischen Botaniker Konstantin Merezhkowsky und unabhängig davon in den 1970er-Jahren von der amerikanischen Biologin Lynn Margulis entwickelt, welche erst später von Merezhkowskys Forschungen erfuhr. Ihre Vorstellung eines ineinander verwobenen Mitwerdens ersetzt die weit verbreitete Evolutionsmetapher des Baums des Lebens durch ein wucherndes Geflecht. An ein solches Bild scheint Alexandra Pirici mit der großen früchtetragenden pflanzlichen Struktur im Zentrum ihrer immersiven Landschaft anzuknüpfen.

Sand Dune Formation

Sand ripples and dunes are among the best-known examples of dynamic self-organizing patterns in nature. They are shaped by the chaotic interaction of their countless tiny particles with one another and with the wind. When the wind drives sand particles across the earth's surface, they gather wherever they are blocked by an obstacle, such as a rock, plant or random accumulation of sand. The particles pile up on the windward side of the obstacle rather than its slipface. This is because the wind accelerates when it flows over an obstacle. The sand that makes it over the ridge lands further afield where it forms the next ripple or ridge in the sequence. The pattern repeats. The forever shifting shape that emerges as a result of this process depends on the size and weight of the grains of sand and the strength of the wind.

Symbiogenesis

Symbiogenesis is a relatively new understanding of the origins of complex life. It considers interdependent, cooperative relationships between organisms to be a driving force of evolution – as well as the combination of natural selection and random mutation proposed by Charles Darwin. This new evolutionary model was developed at the beginning of the 20th century by the Russian botanist Konstantin Merezhkowsky and independently in the 1970s by the American biologist Lynn Margulis, who only later became aware of Merezhkowsky's research. Their idea of an entangled mutual becoming supplants the widespread evolutionary metaphor of the tree of life with a sprawling web or network. The vast fruit-bearing vegetal structure at the center of Alexandra Pirici's immersive landscape would seem to continue their line of thought.

Turing-Muster

Tropische Meeresschnecken, die als Zeltoliven oder Oliva porphyria bekannt sind, gehören zu den vielen Lebewesen, die komplizierte geometrische Muster auf ihren Schalen, ihrem Fell oder ihrer Haut aufweisen. Ihre Schalen sind mit einem dichten Netz aus dunkelrotbraunen, zusammenstoßenden Wellen, ineinandergreifenden Dreiecken, Zickzacklinien und Flecken überzogen. Diese sind anschauliche Beispiele für Turing-Muster. Solche in der Natur wiederkehrenden Erscheinungen sind nach dem britischen Mathematiker und Pionier der Computertechnik Alan Turing benannt, der sie als Erster anhand eines mathematischen Modells zu erklären versuchte. Das System, das er sich vorstellte, bestand aus zwei chemischen Substanzen, die zusammenwirken, um eine bestimmte Reaktion wie etwa Pigmentierung zu aktivieren oder zu hemmen. Die Gleichungen, die er zur Beschreibung dieses sich selbst organisierenden Prozesses entwickelte, wurden häufig in Rechenmodellen – sogenannten zellulären Automaten – für die Bildung von Pigmentmustern angewandt. Die dabei entstehenden Muster haben eine verblüffende Ähnlichkeit mit den Meeresschnecken selbst.

Turing Patterns

Tropical sea snails, known as tent olives or olivae porphyriae, are among the many living creatures to feature intricate geometric patterns on their shells, fur or skin. Their shells are overlaid with a dense network of dark red-brown colliding waves, interlocking triangles, zig-zags, and patches. These are vivid examples of Turing patterns. Such recurring elements in nature are named after the British mathematician and pioneer of computing Alan Turing, who was the first to propose a mathematical model to explain them. The system he imagined was made up of two chemical substances that work together to activate and inhibit a given reaction such as pigmentation. The equations he developed to describe this self-organizing process have been applied in computational models, known as cellular automata, for pigment pattern formation. The artificially generated designs bear a striking resemblance to the sea snails themselves.

Frühere Arbeiten / Previous Works von / by Alexandra Pirici

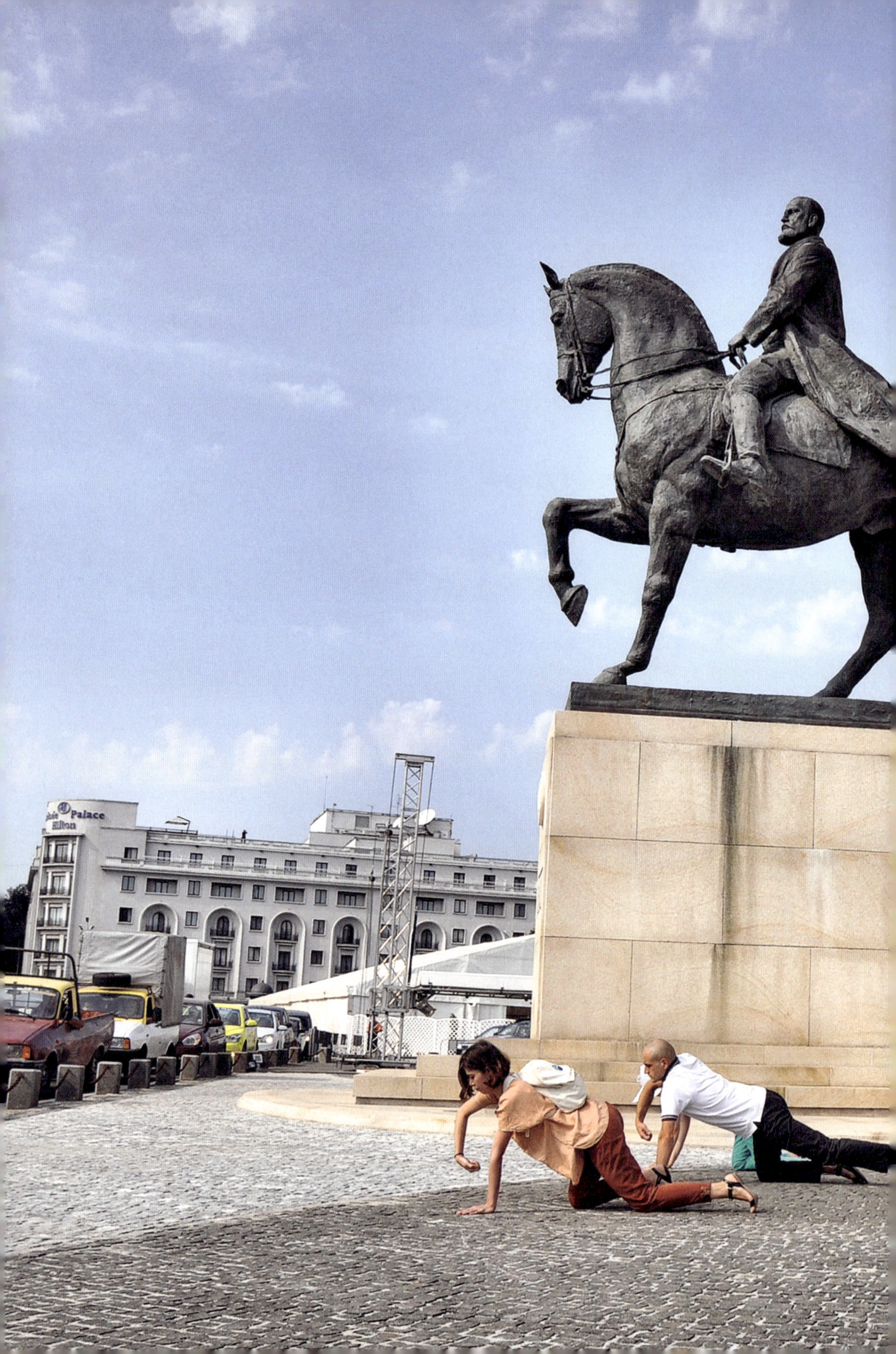

Palace
Hilton

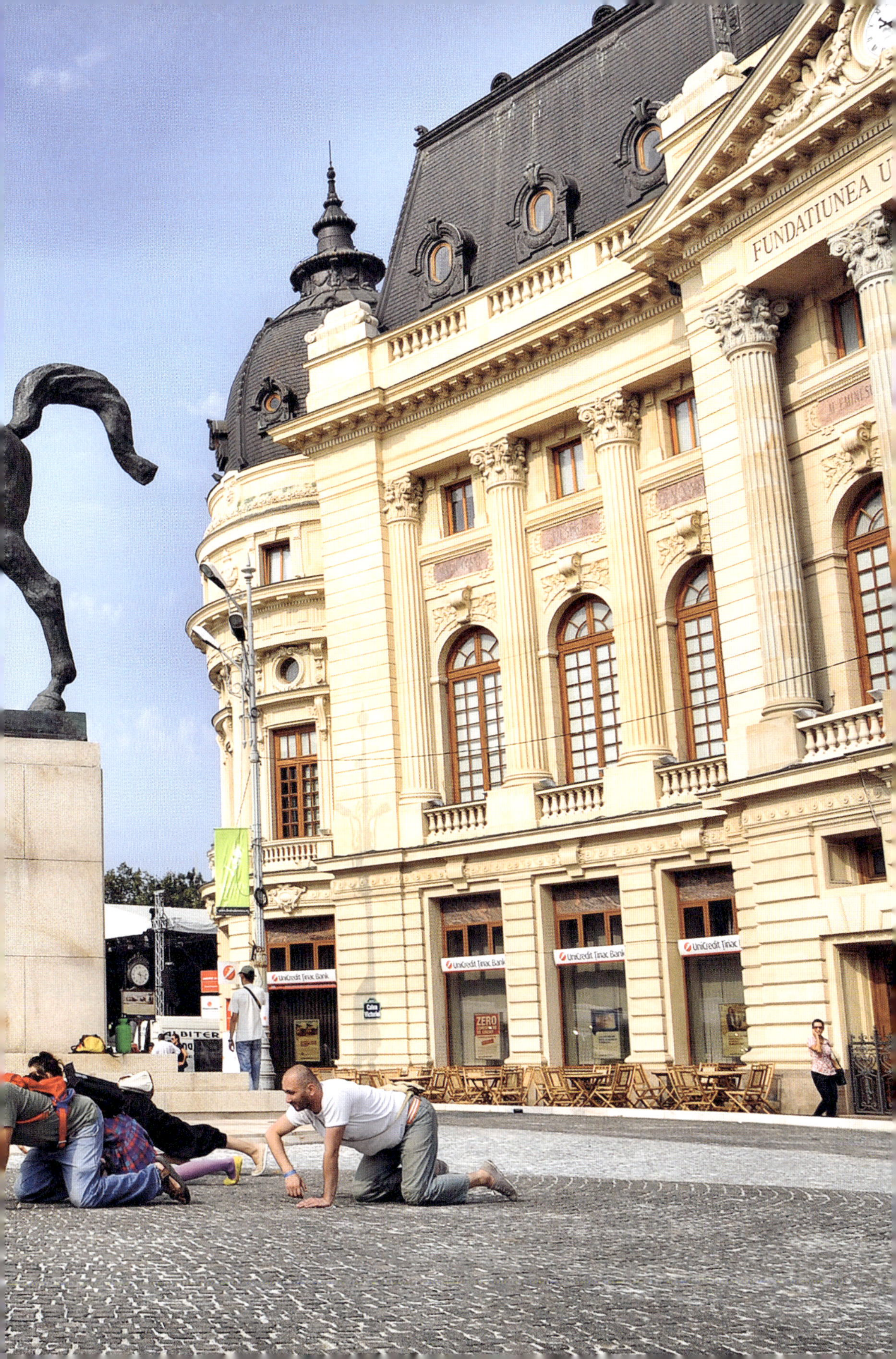

FUNDATIUNEA U
UniCredit Tiriac Bank
UniCredit Tiriac Bank
UniCredit Tiriac Bank
ZERO

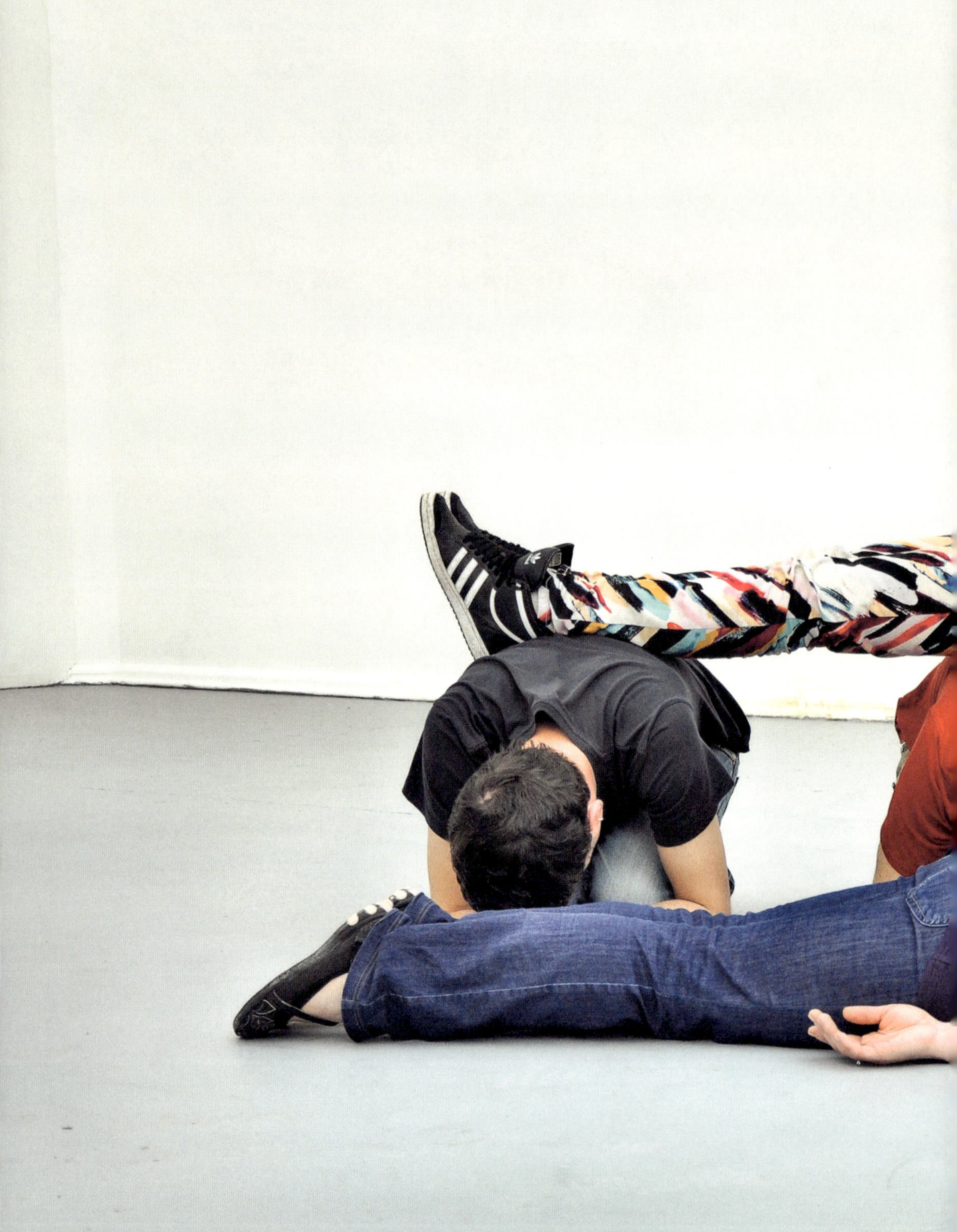

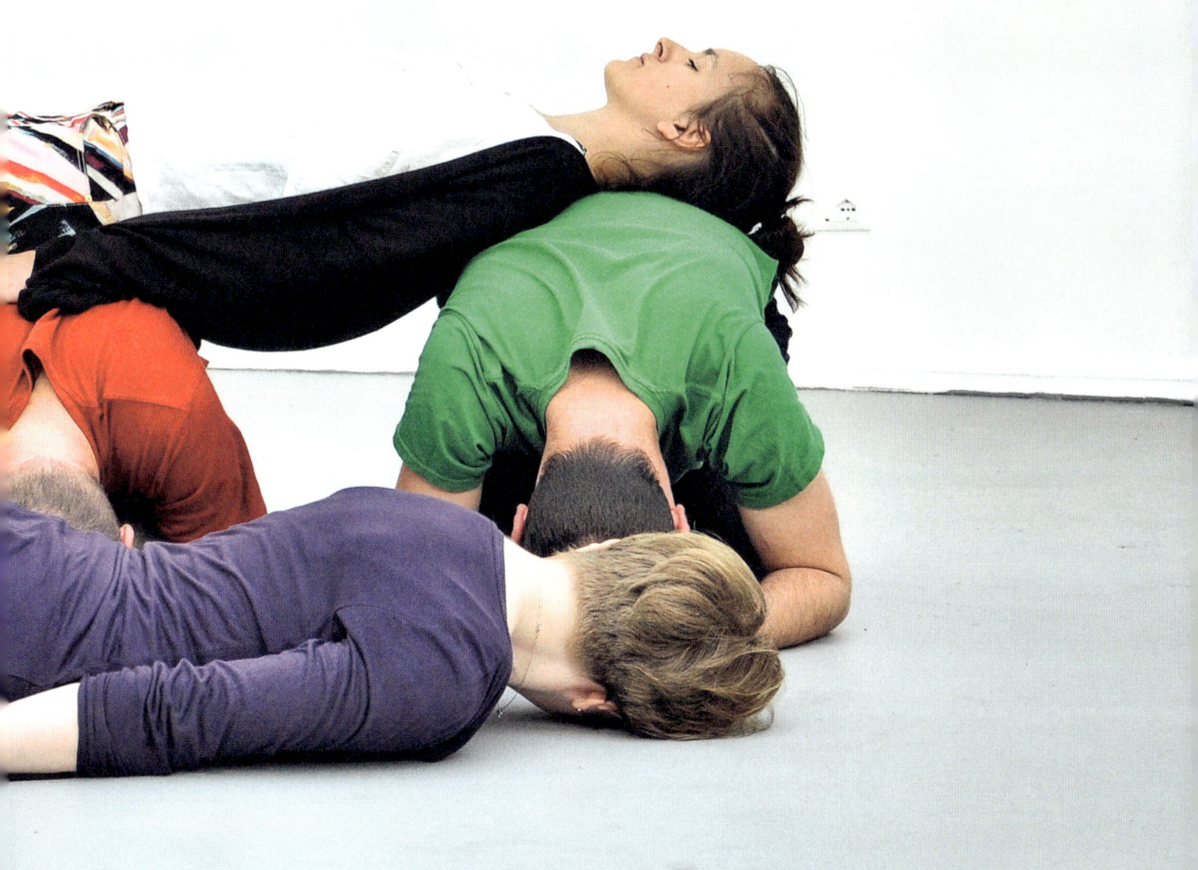

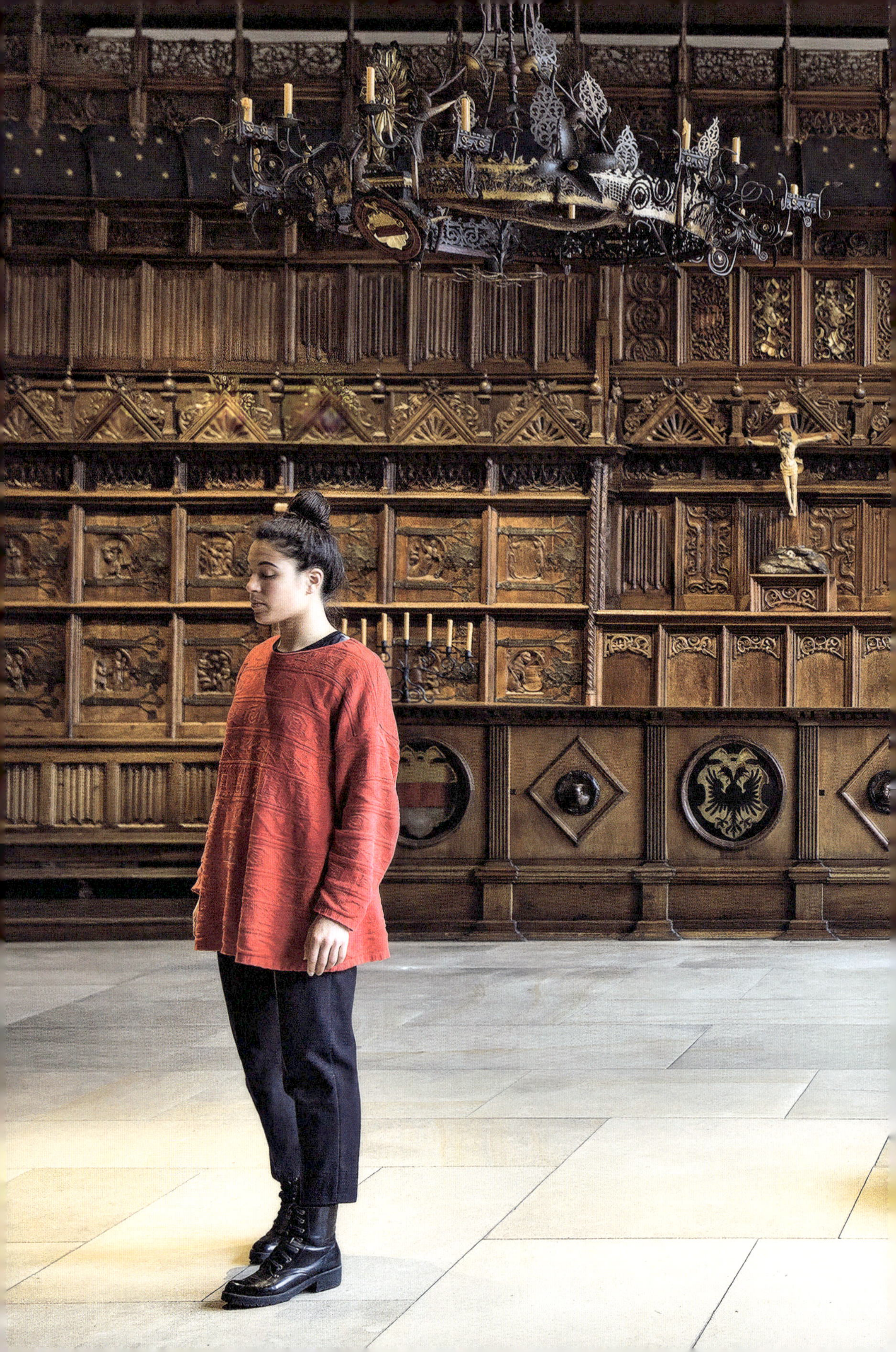

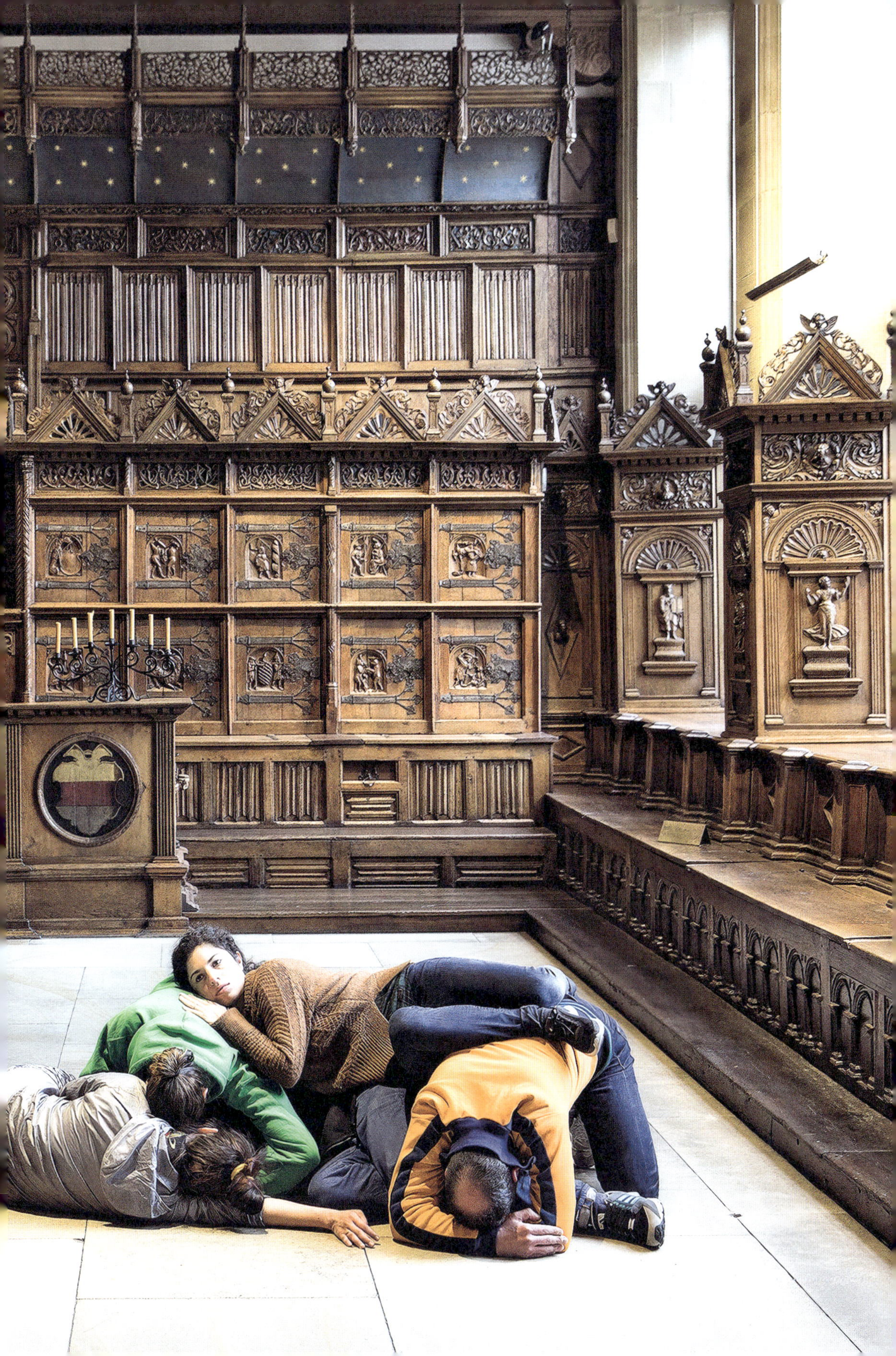

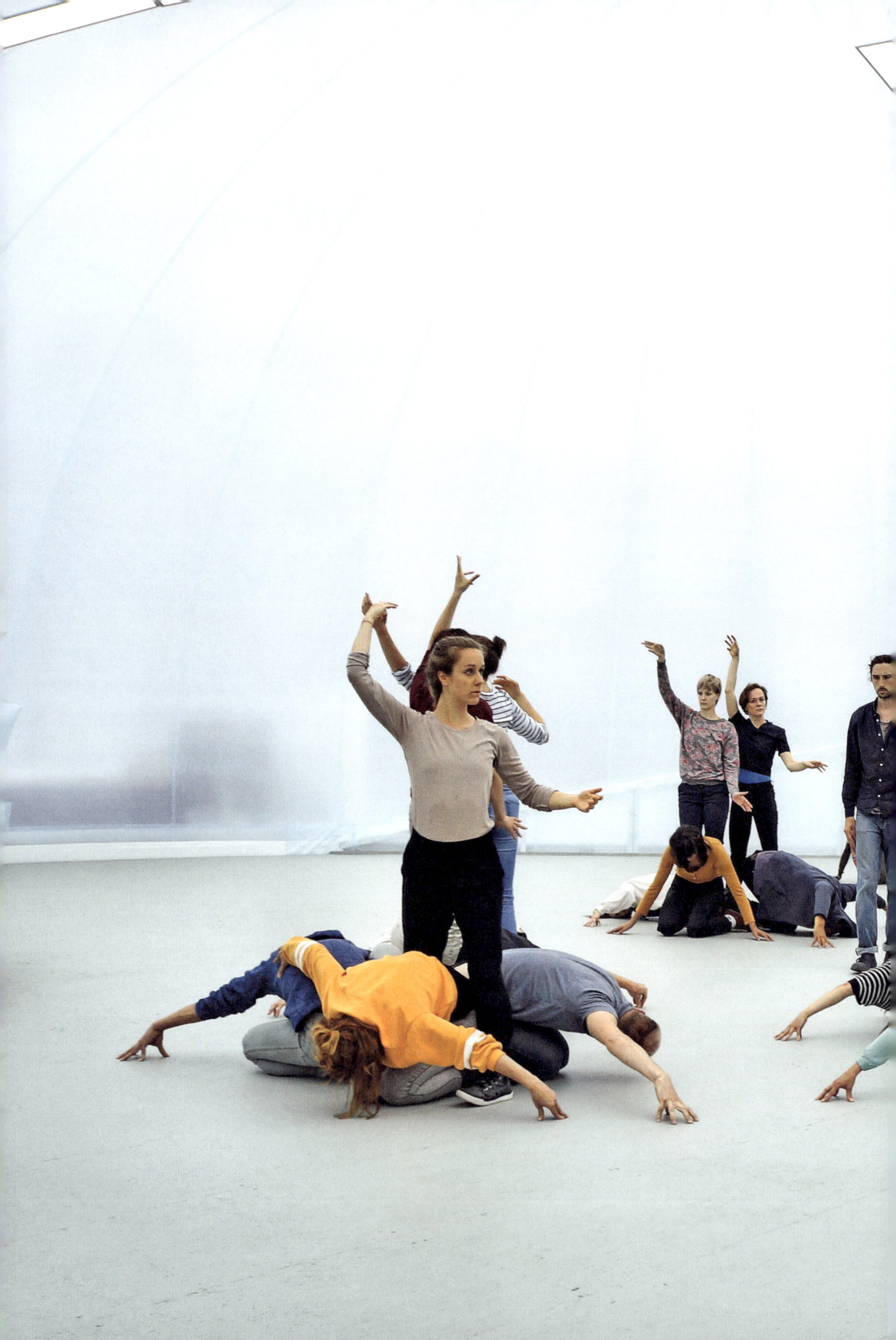

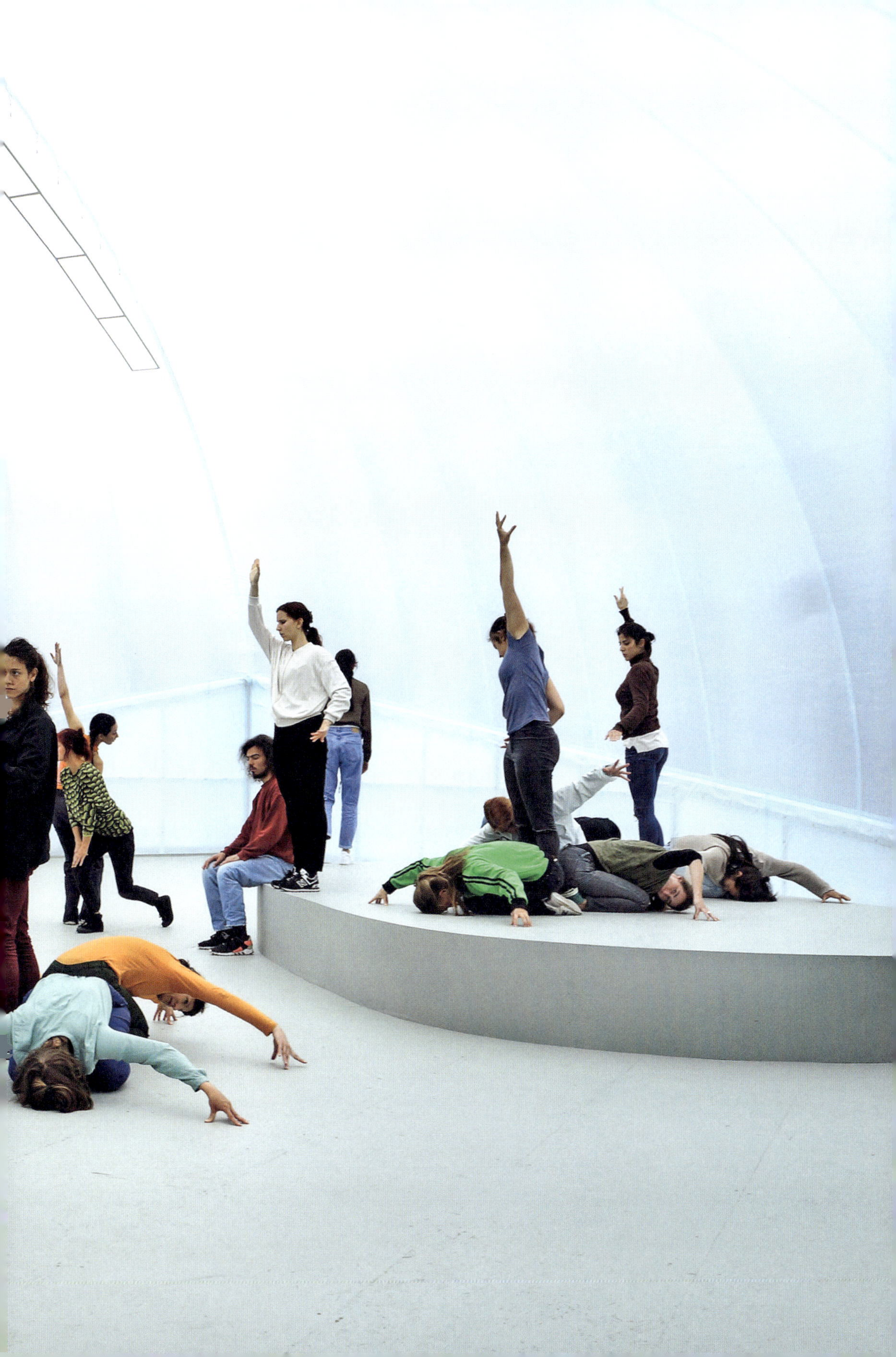

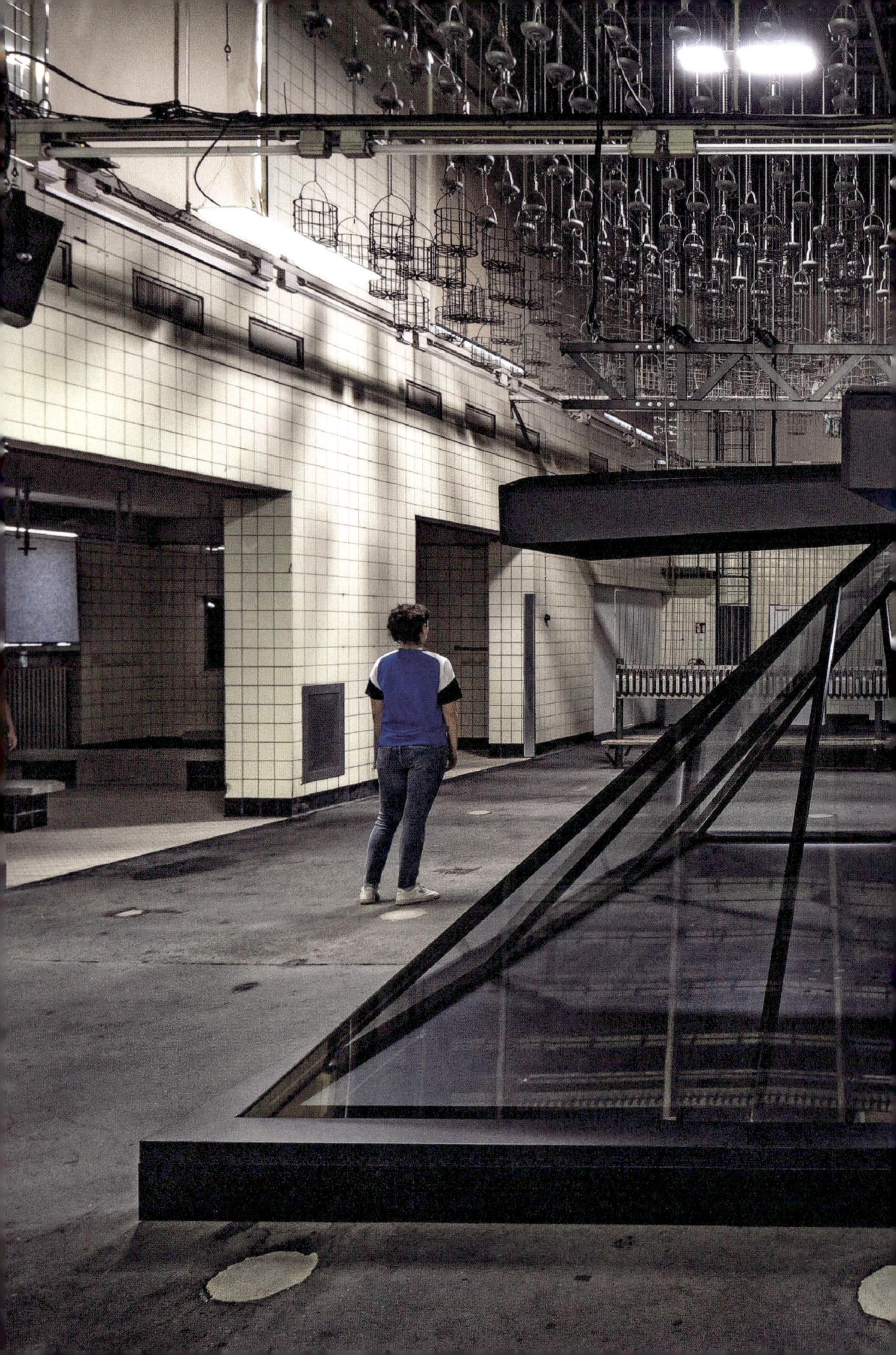

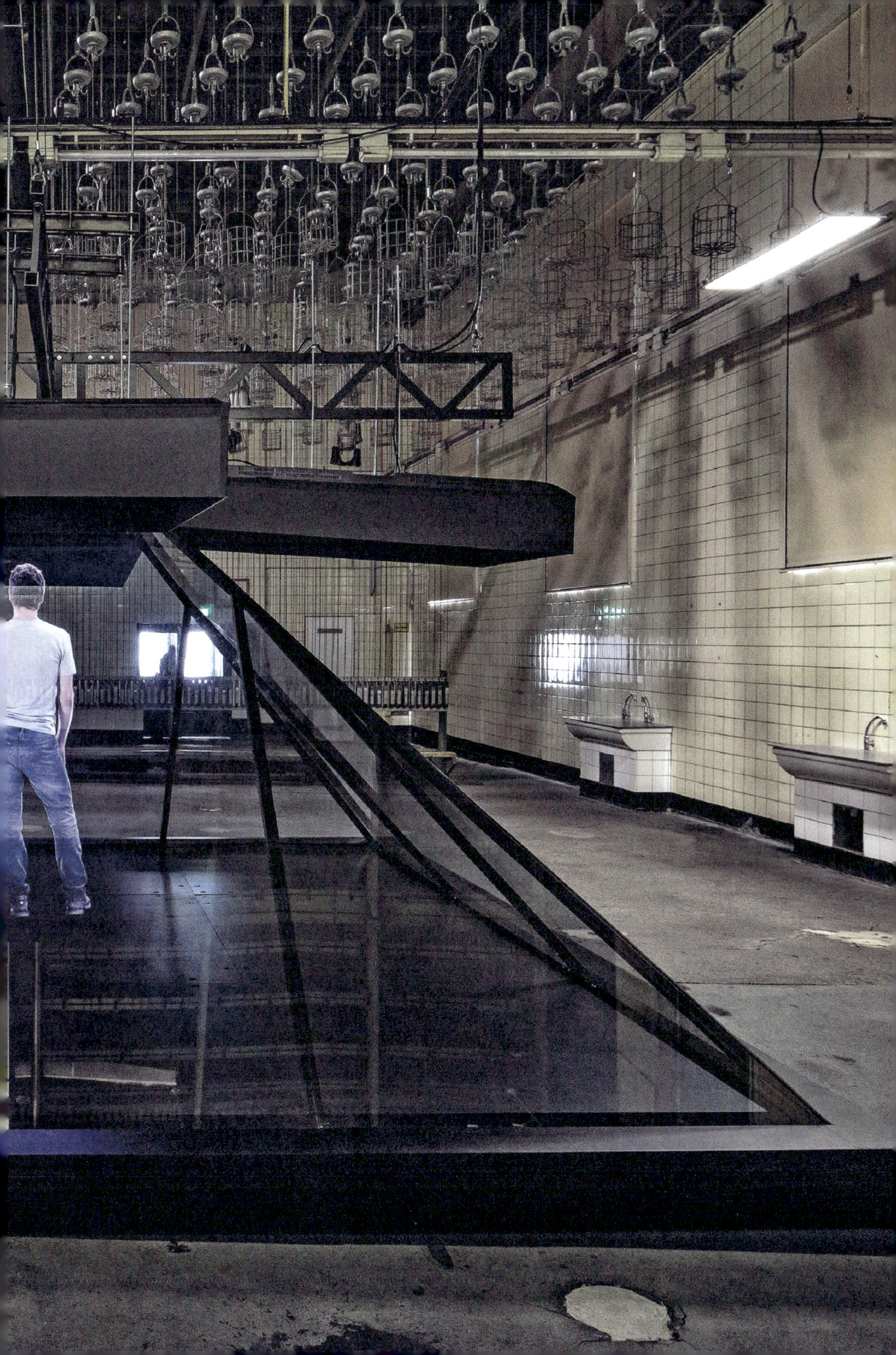

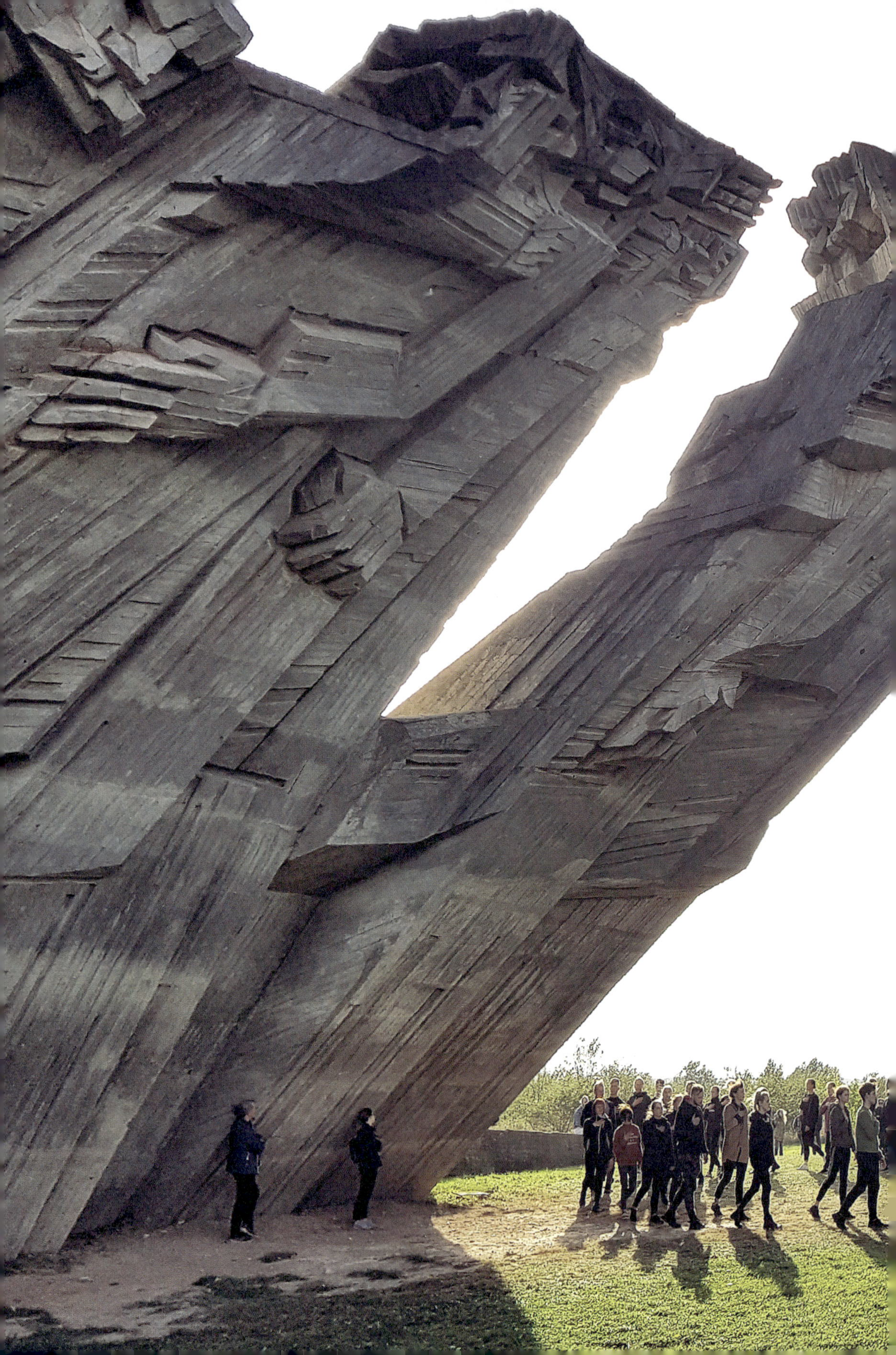

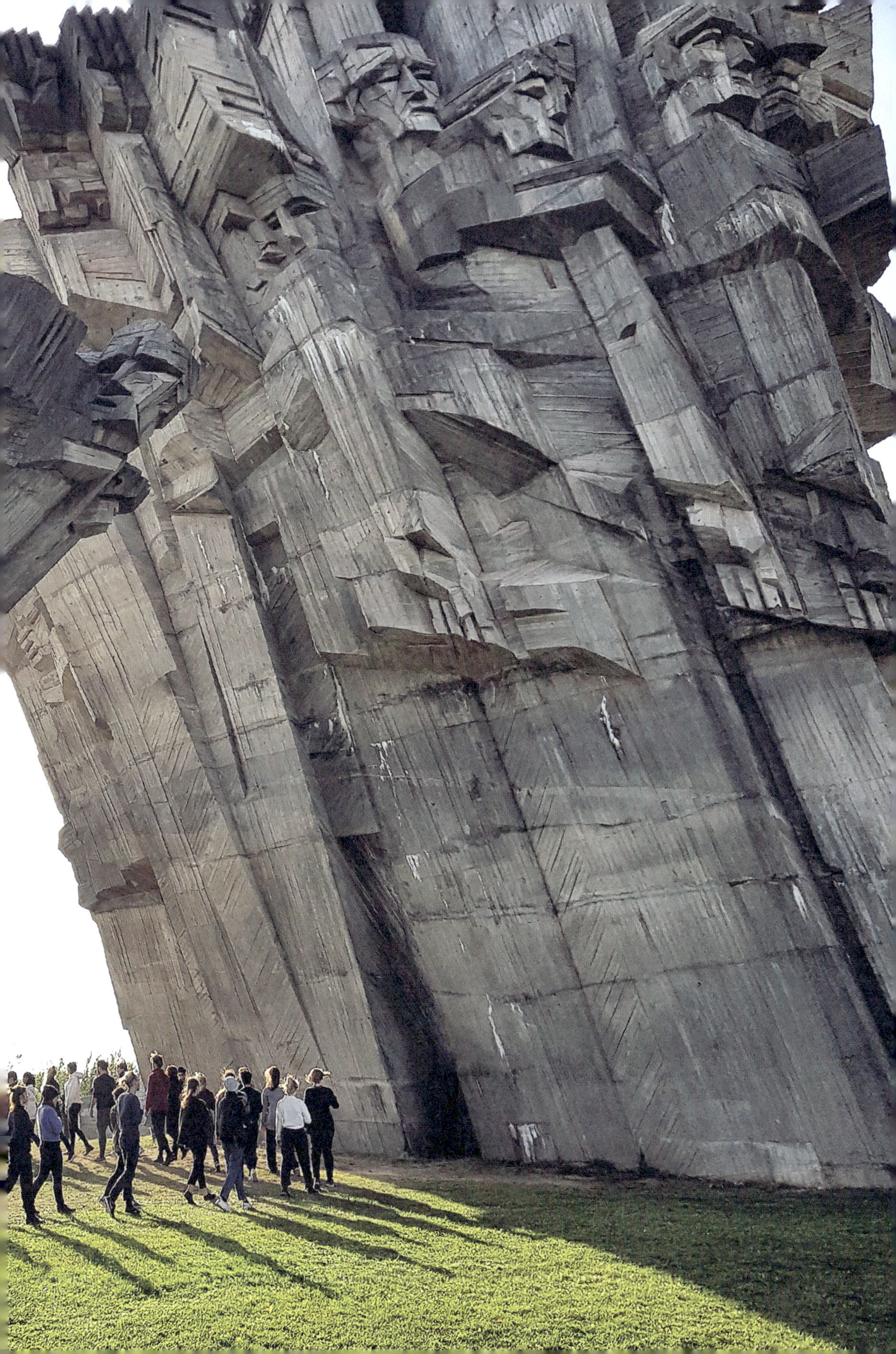

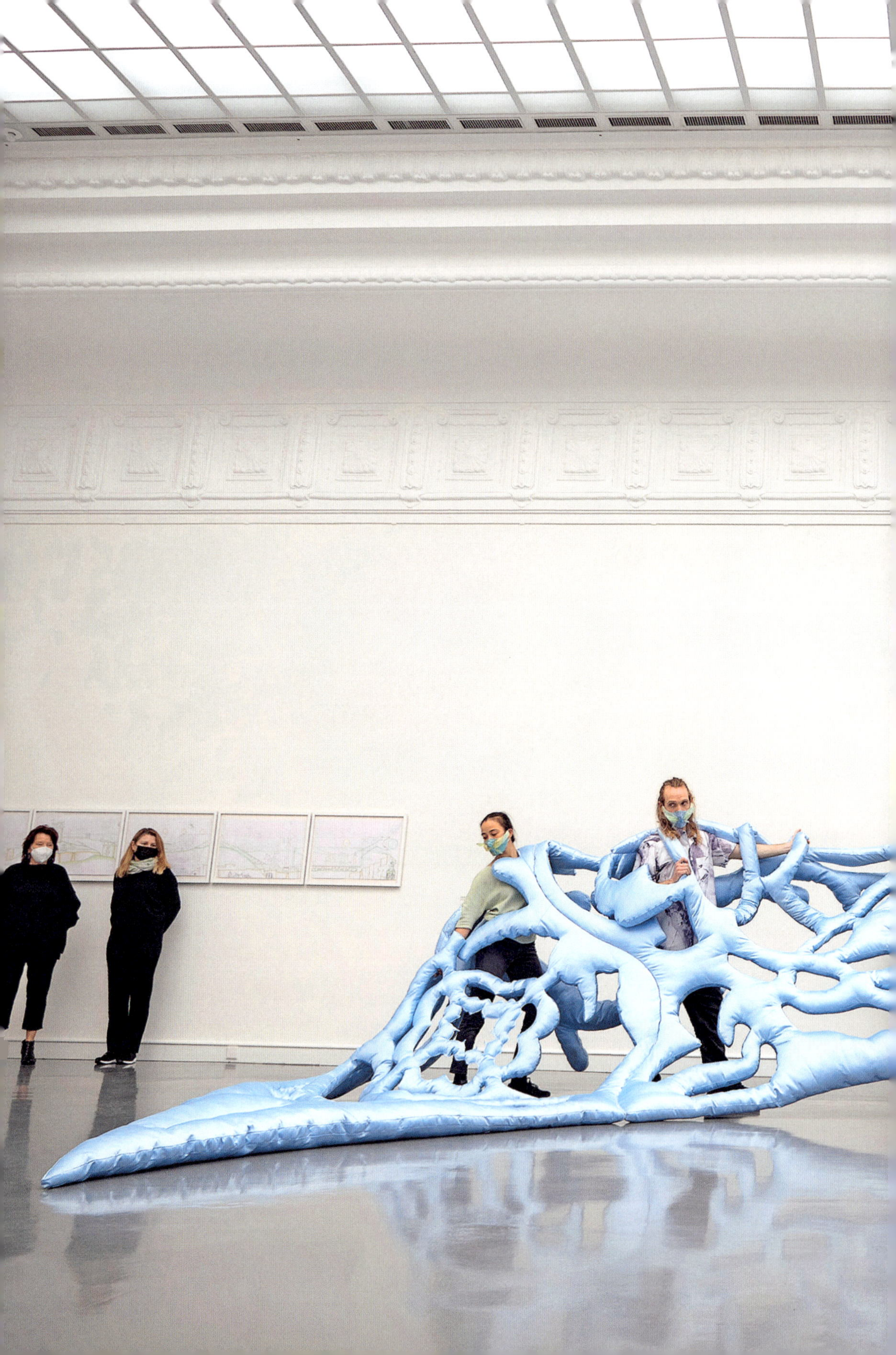

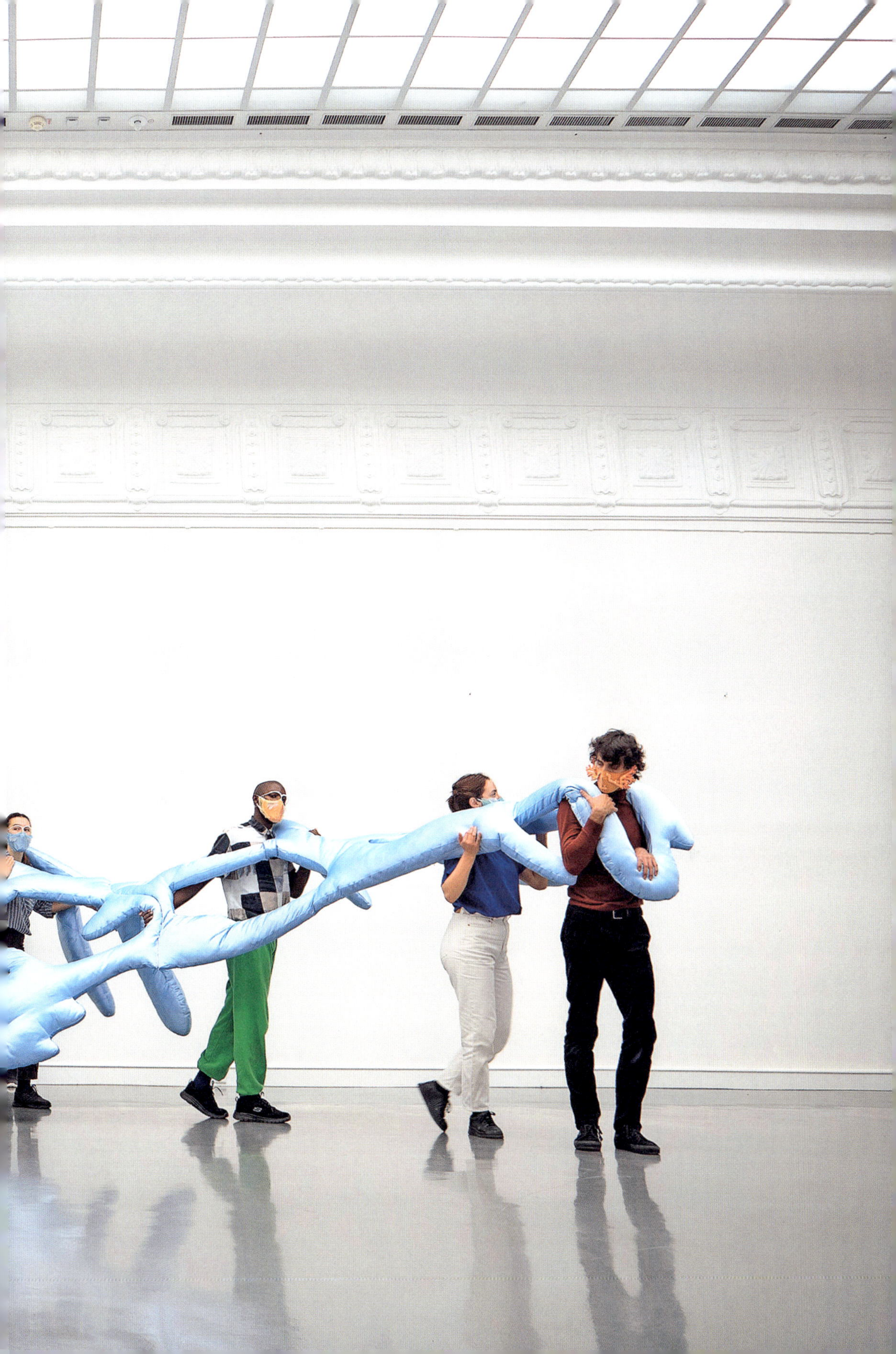

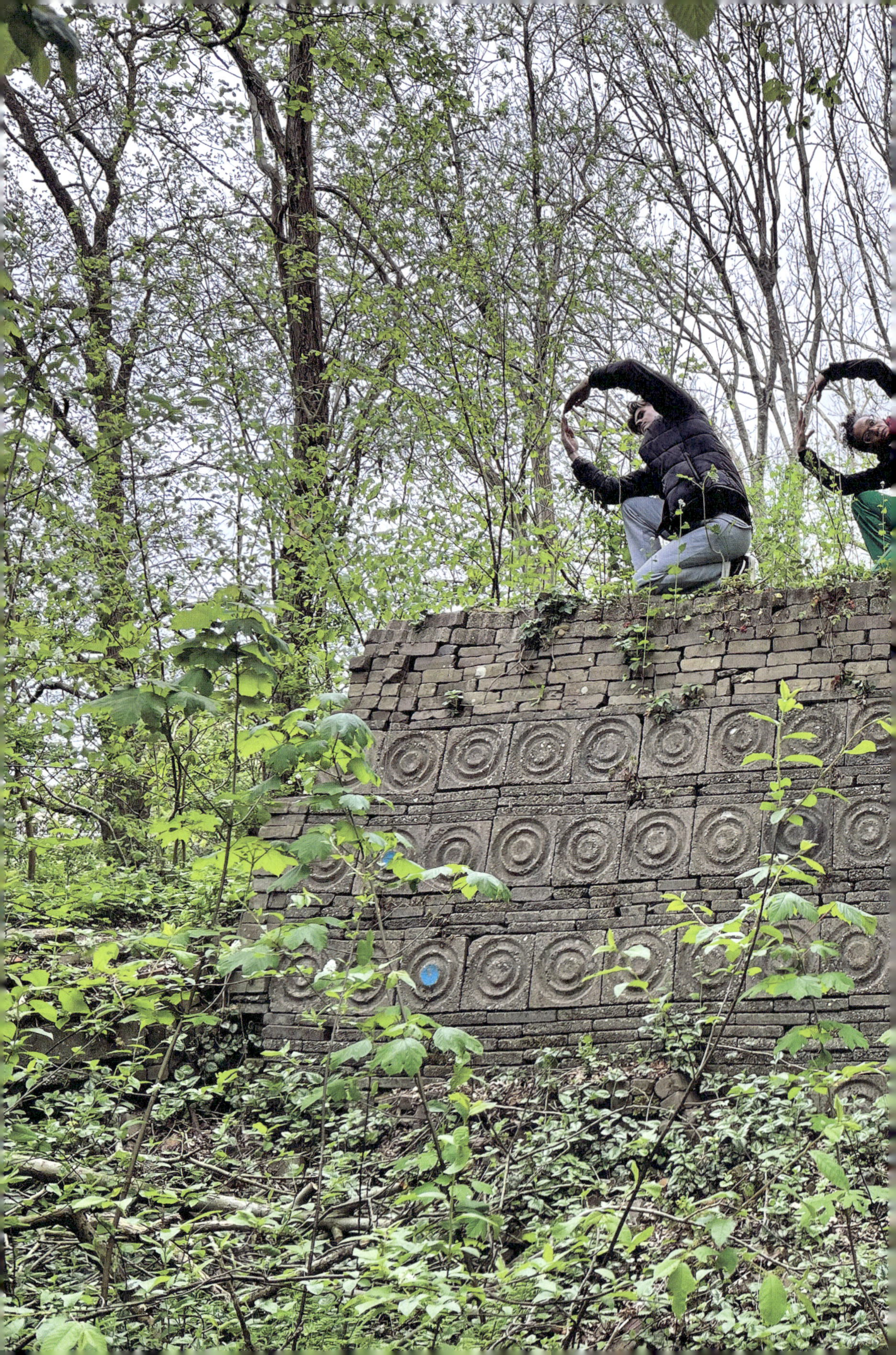

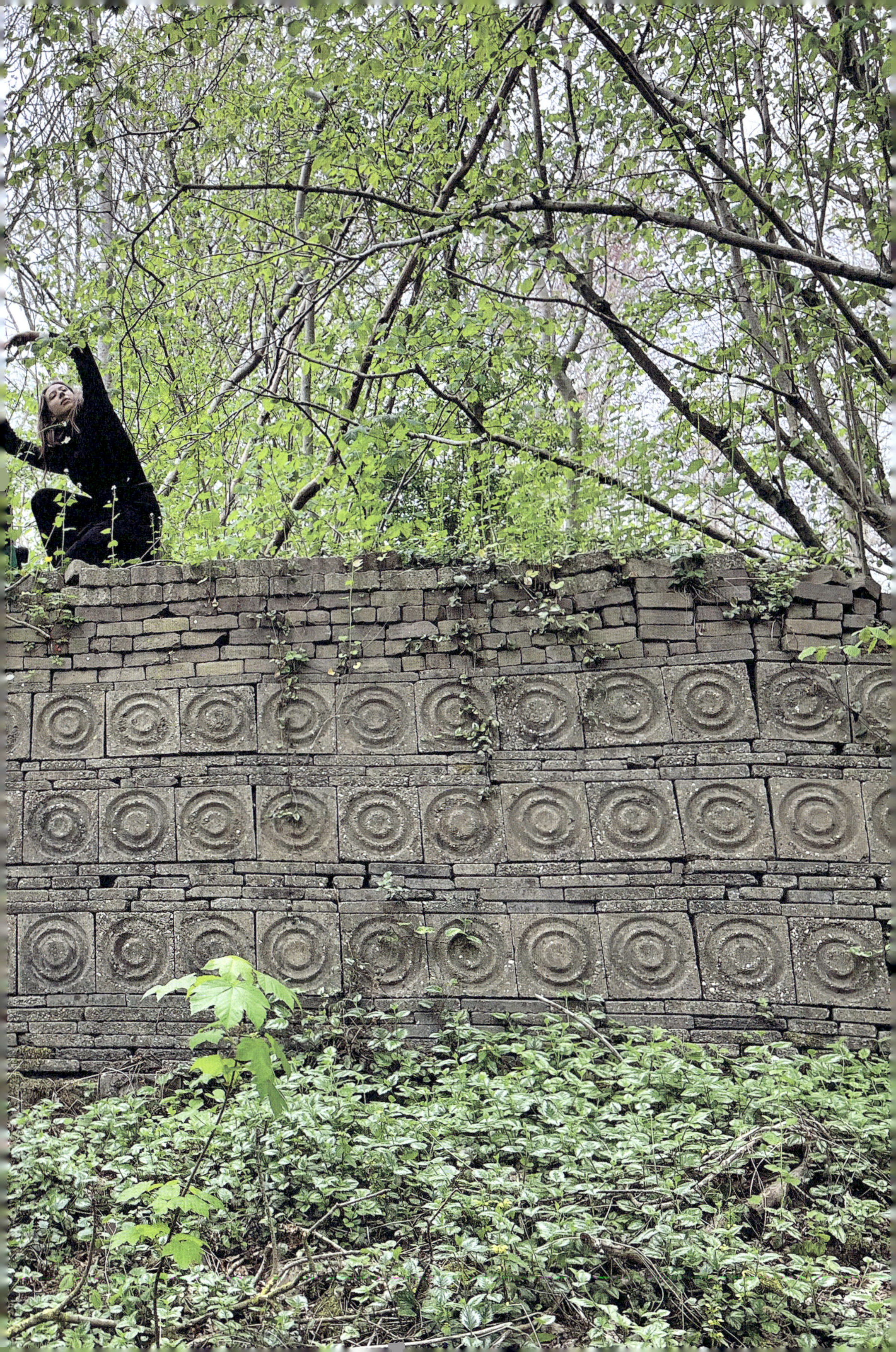

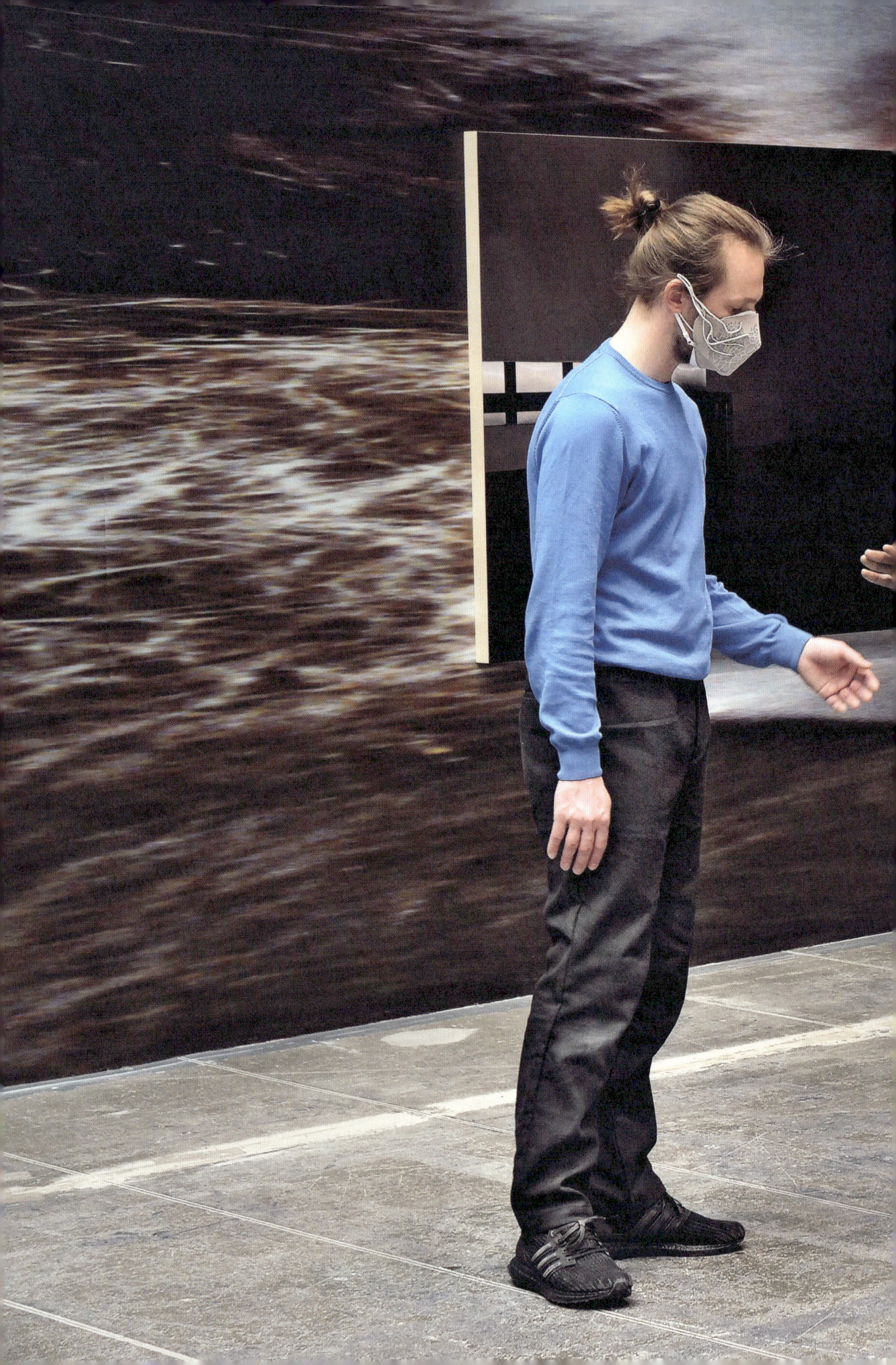

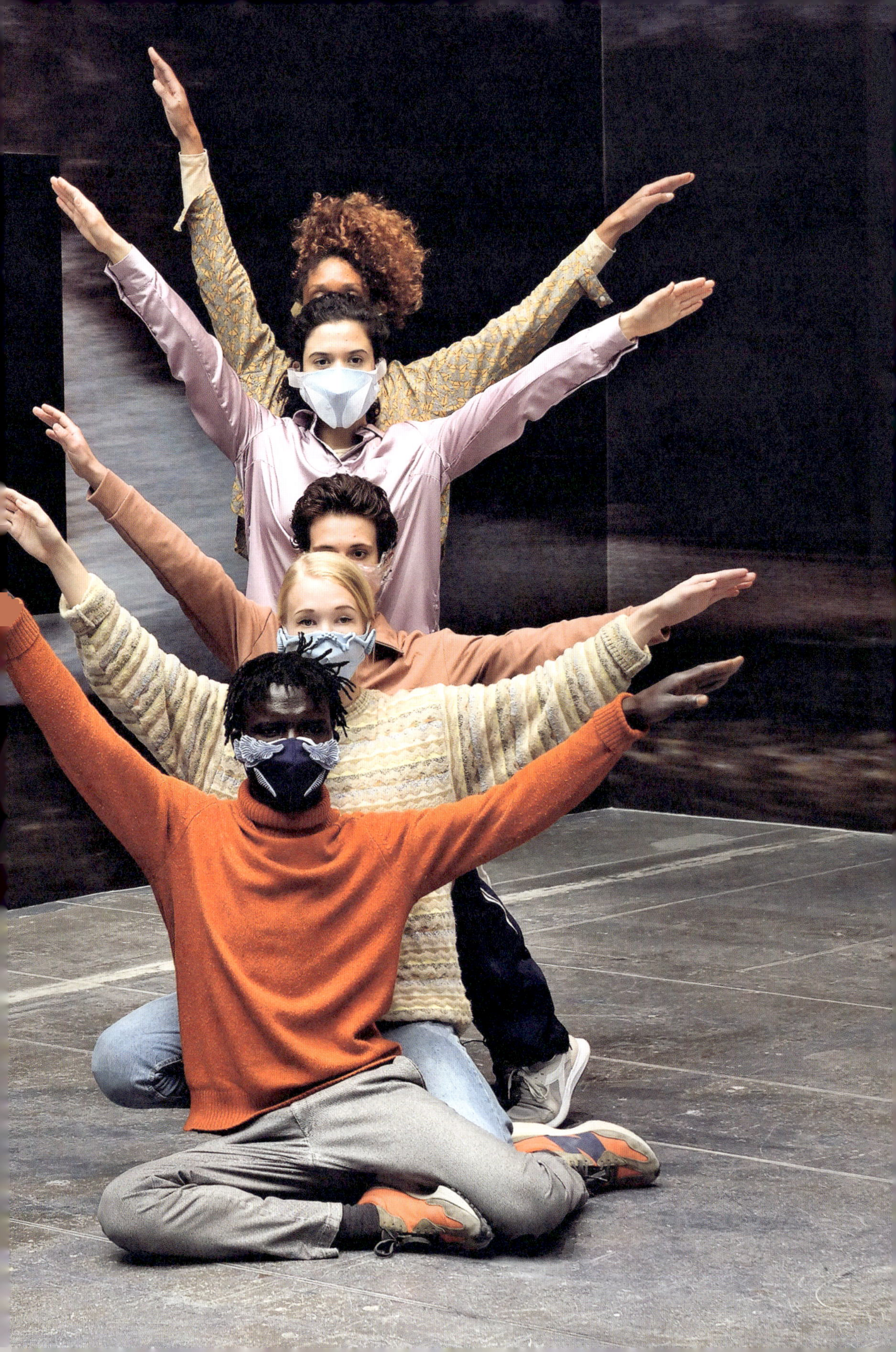

Alexandra Pirici

Geboren / born in Bukarest / Bucharest, RO, 1982
Lebt und arbeitet in Bukarest, RO und München, DE /
lives and works in Bucharest, RO, and Munich, DE

Ausgewählte Einzelausstellungen /
Selected Solo Exhibitions

2024
Alexandra Pirici: Attune.
Hamburger Bahnhof – Nationalgalerie der
Gegenwart, Berlin, DE; Katalog / catalog

2020
Pulse. IX fortas / Ninth Fort, Kaunas, LT
Aggregate. Art Basel Messeplatz, Basel, CH

2018
Co-natural. New Museum, New York, NY, US

2017
Aggregate. Neuer Berliner Kunstverein,
Berlin, DE

2017
Persistent Feebleness. Galerie für
Zeitgenössische Kunst Leipzig, Leipzig, DE
*An Immaterial Retrospective of the Venice
Biennale.* Rumänischer Pavillon / Romanian
pavilion, La Biennale di Venezia, Venedig /
Venice, IT

Ausgewählte Gruppen- ausstellungen /
Selected Group Exhibitions

2022
The Milk of Dreams. La Biennale di Venezia,
Venedig / Venice, IT
The Floating Collection. Museo d'Arte
Moderna di Bologna, Bologna, IT
Paradys – Arcadia. Paradys Oranjewoud,
Oranjewoud, NL

2021
Nature and State. Staatliche Kunsthalle
Baden-Baden, Baden-Baden, DE
Post Nature. Ulsan Museum of Art, Ulsan, KR

2020
Things Entangling. Museum of Contemporary
Art Tokyo, Tokio / Tokyo, JP
Constellation. International Çanakkale
Biennial, Çanakkale, TR
Paranoia TV. steirischer herbst, Graz, AT
Performance / Documentation / Presentation.
Lunds Konsthall, Lund, SE

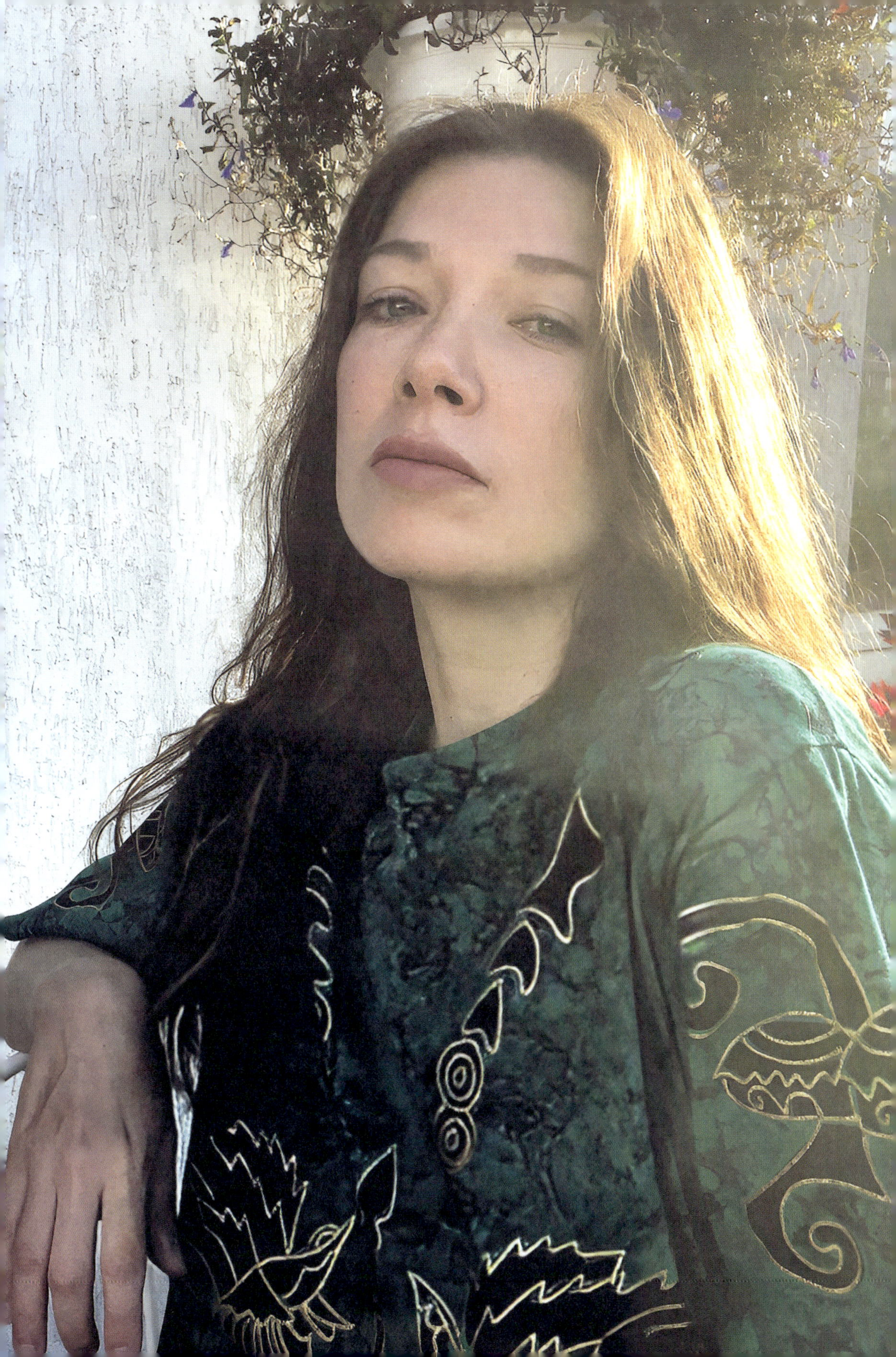

*Nach dem Beaufsichtigen der Maschinen /
After Supervising the Machinery.*
Engelskirchen, DE
Dance first. Think later. Musée d'art et
d'histoire, Genf / Geneva, CH
Umbruch / Upheaval. Kunsthalle Mannheim,
Mannheim, DE

2019
AnoZero'19. Bienal de Arte Contemporânea
de Coimbra, Coimbra, PT
And Other Such Stories. Chicago Architecture
Biennial, Chicago, IL, US
Block Universe. Imperial War Museum,
London, GB
Ruhr Ding: Territories. Public Art Ruhr,
Dortmund, DE

2018
Delicate Instruments of Engagement.
Tanzquartier Wien & Kunsthalle Wien,
Wien / Vienna, AT (weitere Stationen /
traveled to: Nationalgalerie, Prag, CZ /
National Gallery, Prague, CZ; Theatre de la Ville
de Paris, Paris, FR)
Kunstenfestivaldesarts. KANAL –
Centre Pompidou, Brüssel / Brussels, BE
Public Art Munich. München / Munich, DE
Hopscotch-Rayuela. Art Basel Cities,
Buenos Aires, AR
Stagings. Soundings. Readings. Free Jazz II.
NTU CCA Singapore, Singapur / Singapore, SG
General Rehearsal. Museum für Moderne
Kunst, Moskau, RU / Museum of Modern Art,
Moscow, RU (weitere Station / traveled to:
Forum do Futuro, Palacio da Bolsa, Porto, PT)

2017
Skulptur Projekte Münster. Münster, DE
Action! Kunsthaus Zürich, Zürich / Zurich, CH
Impulse Theater Festival. Kunsthalle &
Kunstverein Düsseldorf, Düsseldorf, DE
Access Point. Russisches Museum /
Russian Museum, St. Petersburg, RU
*Future Climates: The School of
Redistributions.* State of Concept, Athen /
Athens, GR (weitere Station / traveled to:
Kadist, Paris, FR)

2016
Berlin Biennale. Kunst-Werke, Berlin, DE
BMW Tate Live. Tate Modern, London, GB
Wisdom of the Earth: This Is Not a Stone.
Nationales Kunstmuseum, Bukarest, RO /
National Museum of Art, Bucharest, RO
A Living Museum. Tate Liverpool, Liverpool GB

2015
STADT/BILD. Nationalgalerie –
Staatliche Museen Berlin, Berlin, DE
Monument to Work. Public Art Agency
Sweden, Göteborg, SE
OFF Biennale. Budapest, HU

2014
Playground Festival. Museum M, Leuven, BE
(weitere Stationen / traveled to: Centre
Pompidou-Metz, Metz, FR; Museum der
Moderne, Salzburg, AT; Museum für Moderne
Kunst, Warschau, PL / Museum of Modern Art,
Warsaw, PL; Fridericianum, Kassel, DE)
*Confessions of the Imperfect.
1848 – 1989 – Today.* Van Abbemuseum,
Eindhoven, NL
imagetanz. brut Wien, Wien / Vienna, AT
The Forgotten Pioneer Movement. DISTRICT
Berlin & HAU Berlin, Berlin, DE
Temps d'Images. Cluj, RO
Le Mouvement. Biel / Bienne, CH
Baltic Circle. Helsinki, FI
Manifesta 10. St. Petersburg, RU
*Just Pompidou It. Rétrospective du Centre
Pompidou.* Centre Pompidou, Paris, FR

2013
TIME. Bass Museum of Art, Miami, FL, US

2012
*Km 0. Representations and Repetitions of
the University Square.* tranzit.ro, Bukarest /
Bucharest, RO
Homefest. Lorgean Theater, Bukarest /
Bucharest, RO

2011
If You Don't Want Us, We Want You.
Bukarest / Bucharest, RO

2010
A Horse Opera. National Dance Center,
Bukarest / Bucharest, RO

2009
*You Should Know What He Drank Like an
Old Whale.* National Dance Center, Bukarest /
Bucharest, RO

2007
Balkan Dance Platform. Athen / Athens, GR

2005
Explore Dance Festival. National Dance
Center, Bukarest / Bucharest, RO

Forschung, Lehre, Vorträge / Research, Teaching, Talks

Seit / since **2023**
Erste Professur für Performance in der zeit-
genössischen Kunst / first appointed professor
for Performance in Contemporary Art, **Akademie
der Bildenden Künste, München** / Munich, **DE**

2022
„Posthuman Feminism". Mit /with
Rosi Braidotti und / and Jeffrey Deitch,
La Biennale di Venezia, Venedig / Venice, IT

2020
*Sensing the Living: Promoting the Perception
of Plants.* In Zusammenarbeit mit / in collab-
oration with **Paco Calvo (Universität Murcia /**
University of Murcia) **für** / for *Studiotopia –
Art Meets Science in the Anthropocene*
(2019–2022)
*Describing in Movement / Observing Through
Embodiment* (fortlaufend / ongoing)
„Sculpture, Alive: Materiality and Mutability
of Form, Structure and Meaning". Yorkshire
Sculpture International, Leeds & Wakefield, GB

„The Transformation of Monumentality.
The Rise and Fall and the Dance of
Monuments". Mit / with Dmitry Vilensky,
School of Mutation, Institute for Radical
Imagination, online

2019
„What We Talk About When We Talk About
Art". SITAC XVI symposium, Mexiko-Stadt /
Mexico City, **MX**
„Operative Power of Art Practices".
Symposium *Mourning Money*, UKK Denmark,
Königlich Dänische Kunstakademie,
Kopenhagen, DK / Royal Danish Academy of
Fine Arts, Copenhagen, DK

2018
„Persistent Feebleness". Symposium
*Mit Denkmälern Sprechen? Monumente:
Vergessen und Aktuell / Talking to
Monuments? Monuments: Forgotten and
Up to Date,* Migros Museum, Zürich / Zurich, DE
„Workers leaving the factory, bodies
becoming the node". transit.sk, Bratislava, SK

2015
„Demonstration-lecture". *Are you alive or not?
Looking at art through the lens of theatre,*
Gerrit Rietveld Academie, Amsterdam, NL

Ausgewählte Bücher und Magazine / Selected Books and Journals

Corina L. Apostol & Nato Thompson (Hg. / eds.), *Making Another World Possible: 10 Creative Time Summits, 10 Global Issues, 100 Art Projects*, Oxford / New York: Routledge, 2020, S. / pp. 203–204.

Bertie Ferdman & Jovana Stokic (Hg. / eds.), *The Methuen Drama Companion to Performance Art*, London / New York: Bloomsbury, 2020 (Cover).

Alexandra Pirici, „I Want My Writing to Be Photographed so as to Explain My Hand" in: *Rosa Mercedes* 2 (Mai / May 2020), https://www.harun-farocki-institut.org/en/2020/05/03/i-want-my-writing-to-be-photographed-so-as-to-explain-my-hand-2/, zuletzt abgerufen am / last accessed on 18.03.2024 (in spanischer Übersetzung erschienen / Spanish translation published in: *Revista Pausa* 43, 2021).

Carolina Magis Weinberg, „Gestos Monumentales: Alexandra Pirici" in: *Revista UNAM* (März / March 2020), https://www.revistadelauniversidad.mx/articles/95bf1036-161a-4511-9c0b-df620a9a40a2/gestos-monumentales-Alexandra-Pirici, zuletzt abgerufen am / last accessed on 18.03.2024.

Christoph F. E. Holzhey & Arnd Wedemeyer (Hg. / eds.), *Re-: An Errant Glossary*, Berlin: ICI Berlin Press, 2019.

Alexandra Pirici, „The Body as Technology for Spectacle in Contemporary Football" in: *Corner (Football and Society)* 1 (2019), S. / pp. 58ff.

Ana Janevski, Roxana Marcoci & Ksenia Nouril (Hg. / eds.), *Art and Theory of Post-1989 Central and Eastern Europe: A Critical Anthology*, Durham: Duke University Press, 2018 (Cover).

Alexandra Pirici, „Performance as Conjuring" in: *Texte zur Kunst* 110 (Juni / June 2018), S. / pp. 75–80.

Alexandra Pirici, „on Caspar David Friedrich's ‚Moonrise Over the Sea' (Old Masters, New Loves)" in: *Monopol Magazin* (Februar / February 2017), https://www.monopol-magazin.de/moonrise-over-sea-caspar-david-friedrich, zuletzt abgerufen am / last accessed on 18.03.2024.

Mélanie Boucher, „Soft Power ou Les corps-monuments d'Alexandra Pirici / Soft Power or Alexandra Pirici's Body-Monuments" in: *Espace* 112 (Winter 2016), S. / pp. 26–35.

Alexandra Pirici, „Actualizing History in the Living Body, as Subject-Object" in: Nick Aikens et al. (Hg. /eds.), *What's the Use – Constellations of Art, History and Knowledge*, Amsterdam: Valiz, 2016.

Julia Kurz, Joanna Warsza & Franciska Zolyom (Hg. / eds.), *Art in Times of Gray Democracy*, Leipzig: GfZK Leipzig, 2015.

Alexandra Pirici & Raluca Voinea, „Manifesto for the Gynecene" in: Armen Avanessian & Helen Hester (Hg. / eds.), *dea ex machina*, Berlin: Merve Verlag, 2015, S. / pp. 35–44 (zahlreiche Übersetzungen veröffentlicht / various translations published).

Amy Bryzgel, *Performing the East: Performance Art in Russia, Latvia and Poland since 1980*, London / New York: Bloomsbury, 2013.

Impressum / Imprint

Diese Publikation erscheint anlässlich der Ausstellung /
Published on the occasion of the exhibition
Alexandra Pirici. Attune
26. April – 6. Oktober 2024 / April 26 – October 6, 2024
im / at Hamburger Bahnhof – Nationalgalerie der
Gegenwart, Staatliche Museen zu Berlin
Direktoren / Directors: Sam Bardaouil & Till Fellrath
smb.museum/hbf

Ausstellung / Exhibition

Konzept, Realisierung, Choreographie und
Komposition / Concept, Realization, Choreography and
Composition: Alexandra Pirici
Design: Andrei Dinu
Performer*innen / Performers: Caroline Beach, Juan
Corres Benito, Noemi Calzavara, Michelle Cheung,
Gabrielle Duval, Miguel Angel Guzmán, Nitsan
Margaliot, Jared Marks, Tatiana Mejía, Emily Ranford,
Asuka Julia Riedl, Robert Schulz, Yurika S. Yamamoto

Kuratorin / Curator: Catherine Nichols
Restauratorische Betreuung / Conservation: Eva Rieß
Ausstellungskoordination / Exhibition Coordination:
Elena Montini
Koordination Live-Aktion / Live Action Coordination:
Robert Schulz
Kommunikation / Communication: Fiona Geuß,
Anna Nike Sohrauer
Kunstvermittlung / Mediation: Claudia Ehgartner
Sekretariat / Office: Katrin Berendsen
Sammlungsverwalter / Collection Management:
Jörg Lange, Thomas Seewald
Haustechnik / Maintenance: Stefan Gösche,
Garry Rogge, Dirk Wagner, Frank Wloka
Praktikantinnen / Interns: Gretchen Sorge,
Anica Tengelmann

Produktion / Production: Björn Alfers
Betreuung der Briggs-Rauscher-Reaktion /
Support for the Briggs-Rauscher Reaction:
Bogdan-Constantin Enache
Chemische Unterstützung / Chemical Support: Microsin
Technik / Engineering: Michael Akstaller, Frank Fietzek,
Robert Kruppa, David Wimmer
Elektrik / Electrical Work: Victor Kégli
Art Handling: Abrell van den Berg Ausstellungsservice
Schlosserarbeiten / Metal Work: Maël Lefrançois /
MaLeWo
Ausstellungsbau / Exhibition Construction:
LICHTblick Bühnentechnik
Ausstellungsgrafik / Exhibition Graphics: Eps51
Produktion Ausstellungsgrafik / Production of Exhibition
Graphics: Annette Herwegh

Publikation / Catalog

Für die / For the Nationalgalerie – Staatliche Museen
zu Berlin herausgegeben von / edited by
Sam Bardaouil & Till Fellrath
Konzept / Concept: Catherine Nichols
Autor*innen / Authors: Cecilia Alemani,
Catherine Nichols, Alexandra Pirici, Raluca Voinea
Redaktion / Editing: Lisa Hörstmann
Übersetzungen / Translations: Sabine Bürger und
Tim Beeby, Harriert Fricke, Jaqueline Todd

Cover:
Ausstellungsansichten / Installation views
Alexandra Pirici. Attune, Hamburger Bahnhof –
Nationalgalerie der Gegenwart, 2024

Silvana Editoriale

Hauptgeschäftsführung / Chief Executive: **Michele Pizzi**
Verlagsleitung / Editorial Director: **Sergio Di Stefano**
Art Director: Giacomo Merli
Redaktionskoordination / Editorial Coordinator:
Chiara Tulli
Korrektorat / Copy Editor: **Cristina Pradella**
Produktionskoordination / Production Coordinator:
Antonio Micelli
Redaktionsassistenz / Editorial Assistant:
Giulia Mercanti
Photo Editor: Silvia Sala
Pressestelle / Press Office: **Lidia Masolini**

Visuelles Konzept und Design / Visual Concept
and Design: Eps51
Layout und Satz / Graphic Design and Typesetting:
Eps51
Druck und Bindung / Printing and Binding:
Tipostampa, Moncalieri
Papier / Paper: Fedrigoni Arena White Rough
Schriften / Typefaces: Bagoss Variable

Erschienen bei / Published by **Silvana Editoriale S.p.A.,**
Mailand / Milano. **www.silvanaeditoriale.it**

Printed in the EU
ISBN: 9788836656578

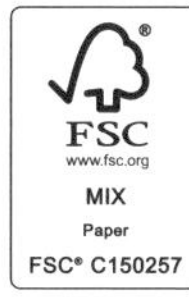

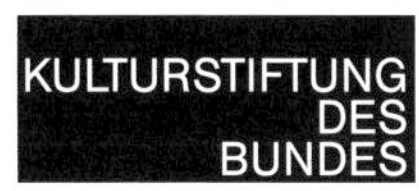

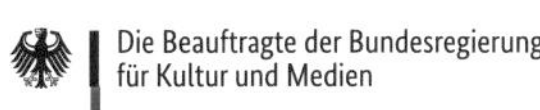

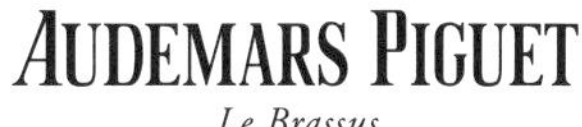

Abbildungsverzeichnis / Photo Credits

Für alle abgebildeten Werke von /
for all reproduced works by **Alexandra Pirici**:
© Alexandra Pirici

Foto / photo **Cover oben** / top, **S.** / pp. 4, 5, 8, 9, 15,
20, 21, 21–31; 34, 35, 38–41, 48, 49, 54, 55, 66, 67,
72–77, 80, 81:
© Alexandra Pirici. VG Bild-Kunst, Bonn 2024 /
by SIAE 2024, Staatliche Museen zu Berlin,
Nationalgalerie / Jacopo La Forgia
Foto / photo **Cover unten** / bottom,
S. / pp. 32, 33, 36, 37:
© Alexandra Pirici. VG Bild-Kunst, Bonn 2024 /
by SIAE 2024, Staatliche Museen zu Berlin,
Nationalgalerie / Laura Fiorio
Foto S. / photo pp. 12, 13:
© Dorling Kindersley ltd / Alamy Stock Photo
Foto / photo **S.** / pp. 63, 65:
© Alexandra Pirici. VG Bild-Kunst, Bonn 2024 /
by SIAE 2024
Foto S. / photo pp. 88, 89, 98, 99, 102, 103:
© Alexandra Pirici
Foto S. / photo pp. 90, 91, 104, 105:
© Eduard Constantin
Foto S. / photo pp. 92, 93, 96, 97:
© Henning Rogge
Foto S. / photo pp. 94, 95, 100, 101, 107:
© Andrei Dinu

Dank / Acknowledgements

Die Ausstellung wurde gemeinsam vom Hamburger Bahnhof – Nationalgalerie der Gegenwart und Audemars Piguet Contemporary in Auftrag gegeben. Die Ausstellung wird von der Kulturstiftung des Bundes kofinanziert. Mit Unterstützung der Hamburger Bahnhof International Companions e.V. / The exhibition is co-commissioned by Hamburger Bahnhof – Nationalgalerie der Gegenwart and Audemars Piguet Contemporary. The exhibition is co-funded by the German Federal Cultural Foundation. With the support of Hamburger Bahnhof International Companions e.V.

Die Publikation wurde ermöglicht durch die Freunde der Nationalgalerie. / The publication was made possible by Freunde der Nationalgalerie.